# Opening Up

## Volume II: My Life in Theatre

### David Clarke

McGeary Media

# Preface to Volume II

This is the second and concluding volume of a shortened and edited version of a memoir I wrote after I retired as a consultant surgeon. The motives for the memoir are summarised in the preface to Volume 1, appended. My background is not unique by any means, but certainly unusual for its time.

The narrative is structured chronologically as an autobiography, but as well as my life I have included anecdotes about interesting people, examples of surgical cases and procedures, as well as digressions, mainly of a historical nature.

Volume 1 (subtitled The Making of a Surgeon) described my early life and education after my birth in 1942, five years of medical school to graduation in 1966, and ends a few years later as I embarked on the first tentative steps as a surgical trainee.

This Volume 2 (subtitled My Life in Theatre) covers the almost ten years of additional training, rotating through various surgical specialties as well as two periods of research, one in the USA, and culminating in a consultant post in Middlesbrough, which ended with my retirement in 2006, after twenty-five years.

A short third volume subtitled A Medical Miscellany consists of a few chapters of additional reflections and reminiscences of a career in surgery, and completes the series.

David Clarke

# Contents

# Chapter One

# Bones and Groans

My wife Mary and I found a two-bedroomed bungalow in Woodlands Park Estate, Wideopen, for £3,950. Wideopen was just off the Great North Road, near the mining village of Seaton Burn. The bungalow was on a corner site and as well as a small front and back garden we had a large triangular area to the side, which we regarded as a bonus. Our old Jesmond flat was furnished, so we had to start from scratch, with a wood-framed three-piece suite with purple cushions, a G Plan bed and wardrobe and a kitchen table and chairs. It took some time to get a black-and-white TV. The estate was attractive to what were later termed 'yuppies'—young urban professionals, including several of my colleagues.

In summer 1969, I started my three-year rotation as a surgical registrar—one year of general surgery and six months in each of four sub-specialties. The first port of call for my friend and fellow graduate George Bone and I was the Department of Orthopaedics in the Royal Victoria Infirmary (RVI), Newcastle-upon Tyne. It remains the major teaching hospital of the Newcastle Medical School, but apart from the beautiful facade, dating from 1906, the building has undergone such extensive modernisation that it is barely recognisable as our well-loved *alma mater* of nearly sixty years ago. In those far-off days, there were two senior orthopaedic surgeons. Jake Stanger—'assisted by Mr P Napier Robson', as it said on the department notepaper, or 'PNR' as the staff called him—had recently been joined by Mr David Stainsby, a newly appointed orthopaedic surgeon, who had his own registrar, a career trainee. The senior registrar was Mr Nargolwala (aka Naggers). Fortunately for George and me, David Stainsby had already produced a comprehensive guide to fractures, a portable and unobtrusive pamphlet to which we could easily refer when necessary.

In my first week I took the x-ray of a patient with a Monteggia fracture-dislocation of the forearm to PNR. This can be difficult to reduce (manipulate) and may need surgery.

'Get one of the registrars to do it,' he said.

I was speechless for a few moments.

'Don't tell me—you *are* one of the registrars. All right, eight-thirty tomorrow morning.'

One thing about PNR, he was a man of his word and was always punctual. He was popular with the nursing sisters because he was always polite (to them!), gave clear instructions and was quick. But he put the fear of God into us juniors and perhaps because of this and the fact that he kept a straight face, it is only retrospectively that I can appreciate his sense of humour. Whenever we admitted a motorcyclist with a fractured femur, which was often, he would say, loud enough for the patient to hear, 'Have you sent for the psychiatrists yet?' Once, in the patient's presence, he said, 'This woman was indulging in that well-known bird game, the extramarital lark, when her boyfriend pushed her through a plate-glass window.'

My favourite expression of his was when a small boy came in one day in autumn with a supracondylar fracture (this is of the upper arm bone just above the elbow).
'Oh my God, the supracondylar season is with us again,' he said. 'These loopies will shin up trees looking for conkers and drop out with dismal regularity.'
He emphasised and prolonged the syllables of *dismal* in a sonorous tone.

One day he asked me to plate a fractured tibia, which for some reason had been left for a week. This meant inserting a metal plate and screws across the bone after manipulating the broken ends together, an action called reduction. Try as I might I was unable to reduce the fracture before plating it. The anaesthetist, Joe Stoddart, asked what the problem was.

'Well, if it's just brute strength you need, I'll help,' he said.

So he left the anaesthetic nurse to take over while he pulled upwards and me downwards, and eventually we succeeded. The next day, when PNR asked how I had got on, he chuckled and said his asthma was playing up and he thought it would be 'a bit sticky', which was why he left it to me! In similar fashion, one weekend I was struggling to reduce a dislocated hip. I had to resort to transferring the man from the table to the floor and get a porter to sit on his pelvis before I heard and felt the satisfying clunk as it reduced, having lifted both patient and porter off the floor with the lower leg bent at the knee over my shoulder. When I told PNR he asked to see the x-ray.

'Well, at least it *was* dislocated,' he confirmed. 'Some years ago I was called in to help out when two registrars couldn't reduce a hip. I told them that before attempting to reduce a dislocated hip, first ascertain that it is, in fact, dislocated.'

One weekend I was on call with the houseman, Rosie. It had poured with rain throughout Sunday. We were both in the Accident Room when she looked at her watch. 'It's midnight,' she said. 'It's been a quiet weekend. I'm going to bed.'
Being of a superstitious nature, I had no sooner told her never to say that again when a breathless porter shot round the corner for a trolley and told us someone had jumped down from ward twenty. The first intensive care unit was being built at the time and the patient had fallen into the gap between ward two and the building site. In the darkness and torrential rain, and stumbling on the builders' rubble, it was a struggle to extricate the victim, especially as we needed to position and carry her gently in case she had sustained a spinal injury. She was a twenty-two-year-old university student who had been admitted under Prof Reg Hall a day or two before with an aspirin overdose severe enough to warrant haemodialysis via a temporary Scribner shunt inserted in the wrist. The treatment was so successful she could leave her bed without being discovered, mount the stairs from her ward to ward twenty on the third storey and jump out for a second suicide attempt. She had, however, landed on her feet and crushed them and her lower legs into multiple comminuted fractures. She had also dislocated her left sacroiliac joint but had no significant injuries above that. After relieving her pain, resuscitating her with plasma and warming her up, she was x-rayed and transferred to a side room on ward eighteen. I intended to take her to theatre in the early hours and simply mould her feet and lower legs into something approaching normality, immobilise them in plaster of Paris (POP), place a Steinmann pin in the left knee, reduce the dislocation and maintain it in traction. Nowadays she would have been placed on a dedicated trauma list during working hours, but woe betide anyone who delayed a Monday morning list in the 1960s.

I was sitting in her room monitoring her progress when who should walk in but the medical registrar, accompanied by Prof Hall himself, carrying a small wooden box. Reg opened the box and much to my amazement conducted a full (as far as was possible) neurological examination, starting with the cranial nerves, testing that of smell, the olfactory nerve, with oil of cloves. When he had satisfied himself that the only injuries were orthopaedic, he turned to me and asked who was on call. I must have looked taken aback for a moment because he added he was referring to the consultant. On being informed that it was PNR, he said he was sure I would let him know about such a serious case. Of course, I had had no intention of doing so—but now had no alternative. The prospect filled me with anxiety, so when PNR answered the phone I quickly blurted out that Professor Hall had asked me to let him know. He calmly listened and finally responded.'

Do you have a car?'

'Yes, sir.'

'Well, it's absolutely pissing down outside and, as you may know, my garage is some distance from my house. Bring the x-rays and I'll be waiting for you.'

The light was on in the front room, which was used as a consulting room, and the door opened as I arrived. He looked like Noel Coward in *Private Lives*, except for the absence of a cigarette holder. He was in a Paisley-patterned silk dressing gown, his blond hair slicked back, and he looked as if he was about to dress for dinner rather than having just got out of bed. An x-ray viewing box was already lit. As usual, he was brief and to the point. Taking the films from me, he opined, 'That's buggered, that's buggered and that's buggered. Don't try too hard, Clarke. In my experience, these kidney patients don't do very well.'

And that was it. I think he must have got muddled and thought she was on chronic dialysis. Anyway, I did what I had planned and in the short-term she was all right, but I left the unit shortly afterwards. I never did find out why she wanted to take her own life, but she spent most of her time in bed wading through Bertrand Russell's *History of Western Philosophy*, and having attempted to do so myself, I can confirm that it induces deep depression. Black humour aside, I can still see her as I write and I hope she was able, with help, to overcome her self-destructive urges and eventually lead a fulfilling life.

The wards were mainly devoted to trauma by necessity. The female ward contained mostly elderly women with fractured neck of femur, treated either by McMurray pin and plates for the pertrochanteric type, or Austin-Moore prostheses for those just below the head itself (because in these the blood supply of the head of femur is torn off and the head dies, so needs replacing). We registrars did many pin and plate operations, but either the senior registrar or the consultants did the Austin-Moores. There was a small paediatric annex and PNR did a few cases of scoliosis, one of his interests. Similarly, the male ward contained mostly trauma. I can remember the occasional meniscectomy (removal of knee cartilage, as in miners and footballers), and PNR did a few Charnley hip replacements, but they were not routine as they are today. There simply weren't the beds. I recall being chastised for admitting an old man with a fractured humerus who lived alone and was found by neighbours after lying for hours on his kitchen floor. I had used the last precious bed that was booked for an elective case.

Fractured neck of femur was not common in men, although I had one who was fifty-eight but looked seventy-eighty. He had been a boxer in the fairground booths and told me he had had more than 600 fights! When doing a pin and plate procedure, one had to first reduce the fracture and then find the path for the pin 'blindly', using guide wires. There was no image-intensifier then, so a standard x-ray plate was used and when developed was displayed by the radiographer on a screen in a window of the theatre door for all to see. Sometimes it took several attempts to get right, with some guide wires taking bizarre paths, to the amusement of the staff. It was said that PNR once passed by just as an x-ray was being placed in the screen and he sent in a message.

'Tell Mr X that the one in the bladder seems the most suitable.'

It was also rumoured that some previous registrars ferreted through the x-ray packets before ward rounds, removing all the embarrassing ones! We did not see Jake Stanger very often, which was a pity because he had a reputation as a skilled surgeon with excellent judgement. I won't easily forget the embarrassment I suffered when I was left to do one of his clinics. The large consulting room had two doors, from which either a male or female would emerge, usually in a dressing gown and ready for examination. I asked the nurse to send in the next patient. Both doors swung open simultaneously and from one emerged a boy of about eight, lurching in like a robot with both legs encased in full-length callipers and with two sticks and a back brace. He was accompanied by his mother. From the other came his father, who had been behind the male door to avoid being in the same room as an undressing woman. They had come all the way from Carlisle to seek the expert opinion of a senior orthopaedic surgeon—and they saw me!

Shortly before Christmas I was strolling through the department in my white coat when Jake approached.

'Who are you?' he asked.

'Your registrar, Mr Stanger.'

'Ah, good. Are you a bird man or a drinking man?'

Not sure whether his idea of a bird man and mine were identical, I played safe and declared myself to be a drinking man. Like Santa Claus he reached into a large sack and produced a bottle of sherry for me as a Christmas gift. The sisters and staff nurses seemed to get 200 Embassy cigarettes each, irrespective of whether they smoked, although in those days they probably did. I soon found out what a bird man was. There was a flu epidemic that Christmas and I was one of the few to remain free of it. Over the holiday period I came in each day to do ward rounds. The ancient Meccano-like metal-framed lift was adjacent to and contained within the staircase that wound round it up three storeys to wards seventeen and eighteen and finally the operating theatre. At the other side of the lift at ground-floor level was the secretaries' office, which also housed several personal lockers. On the first day I came in there was a foul smell emanating from the lift, but I couldn't detect the cause. Over succeeding days the smell got worse, and I thought there must be a blocked drain somewhere. The mystery was solved after the holidays. When Jake distributed his Christmas gifts, his senior registrar, Naggers, was ill with the flu. The secretary telephoned Naggers at home to say that Mr Stanger had left a couple of pheasants for him. But thinking she said 'presents', he replied he was too ill to collect them and to put them in his locker until he returned. Amazingly, she obeyed his instruction, even though his locker stood directly in front of a radiator! I know that game is supposed to be hung, but this was taking it a bit too far.

The senior house officer was Harry Carr, a man in his fifties. Harry must have qualified either during the Second World War or just after but had been out of medicine for about twenty years to run the family business, I believe, and had just returned. Naggers took him under his wing and guided him, not just in orthopaedics but in various procedures and prescribing. Harry was undoubtedly eccentric, but he had a natural curiosity and an original mind and took very little at face value, always questioning the established view. He was always coming up with new ideas of traction and would rig up Heath Robinson-type contraptions. He was unfailingly cheerful, friendly and keen to please. Harry had a Chaplinesque walk, with his feet out at obtuse angles. This seemed exaggerated and amusing on hot days when he appeared in the fracture clinic in matching olive-green shorts and shirt and white rubber theatre boots. The rest of us, of course, sweated in our long-sleeved shirts, ties and white coats.

'Where did you get those?' I asked him.

'These,' he replied, 'are my IWTs.'

'IWTs?' I queried.

'Yes, *I Was Theres*—I wore them in the jungle in Burma during the war.'

One day Harry was assisting Naggers with a difficult manipulation of an unstable fracture of the lower leg. While applying the POP, Naggers told Harry to hold the leg as steadily as possible and not to move. Halfway through the procedure Harry's trousers fell down and he had nothing on underneath. He remained like a statue, legs akimbo to spread the weight of the limb. Two or three nurses who were there as observers suddenly, as one, turned on their heels, put their noses in the air and marched out with military precision.

The purpose of a POP cast is, of course, to immobilise the fracture. Harry's early casts certainly succeeded in this regard—in fact they were so heavy they often immobilised the patient. Once in casual conversation Harry told me he had a Bugatti in his garage and was determined to get it back on the road again. I knew next to nothing about cars but I did know Bugattis were special and over the years I noticed they can fetch a lot of money. Harry was a bachelor with a housekeeper and lived in Gosforth opposite Ian McNeill, the surgeon, who told me he often saw him tinkering with a car on the drive. He later became a clinical assistant in Gateshead. I last saw him outside the Royal Victoria Infirmary in 1980, the week I left to take up my consultant post in Middlesbrough. He was his usual ebullient self and had that infectious, broad beam of a smile that lit up his whole face, making one feel so much better for having seen him. He told me he had to retire but did not want to. I sadly bade him farewell, thinking, correctly, that I would not see him again. Over the years I occasionally thought of him and the Bugatti. Then, lo-and-behold, he popped up in the national papers after his death at eighty-nine. His next-of-kin, nephews and nieces, found the Bugatti in his garage. It was one of only seventeen ever made and sold for three million pounds at auction by Bonhams in Paris. I gather there was an E-type Jaguar and an Aston Martin too, but they were only fit for scrap. Interestingly, I read a review of a biography of Field Marshal Bill Slim, who led the army in Burma that eventually drove the Japanese back at the end of the war. They were still fighting long after VE Day. Often termed 'the forgotten army', Slim gave his men a Patten-type speech, telling them one day they could tell their grandchildren, 'I was there'—hence Harry's name for his jungle greens. Good old Harry! One of life's characters.

Another character was Mac (McGuinness), the plaster technician. The skill in applying POP casts takes time to acquire and we all had to apply them out of hours, but from nine-to-five in the Fracture Clinic it was Mac's job. He was a curmudgeon whose co-operation had to be slowly earned over time. We got on all right but I approached him with caution. He always called the doctors 'Sir', but like a RSM with young officers, I doubt if he often meant it. He was, however, highly skilled at his job and he seemed to have made himself indispensable by a reluctance to train anyone to replace him. A few assistants were sent to him over the years, but he simply ignored them until they lost interest. When he took a holiday there was an arrangement whereby a senior male nurse filled the gap for a fortnight and refreshed his skills. Over the years Mac had picked up a fair knowledge of orthopaedics and one of his infuriating habits was to stand next to the x-ray screens and watch as junior doctors puzzled over what to do with a particular fracture. He would shuffle around with a poker face doing a soft, tuneless whistle and out of the corner of his mouth, like an amateur ventriloquist, mutter *sotto voce* something like, 'Needs a plate.' It was aimed at the nurses and not meant as advice to the doctor, but simply as a demonstration of his superior knowledge over the tyro. On one occasion though, he and the nursing sisters were hoist on their own petard. It had happened three years earlier when I was on the unit as a houseman. We were told a gynaecologist was coming to be a locum senior house officer for two weeks. They were rubbing their hands with glee at the prospect of such a novice floundering, but on the Monday morning who should bounce in, full of bonhomie and confidence, but Tom Lind, later a professor of gynaecology. Unknown to them he had served with the forces in Germany and knew plenty of orthopaedics, as well as gynaecology. He soon charmed them and seemed to thoroughly enjoy himself, and as a lonely houseman I had a friend for a fortnight. I heard that when Mac retired, nobody other than the personnel department knew, and he simply failed to turn up for work one day. If true it would be in character, and I can imagine him cackling away at home at the chaos he had created, like one of Harry Enfield's 'old gits'. On the other hand, he had worked in the RVI since he was about fourteen and one would like to think he would welcome a small celebration of his long service. Perhaps he just gave very short notice.

One afternoon shortly before Christmas, I was relaxing alone in the Fracture Clinic when I heard the trip, trip, trip of footsteps in the corridor. This was shortly followed by the sight of a wheelchair pushed by Matron Freda Shaw, her back ramrod straight, resplendent in bottle-green dress with lace collar and cap. The occupant of the wheel-chair was a friend of Matron, a lady in her sixties, and a double-barrelled member of Northumberland gentry. This lady was making her Christmas cake and somehow fell onto the points of her elbows, fracturing both olecranons. I have tried to replicate this manoeuvre on a soft landing and it's not easy. Most of the rum or brandy that should have gone into the cake had clearly gone down her throat instead, because her cut-glass accent was decidedly slurred. I naturally felt slightly intimidated by the combination of Matron and a forceful upper-class lady, so was relieved when she said, 'Of course, I shall be going privately.' I phoned PNR, admitted her, found a private anaesthetist and listed her for bilateral Danis screws on Monday. Come Monday morning, at eight-thirty precisely, patient in anaesthetic room, Sister scrubbed up and ready, anaesthetist Johnnie Wheldon and me there, but no PNR. PNR was always punctual. I soon began panicking, for I was sure to get the blame. Had I forgotten something? Ten minutes passed. Furtive looks all round. Then, at eight-fifty am, the clanking of the lift down below, the welcome whirr of the electric motor, followed by the clunk as it arrived. What a relief! To our surprise, Jake Stanger poked his head around the theatre door.

'Mr Robson has the flu and has asked me to take over, and I'm not feeling very well myself,' he announced.

He changed, scrubbed up, came to the table, picked up the knife and put it down again.

'Sister,' he said. 'Can you arrange for some tea? I feel quite faint.'

At this he left. There was no alternative but to do the procedure myself. Quite straight-forward. Every time I tell this story I say I'm still waiting for the fee!

The aforementioned Tom Lind was renowned for an irreverent sense of humour. One requirement for the membership diploma in obstetrics was six months of general surgery and Tom was seconded to the Professorial unit. He was late for one of Brian Fleming's ward rounds on the female side, and as he dashed up the corridor he came across the ward maid's electrical floor sweeper, a device with handlebars and a large rotating brush on the end. Obviously with the intention of amusing the ladies, Tom trotted up the ward pushing this object, making the sound of a motorcycle, and as he reached Brian he made the 'engine' stutter to a stop and then cocked his leg over as if dismounting, all the while the patients giggling behind their hands. Brian remained unmoved.

'Lind, this is a ward, not a madhouse,' he said, maintaining his dignity.

'Oh, well in that case,' Tom replied, 'I've got the wrong place.'

He then started up his engine, cocked his leg over, about turned and disappeared off the ward.

When the Minister of Health visited the MRC Research Unit, which was led by Angus Thomson, Tom was urged to be present and look busy. As he peered down a microscope, the minister asked what he was doing.

'I'm learning to be a genius,' replied Tom.

Somewhat bemused, or amused, the minister asked what would happen should he not succeed.

'I'll be the best qualified idiot in the building,' was the almost unanswerable response.

# Chapter Two

# A Crash Course in Accidents

My next placement was Accident and Emergency. My colleague here was Eric Butchart, a year ahead of me, who became a cardiothoracic surgeon in Cardiff. We alternated duties. Of course, Friday and Saturday nights were the busiest of the week due to a mixture of drunken brawling, sporting injuries and domestic violence. The latter is exemplified by the instance when a wife with a bleeding scalp was accompanied by a sheepish-looking husband late on a Saturday night, the wife confiding to the person stitching her wound that hubby was responsible, only for the latter to present himself at 3am with a similar injury inflicted with a cricket bat wielded by the revengeful spouse. The Accident Room was the shop window of the hospital but also the Cinderella. When Eric and I were there, Hugh Brown had just been appointed as consultant in charge, but he was really a plastic surgeon whose main interest was hand surgery, until then a neglected sub-specialty dealt with by the general surgeons when they were emergencies. However, despite the comparative lack of major trauma, the post was a rewarding one for a surgical trainee. We saw a wide variety of cases and, apart from the GP, were the first point of contact, able to do a full assessment and responsible for the decision to admit or not. We became slick at minor surgery and helped Hugh with his more difficult hand cases. He had an extensive repertoire of filthy jokes, which seemed unusual for such a senior and dignified looking man, and although pleasant and cheerful when teaching us, he was a tough examiner in vivas. His anatomical knowledge served him in good stead, for at some stage in his career he met John Converse, chief plastic surgeon at New York University Medical Center, who asked him to conduct a two-week course in the subject at this institution, an arrangement that continued for several years. Converse was internationally famous and edited a seven-volume treatise on plastic surgery. In 1959 he was consulted by Hollywood heartthrob Gary Cooper, star of *High Noon* opposite the young Grace Kelly. After Cooper's death in 1961 Converse married the star's widow, Veronica, herself a former actress and socialite. With the combination of Converse's high earnings and Veronica's legacy, the couple lived in splendour in a penthouse duplex on Park Avenue, New York. Hugh delighted in describing his first visit there and how out of his depth he felt, especially on hearing his hostess telling someone on the telephone that an English guest was staying, and that someone was Jackie Kennedy. Converse seemed to mix capitalism with philanthropy. He made the bulk of his money from cosmetic surgery on the wealthy, such as film stars, but offered complex facial reconstructions that challenged his skills to patients who were poor. One example quoted was a small boy from Harlem who was savaged by a dog. As well as offering his services for free, he apparently paid the hospital charges also, otherwise the procedure would not have gone ahead.

***

I was only two months into the job when our first son, Michael, was born, on March 26th 1970. I dropped Mary off at the Princess Mary Maternity Hospital in the early hours and had fully expected to sit with her in the afternoon and at the birth. But life not being fair, Eric was indisposed by one of his infrequent, but severe, attacks of migraine and could not relieve me. By the time I arrived at the hospital after my shift Michael was already in the nursery (the customary practice of the time), having been born at 5.30pm, and Mary was still sleepy and confused after a large dose of pethidine. The resident anaesthetist, the late Ed Charlton, from the year above, saw me and showed me the nursery, where Michael was easy to spot. He had a shock of black hair and alone among his fellow neonates, it seemed to me, was moving his head from side to side, eyes wide open, as if he was adjusting his bearings, having clearly 'been here before', as the attending staff midwife observed.

Mary had tearfully left her position as staff midwife at Newcastle General Hospital only two weeks before. She intended to be a full-time mother to our children unless our financial situation prevented it, and she remained so until the early 1980s.

Here are a few reminiscences about my six months in A&E, where one of our colleagues, a senior house officer from the Sudan, was a chain-smoker, and as his first name was Mustapha, the nurses understandably nicknamed him Mustapha Fag.

I have not so far mentioned attempts at resuscitation following cardiac arrest. As students, we practised several methods of artificial respiration to be used in cases of drowning, but cardiac massage was not yet routine, becoming gradually so over the next few years. I cannot recall any attempts during my year as a houseman and, indeed, there was no such thing as a Crash trolley, now present on every ward, which possesses all the equipment, drugs and defibrillator for resuscitation. Coronary care units (CCUs) were introduced in the early sixties, and the one in the RVI in 1968. Professor Frank Pantridge of Belfast introduced an alternative form of emergency treatment in 1966, a 'coronary ambulance', in which a doctor and nurse drove to the patient and attempted to stabilise them before transfer to hospital. The one at the RVI was started by the cardiologist Dr Hewan Dewar and funded by donations. An old ambulance was purchased for £100 (!) and fitted out with the equipment. It was staffed and driven by volunteers and, except for Dr Dewar, all juniors, who slept in the hospital. One evening Dr Dewar got up to go to the toilet. A nurse who worked permanent night shifts and hence did not recognise him, mistook him for a confused patient and gently put an arm around his waist.

'Now then, pet,' she said. 'Where do you think you're going?'

The bewilderment of both parties continued until his identity was revealed. This episode created mirth around the hospital within hours, because Dr Dewar was a punctilious, stern, apparently humourless little man with a meticulously waxed moustache, and was the last person whom one would expect to see the funny side. I seem to recall from my friends who were involved that the most difficult task was driving the blessed ambulance, which had heavy steering and required double-declutching on changing gear.

One Saturday evening the ambulance was called to the Students' Union, very close to the RVI. I was on call in the Accident Room and a little later was told the resuscitation had been unsuccessful and the deceased was in the BID (Brought In Dead) room. I entered, unaccompanied, and there was the body of a handsome youth of nineteen, with almost shoulder-length blond hair. He had been electrocuted by an electric guitar. It was an eerie, discomfiting experience, going through the pockets of his still-warm body searching for identification, and even more so when I found he had listed his next of kin as his grandmother. My reaction was of profound sadness at the waste of such a young life, and also for the grief on the morrow suffered by Grandma, who even at this moment might have him in her thoughts in her ignorance of the tragedy.

On another busy evening a staff nurse walked briskly past and said quite abruptly and without stopping, 'See what you can do with that in room two.' The 'that' seemed somehow inappropriate, but within seconds I discovered why. On opening the door I was confronted with what looked like a brown, charred sculpture of a Buddha, sitting cross-legged on the couch, but with arms and fists up like those of a boxer. The strong, sickly smell of burnt flesh accompanied the sight. Firemen had retrieved the 'patient' at a house fire and the ambulance men dumped 'her' (it was a her, though not easily discernible) in room two, told a nurse, and beetled off, presumably because the victim was obviously dead. The so-called 'pugilist's position' is well known in cases of burns, caused by contracture of muscles and tendons.

***

An anxious mother dashed in just before noon with her toddler son in hand.

'He's swallowed a battleship,' she blurted out, creating temporary amusement among the staff.

She was ironing in the kitchen while the boy played with his Matchbox toys in the next room. Suddenly she heard him cough and choke and on rushing in found him blue in the face and gasping. After a sharp blow to the back he gulped and recovered. Panic over, she searched through the toys and was dismayed to find the battleship missing, so naturally she brought him to us. The little chap seemed fine, but clearly an x-ray was warranted. In those days, we in A&E could send patients for x-rays of bones, chest or abdomen, but the developed films would return with the patient, unreported by a radiologist. We could interpret the majority without help and decide on further management using our own judgement. We returned the x-rays to the department for a formal typewritten report to be sent back a day or two later, as a backup against a misdiagnosis. On this occasion I wrote on the request form, '?swallowed battleship'. When Mum returned with her offspring I could see a report in the transparent folder with the film. This was not the custom, but the radiologist obviously couldn't resist responding to my query, for the report said, 'Sorry, old chap, E-type Jag.' Such objects always look huge in a child, and mother nearly had a fit, but from its position one could see it had already left the stomach and would probably pass naturally. Unless the child developed abdominal pain, the mother simply had the unpleasant task of examining his stools for the next couple of days, and indeed he did pass it satisfactorily.

***

A sweet old lady in her eighties arrived with abdominal pain due to diverticulitis and was lying on the trolley in a lovely white nightie with lace collar and cuffs, quite comfortable. After introducing myself, I noticed on her particulars that she was a retired nurse and commented on the fact. With a quizzical smile she asked me who I thought had advised her to study nursing. Looking at her age and facial expression there was only one answer. It was indeed Florence Nightingale, who was a friend of the family.

***

A single man in his thirties was accompanied by his widowed mother, who was dressed up to the nines and could have doubled for the actress Patricia Routledge in the role of Hyacinth Bucket. In keeping with this comparison, she refused to let him get a word in edgeways. He was pale, thin, had long-standing diarrhoea and a palpable lump in his right lower abdomen. The history was weeks if not months, and I was pretty sure he had Crohn's disease, a chronic inflammatory disease of unknown cause. It can affect anywhere in the gastrointestinal tract but most commonly the small bowel where it joins the large bowel at the caecum, from which dangles the appendix. I arranged routine tests and admitted him to the surgical ward. About a week later I asked a colleague on the ward if my diagnosis had been confirmed. He said everyone had agreed with the clinical diagnosis, but further investigation revealed ileocaecal tuberculosis, a most unusual condition in the indigenous population. The few cases we saw were in immigrants from the Indian subcontinent. But this man's mother was especially protective, and mistakenly so, for she was obtaining her milk from the farm adjoining her house in a posh new private estate on the outskirts of Newcastle, before they sent the milk for pasteurisation. In those days a small number of herds were not tuberculin-tested; why, I do not know, but I remember this fact from my public health textbook. At least the condition was eminently treatable by combination drug therapy, unlike Crohn's, which can be unpredictable.

***

One Saturday night I got to my bed on the floor of a room adjoining the Accident Room at about 4am, only to be roused from a deep sleep by an excited porter shaking me.

'We've got a Newcastle United footballer in,' he said.

I reluctantly got up, still half asleep, and not in the best of tempers, and was shown to a Scotsman called Tony Green, a recent signing from Blackpool for £150,000, a princely sum then. Earlier in the day he had played in a home game in which he was particularly anxious to do well. However, not only had he performed indifferently, but a few days earlier he had sustained a cut ankle in training, which was stitched by the club doctor. He was invited to a party in the evening and being a little depressed about his performance, as well as feeling lonely because his family were still in Glasgow, he agreed to go to cheer himself up. The reason for his attendance was he could no longer tolerate the pain in the cut. As well as playing football he had been standing at the party and was not inebriated, having only had one or two drinks. The cut was directly over the medial malleolus, or ankle bone, a very tender spot, and it was badly infected; red, exquisitely tender and discharging profuse amounts of pus. The black silk stitches were large and crudely inserted. I was appalled and very sympathetic, especially as he wouldn't stop apologising. I was surprised he had been able or allowed to play—the slightest tap would have been agonising. I know times have changed, but this expensive professional footballer seemed to have been subjected to very amateurish treatment.

***

If there was ever any trouble due to drunkenness in the Accident Room, we usually found the police helpful and prompt in their response. This was in the days before hospital security staff. When I came on duty one Saturday night there was already a young man handcuffed to the base of the metal support of a cubicle, under the custody of two police constables, one a fiery redhead, the other a more laid-back man of dark hair. I no longer recall the prisoner's injuries, although they were certainly minor, nor the reason for his arrest, but he poured out a continuous torrent of obscenities aimed at his custodians, while I attended to patients in adjoining cubicles. The dark-haired copper took no notice, but I could see the redhead was restraining himself with difficulty. Eventually he could take it no longer and started beating the lad up, aiming all his punches to the body but without attempting to conceal his attack from onlookers by closing the curtain. After a short time his companion restrained him and he desisted. I felt embarrassed, partly because I felt I should have intervened—I thought it unlikely they would turn on me if I did so. But despite being a witness to 'police brutality', I had always been grateful to them in the past and to be honest, I thought the victim deserved a bit of softening up. After a short pause he started up again, and once more the redhead had a go, only to be held back by his mate. Finally, the invective rose to a crescendo and at long last, the dark one joined in.

One saw some curious things that defied explanation. For example, a middle-aged woman presented with a moist, smelly completely gangrenous middle finger, the infarction demarcating abruptly at the base. There was no evidence of vascular disease or source of an embolus, so the cause was a mystery, but the finger was dead and had to be amputated. To my amazement I found an elastic band, deeply embedded within tissue and invisible before operation, wound round several times and obviously applied intentionally to obtain the desired result. The woman's reaction was an unemotional, 'I wonder how that got there?' Her motive remained undiscovered, but she didn't seem at all upset at losing the finger.

In a similar vein, a pale, thin, obviously ill man attended as a casual patient. He had a long-standing high mid-thigh amputation as a result of an accident in youth. He revealed a massive, fungating cauliflower-like cancer of the penis, the most advanced I have ever seen. He maintained it had only recently appeared after he inadvertently trapped his penis when applying his artificial limb, a most ingenious lie. It had obviously been present for at least months, if not years. He was so thin one could feel enlarged lymph nodes in his pelvis. indicating widespread disease. I suspect he was either too embarrassed until forced to seek medical attention, or possibly mistook it for venereal disease, but it was a mystery why he delayed so long.

One of our night theatre sisters, who I had known for years, turned up with an ulcerating advanced cancer of the breast that she had kept to herself; a difficult task, I expect, especially for a married woman in her late forties.

Another strange case was a young man who said he had been to Philadelphia the previous week. While walking along, a car drove past that he thought had backfired, but simultaneously he felt a jolt in his shoulder. On returning to his hotel he found a bloodstain and narrow entry wound in the shirt and underlying skin. It beggars belief that he felt discomfort only, but he seemed sensible and plausible, and had come because he thought he had been shot. Sure enough, an x-ray showed a 0.22 slug in the shoulder, but whether the true story was given I never discovered.

***

In Newcastle we never saw gunshot wounds, apart from the occasional shotgun accident. Neither, in those days, did we see stab wounds, which are commonplace today. But Nick Batey, once my senior registrar, collected more than a hundred during a year in Glasgow and Greenock and published them in a paper in 1967. Sociologists and criminologists will have theories as to this geographic difference. The socioeconomic backgrounds were and remain similar, although the population of Glasgow is far bigger, and I seem to recall the city was renowned for razor gangs as long ago as the 1950s.

Perforated peptic ulcers were common. Usually, the victim suffered from indigestion, which became worse before the sudden perforation, when they would be felled by agonising upper abdominal pain. This rapidly became generalised, causing peritonitis and a board-like rigidity of the abdomen on examination. Occasionally, they would have few, or no, premonitory symptoms. I admitted one patient who was a Trident jet airliner pilot approaching to land at Newcastle Airport when he suddenly perforated. He handed over to his twenty-one-year-old co-pilot, who won his spurs and touched down safely. Another was an ex-paratrooper who had just left the army and was working as a navvy. He wandered into A&E quite casually but gave a classical history of a perforation. Puzzled, I asked him how bad the pain had been.

'Oh, quite bad,' he said. 'I had to lean on my shovel for a few minutes.'

It took considerable persuasion to get him to sit in a wheelchair and be pushed to x-ray—he felt humiliated. But sure enough, there was gas under the diaphragm, diagnostic of a perf, and he reluctantly agreed to be admitted for surgery.

***

A GP sent in a farmer who sustained a dislocated shoulder after the tailgate of a lorry dropped onto it. With the patient was a letter apologising for troubling us, 'But despite 20mg of morphine and 100mg of pethidine, I am unable to reduce the dislocation in the farmyard.' On the one hand this seemed to be an example of excellent family medicine, trying to treat the man on site without recourse to the hospital. On the other, despite the farmer being a large, muscular fellow, not only could that dose of opiates render him comatose, but without an x-ray one couldn't exclude the presence of a fracture as well as the dislocation. However, it seems invidious to criticise a man doing his best.

Another farmer owed his life to what the racing fraternity refer to as 'soft going'. He was working on his combined harvester when he dismounted to inspect the front underside. The continuous vibration of the engine shook the machine into gear, and it slowly rolled over him. Fortunately, the ground was so soft he was driven into it, and although he sustained a posterior dislocation of one hip, his pelvic organs were unscathed. Demonstrative of the stoicism typical of his type, his main concern was embarrassment because of the pressure sustained having evacuated the contents of his bowels into his trousers.

# Chapter Three

# Testing the Waters

M y next port of call was Urology at Newcastle General, where I spent six months as a registrar from August 1970 and February 1971. At its peak Newcastle General had more than 1,000 beds. It began as a workhouse in 1839 and a hospital was added in 1870. It was known as the Wingrove Hospital, this name persisting with locals in my time. Further wards were added in 1902, one of which was for 'Itch and Venereal', later becoming the Department of Prostatic Surgery, the forerunner of the Department of Urology. The complex was renamed Newcastle General Hospital in 1930.

No surgery was performed there until 1922. In 1927, WEM Wardill was appointed to the staff as a general surgeon. His initial interest was in plastic surgery, and cleft palates in particular, but for some reason he switched to prostatic surgery, specifically transurethral resection, in which the prostate gland is chipped away piecemeal via the penis, rather than removed by the abdominal route. In 1938 he visited Gershom Thompson at the Mayo Clinic, Rochester, Minnesota, and returned with a 'cold punch' resectoscope. With this instrument, the prostate gland was resected using a cylindrical steel knife blade and bleeding was stopped by spot coagulation using a diathermy electrode. This technique started to replace removing the enlarged prostate through the abdomen, except for the largest glands, significantly reducing the operative mortality from about fifteen per cent to just 1.5 per cent. Wardill was enthusiastically supported by the local medical officer of health in creating the new Department of Prostatic Surgery and was soon performing 250 resections annually, with few open procedures. The main problem was the operative technique was difficult to learn, and although the 'cold punch' was potentially less dangerous than the 'hot loop', so named because it was heated by electrical diathermy, Thompson himself said that 'to put a resectoscope in the hands of a man who is not prepared to study its use is like giving a sub-machine gun to a small boy who has been reading Deadwood Dick.'

In 1948, with the introduction of the NHS, Wardill retired and emigrated to South Africa. I presume he had not reached the usual retirement age because I heard his decision was an impulsive one, accompanied by, 'I'm not going to be dictated to by bloody miners.' Retrospectively, I wonder if it was prompted by AJ Cronin's novel *The Citadel*, which had a major influence on the perception of medicine and was based on his real-life experience as a doctor in a Welsh mining community. Wardill was succeeded by John Swinney, a Newcastle graduate with a Military Cross from the Second World War, who had been practising urology in New Mexico. In view of the wider interest of the department beyond the prostate, it was renamed the Regional Centre for Urological Surgery. Keith Yeates joined Swinney in 1951. Another twenty-six beds were situated fifteen miles away at Shotley Bridge.

During my six months as a rotating registrar I worked for Swinney, who now had a personal chair, and Yeates, both of whom I liked and admired, and I owe them a lot. They were very different personalities. Swinney was the elder by about eight years and officially the head of department. He had pleasant, rounded features, with twinkling eyes, plump red cheeks and was friendly and courteous and often smiling. But the smile could be misleading—if flushing of the back of the neck accompanied it, you knew to watch out for trouble. He had the nickname 'Smiling Tiger', created no doubt by those who had the misfortune to cross him. He was clearly a dominant personality, but not overbearingly. He was simply firm in his views and reluctant to take no for an answer. He had a somewhat mannered walk because of his inability to fully extend one elbow as the result of an accident. He was a fast, skilful surgeon who could do a total removal of the bladder (cystectomy) for cancer, and ileal conduit (implantation of the ureters into a loop of small bowel brought to the skin surface to replace the bladder) in an hour and a half. The following day, however, the patient looked as if they had had an operation. He got on well with the nursing staff (one sister revered him after he performed an ileal conduit on her for some form of congenital incontinence). He had a sense of humour, and there was mutual respect and loyalty.

Keith Yeates was similarly pleasant, but more introverted and cerebral. He had angular features, sleeked silver hair and walked with a slight stoop. He was softly spoken, often appeared shy and hid his light under a bushel because he was a highly cultured man who thought long and hard about everything. In keeping with this side of his personality he was a slow, careful surgeon, who seemed to caress the tissues. Unlike his colleague he would take four hours to do the same cystectomy operation, but the following day the patient would be sitting up in bed with colour in his cheeks and reading the newspaper as if nothing had happened. But his tardiness could be irritating—I remember him taking forty-five minutes to do a cystoscopy on a private patient and this was one reason the theatre sister, a small, rodent-faced harridan, could be cold and abrupt with him, whereas she worshipped Swinney.

How times change! The secretaries had a communal room but as head of department, Professor Swinney used the one remaining spare room as his personal office. If Keith Yeates wanted to do any work in the department, such as dictating letters or assessing publications when he was editor of the *British Journal of Urology*, he had to use a consulting room in the outpatient clinic. This state of affairs continued until the move to the new ninety-bed unit at the Freeman Hospital in 1978. His lack of an office came to mind in January 2010 when an Asian assistant director of nursing won £300,000 in damages from the North Cumbria NHS Trust in a racial discrimination case because she didn't have a desk. And yet Yeates was a man who had an international reputation in urology, with invitations from several countries to be a visiting professor.

Newcastle General was on an oval-shaped site, with the nondescript Urology block halfway along on the western side. A large central ward block contained Casualty. The only modern building was the Regional Neurosciences block. Opened in 1962, it cost £330,000. Although I confess to bias, the contrast between this and our building was stark. In urology we worked extremely long hours, getting through an enormous volume of cases, in cramped conditions. One crossed the short distance to Neurosciences to find a fat, arrogant neuroradiologist in pinstriped trousers and red braces, swanning about on his mobile stool in a huge room, scooting from one end to the other and pointing out a series of x-rays on a screen. And yet, at the risk of offending all my ex-colleagues in the neurosciences, if one had closed down the department, one would hardly have noticed the overall impact on the wellbeing of the population. Of course, this is a grossly unfair, reactionary view, but is frequently expressed by others also, no doubt in envy at the disproportionate influence wielded by the specialty.

***

At some stage during this first six months I sat the Final FRCS examination with three others, George Bone and Mike Black from my year and Michael Burke of the year above. The exam was in two parts. One could take the written papers in Sheffield, with the clinicals and vivas in London. Taffy Jones, one of the senior surgeons in the RVI, was a former chairman of the board of examiners and 'kindly' agreed to grill us on examination technique, especially with regard to the operative surgery viva. I add the quotation marks because Taff was a tough character who possessed fearsome bristly eyebrows that were threateningly mobile, and he made us sweat. But it was all for our benefit and at least we knew what to expect. I was never a student of his nor worked for him, so knew him only by reputation. There were several tales of his ferocity. He once blasted a registrar off the ward and told him never to darken the portals again, and the next we knew the poor chap was in general practice.

On one teaching round he asked a student to present his patient.

'This is Mr Cockburn, sir,' said the lad, pronouncing the surname as it is spelled.

Taff exploded.

'It's not *Cockburn*, it's *Co-burn*—have you never heard of *Cockburn's* Port?' (omitting to pronounce the 'ck' component).

'No, sir.'

'Well, it's *Co-burn*.'

Then, turning to the patient, he asked, 'How do you pronounce your name?'

'*Cockburn*, Mr Jones,' came the reply.

Taff grunted, paused and told the student to continue.

'This is Mr Cockburn, sir, and he complains of pain on passing his water.'

The pass rate for the Final FRCS was about fifteen per cent. We were all reasonably content about the written papers—at least nobody felt they were a disaster. The clinicals and vivas were a different proposition. The four of us being called on the same day was ominous. Statistically, it seemed unlikely we would all pass.

The clinical exam was in Queen Square, near the National Hospital for Nervous Diseases, Great Ormond Street (known as GOSH, or simply 'sick kids'), and the Italian Hospital. The patients were volunteers, almost professionals, and this counted to my advantage. My patient, for whom I was allocated about half an hour, was a tiny man, a friendly, garrulous Cockney. He knew his history backwards and I hardly needed to ask any leading questions. The poor chap had suffered from ulcerative colitis for many years, culminating in removal of his colon but preservation of the rectum and the small bowel joined to it. Such a procedure was controversial even then but was championed by a surgeon at the old Westminster Hospital. It prevented an artificial anus, or ileostomy, and the wearing of a bag. But ulcerative colitis is a contiguous disease of the large bowel, and although the rectum may sometimes appear relatively spared, it is always involved. Not only may symptoms persist, but the condition is premalignant. My patient had, indeed, later developed cancer of the rectum, which required its removal, so he ended up with an ileostomy after all. To complicate matters further he got a large perineal hernia through where his bottom had been closed off, the only one I have ever seen. When he stood up this hernia containing his bladder dropped down, so that the only way he could pass urine was to elevate the whole shebang with one hand and aim his penis with the other. Quite a performance. But he was uncomplaining, and glad to be alive. I was relieved because I knew enough about ulcerative colitis. With a few minutes left I asked if he had any other problems, and he said his left hand sometimes became cold. I had already taken his pulse from the right and so went round to his left side, where all the pulses in his arm were absent. He was a skinny little man and above his collar bone I easily felt a bony cervical rib. These extra ribs, above the usual first rib, occur in about one in two hundred of the population and can compress the artery in the neck, eventually causing it to clot off. This is usually gradual and often with surprisingly few symptoms, but it can present as an emergency with a threat to the limb. He must have seen the look of triumph on my face, because he wagged his finger as if talking to a naughty schoolboy.

'You would have missed that—you're always told to examine both sides,' he said.

But I could tell he was just as pleased as I was.

As expected, the examiners concentrated on his main problem, but they also asked if I had found anything else and seemed pleased about the cervical rib. Months later I encountered someone who had been examined on the same patient and was dismayed to find his examiners quickly swept away the colitis and roughed him up about the cervical rib, which he had missed.

No matter how much one knows, there's always an element of luck. One of the best surgeons I knew, Roger Allsopp, two years ahead of me in Newcastle, passed at the third attempt, somewhat to his surprise, having been disappointed to see the same set of examiners on this final occasion as he had faced on the two previous ones. Roger became a consultant in Guernsey, where he took up sea-swimming as a relaxation. At sixty-five he swam the Channel for charity, becoming the oldest Briton to do so. As he drank the traditional pint in the pub at Dover afterwards, he noticed among all the names chalked on a blackboard, the name and age of an American, the then oldest person to succeed. Thus stimulated into a further attempt, when he was seventy he broke the record, raising £750,000 for charity, including £250,000 from a single donor (Guernsey has some wealthy residents). I was dismayed to see how little national recognition this remarkable achievement received in the media. A South African heart surgeon named Otto Thaning now holds the record.

Speaking of luck, there is a well-known story about an examiner called Sir Stanford Cade. He was a Russian Jew whose father was a diamond merchant in St Petersburg and who Anglicised his name from Kadinski. As well as being a surgeon he was a pioneer radiotherapist and had a reputation as a stern, tough examiner. One young man had failed the FRCS a few times and attributed his lack of success to having repeatedly faced Cade. It was said that unsuccessful candidates with a grievance could express their concerns to the college and request them to be addressed if deemed to be valid. This particular chap had done so and asked not to be examined by Cade in the future. In fact, candidates were known only to the examiners as a number. Apparently, he received a reply to the effect that the college was prepared to abide by his request but should point out that on investigating his case, Sir Stanford was the only examiner who had passed him!

***

The surgical pathology and operative surgery vivas were held in the nearby Royal College of Surgeons in Lincoln's Inn Fields. The former centred around preserved specimens, some of which were ancient. The first one shown to me by a somewhat irritable examiner looked like an upturned mushroom in a glass case, partly obscured by floating debris, like a child's snow globe. It turned out to be a nineteenth-century guillotine amputation, the stem of the mushroom being bone and the cap being a disc of parchment-like skin. Fortunately, he moved onto other things.

What irritated all four of us was that on entering the men's toilets in the college basement before going upstairs to face our ordeal, we found a large porcelain receptacle placed centrally away from the urinals and surrounded by ice cubes. A notice propped up against it said: 'Examination candidates please urinate here.' The cheeky so-and-sos were collecting urine to measure catecholamines (adrenaline and noradrenaline) which, being stress hormones, should be raised in such as us. We felt this was a sadistic intrusion on our dignity and repaid it by peeing on the ice cubes.

For the operative surgery two examiners took turns, but separately. The first went well, but the second was Professor Tony Harding Rains, who asked me about oesophagectomy for cancer. After my description he asked what I would do if a few days postoperatively the patient showed signs of a major leak at the anastomosis. Rightly or wrongly, we were advised by our seniors not to give various options, which might indicate indecisiveness, but to state our treatment of choice and take things from there. I said I would re-explore the chest, refresh and redo the join. He leant back and paused.

'Are you really trying to tell me, that in a seriously ill patient, you are going to re-operate?'

I realised I had to stick to my guns, so replied that if one didn't do so the patient would certainly die. Once again, he leant back, and after what seemed a long time, but was probably only seconds, said, 'I think I would agree with you there.' What a relief!
I only came across Professor Harding Rains once again, a few years later, at a meeting of the Surgical Research Society. The brand-new Charing Cross Hospital had just been opened and a group of us were shown round. The hospital was ground-breaking for the UK, with a foyer containing a florist, bank and shops. It was extensively cubicalised, a major move away from Nightingale wards, with a novel system of demonstrating where every nurse was. There was a swimming pool for staff. The operating theatres had a tiered gallery of black leather seats above a glass ceiling so operations could be observed (impressive, but useless as it turned out). Professor Harding Rains proudly showed us the research facilities in the department of surgery. It was lunchtime, with fewer people around. He opened each door in turn, explaining the function of each room, pointing out the various pieces of apparatus and positively beaming at his good fortune in acquiring such a no-expenses-spared unit. He relished the complimentary remarks of senior members of the group, one of whom was a Scottish transplant surgeon. Finally, he opened a door, everyone peered in, and a sight straight out of one of the Doctor or Carry On films greeted us. A senior registrar, in white coat with upturned collar, was sitting on a rotating chair behind a desk. On his lap, with her arms around his neck, was the pretty blonde secretary to whom the chair belonged. Both gave a shy smile, and Professor Harding Rains closed the door without a word and set off down the corridor. After a few seconds the Scotsman piped up. 'Is that available on the NHS as well, Professor Rains?' he asked. No reply.

Anyway, we all passed. Our numbers were read out and we were immediately invited to shake hands with the examiners in an adjoining room. I arrived home and went to bed at about 1am, inadvertently waking Mary. I recall lying on my back looking up at the ceiling and saying I had just taken the last exam in my life. My mind went back to the many occasions at Hymers when I had gazed in assembly at the gilt letters of JH Farbstein FRCS on the black honours board and wondered whether those letters would ever appear after my name. They would now, but despite my pride, I felt a fraud, knowing I was not really a surgeon at only twenty-eight. That would take years yet.

Weeks later my diploma arrived, signed by the president and council of the college, most of them distinguished surgeons of national and international repute. I cannot forgive the late Rex Lawrie, of Guy's Hospital, for leaving his florid signature in vulgar, felt-tipped pen, a blot on the manuscript. I didn't attend the ceremony in London. When I tentatively suggested it, Professor Swinney knocked it on the head.

'Oh, you don't want to go to that.'

***

Urology largely consisted of diseases of the prostate (hence the large disparity in male:female bed ratio), stones (calculi) of the urinary tract, tumours of the bladder and, to a lesser extent, of the kidney.As well as routine examination of the patient and microscopic and bacteriological examination of the urine, the two commonest investigations were intravenous pyelogram (IVP) and cystoscopy (visual inspection of the bladder using an illuminated telescope), usually under general anaesthesia as an outpatient.

An IVP is an x-ray of the drainage system of the kidneys. An intravenous injection of an iodine-based liquid enters the bloodstream and is excreted by the kidneys. The iodine component, being radio-opaque, shows up the pelvis (upper drainage part) of the kidneys, ureters and bladder in white against the black background of the x-ray plate. Normally, excretion is rapid, and films are taken at intervals of five, ten and fifteen minutes. Delayed films may be required if there is obstruction or renal dysfunction.

Kidney stones are quite common but rarely cause symptoms unless they leave the kidney and block the ureter, the narrow muscular tube leading from the kidney to the bladder, in which case they cause renal colic, a most excruciating pain passing from loin to groin, making the victim roll around in agony. Around ninety-five per cent of such stones are radio-opaque and hence are revealed on a plain x-ray, but other calcifications are common in adults and can mislead, so an IVP that would outline any stone and show any degree of obstruction, if present, was routinely requested. Nowadays, an ultrasound scan is the first investigation as it is non-invasive, cheaper, gives no radiation dose and prevents the occasional allergy to iodine, which could cause an alarming drop in blood pressure. But this was not available in 1970. Fortunately, despite the agony of renal colic, most stones pass naturally. Bladder stones are now rare in the UK but were common until the nineteenth century and still are in some countries, especially in the Middle East.

The second most useful investigation was cystoscopy. There were lists of these every day, all under general anaesthesia. Several types of cystoscope were available, but the department favoured the Braasch scope. This was the simplest and offered direct vision (most other types produced an inverted image). It was a hollow metal tube, curved at the tip, with a glass lens system and a tiny electric light bulb. The lubricated scope was passed along the urethra to the bladder, which was filled with fluid to enable visual inspection. The fluid was sterile glycine, a simple amino acid, which was stored in a large overhead tank. An electrolyte solution such as saline could not be used if diathermy was required (it dissipates the current), and water becomes absorbed if used for long periods, such as in prostatic resection requiring several instillations and evacuations, causing haemodilution, which can be dangerous.

In charge of the cystoscopy unit was Jack Dodds, a middle-aged ex-naval man, who, as one would expect, kept it shipshape. Like Mac in orthopaedics, he called all doctors 'sir', presumably a relic of his naval years, but unlike Mac, he seemed more sincere. He was a hyperactive, fast-talking Geordie. If a light bulb expired during a cystoscopy, either a replacement was immediately inserted, or a different instrument supplied. He treated complex urological instruments like a young girl would her dolls, and this extended to the resectoscopes in the main theatre, to which he had been transferred when I returned to the department as a senior registrar. In his book *Transurethral Resection*, the late, internationally renowned urologist John Blandy states that, 'Ideally the surgeon should look after these instruments himself. The next best thing is to entrust them to a theatre technician with a natural propensity for gadgets—talent rare enough in men, and almost unheard of in women. Since theatre personnel are often female it is often better for the surgeon to look after instruments himself. A telescope snatched up roughly by a pretty blonde with a Cheatle's forceps or pushed firmly into its metal box for sterilisation may be ruined beyond repair.' A somewhat sexist statement. Luckily for us we had Jack Dodds, but this good fortune was relatively short-lived because of implementation of the *Salmon Report*. This document recommended restructuring of the nursing profession, which up to this time was hierarchical, with strict discipline and control from above by matron and ward sisters. However, there was little nursing feedback to management and the profession understandably felt neglected. With advances in medicine came increased specialisation and the extended role of the nurse. In some respects the *Salmon Report* provided increased status to senior nurses, by whom it was generally welcomed. It was unpopular with the medical profession, who felt the skills and dedication of the ward sisters, with whom they worked closely, were being overlooked. The role of matron was abolished to be replaced by a chief nursing officer, reporting to management, cascading down primary nursing officer, senior nursing officer, nursing officer and finally ward sister/charge nurse. It was a disaster in every respect bar one—it enabled a time-server to reduce their work and increase their salary and pension, but it seemed to the outsider to give someone a fancy job title without a job description. Why on earth do we have a system in which a successful businessman who knows nothing about the subject can submit a report with such profound effects? Is it because the NHS is funded by taxpayers, and its employees are perceived as self-interested and biased and hence an outsider must be employed to counter such views? Anyway, people like Jack were in an invidious situation. He loved and excelled at his job, but he was middle-aged and here was a chance to improve his salary and pension. If he didn't apply, the post would go to someone younger, who might try to make life difficult for him. So within a few weeks Jack was seen wandering around the hospital in a new uniform—a long white coat with navy blue epaulettes—furiously fiddling with a string of 'worry beads' in one hand and carrying a clipboard in the other. Whenever I bumped into him it was always, 'I don't know what I'm supposed to be doing.' The same happened to a wonderful orthopaedic sister who revelled in the crucial role she played in joint replacement surgery. But as a widow with three teenage children to support, the decision to change roles was a no-brainer, to use modern parlance. There must be many others who had to create roles for themselves, each in their own way, but who were perceived as either interfering busybodies or just another tier of devolving the raft of personal (and personnel!) problems that nursing, like any other high stress occupation, produces.

Keith Yeates said John Swinney ran the department like a family business. The atmosphere was so happy that between my two stints there, firstly in 1970 and later as a senior registrar in 1976-77, the nursing and secretarial staff barely changed. As a registrar I became adept at cystoscopies, open prostatectomies and ureterolithotomies (removal of stones from the ureter), but use of the punch resectoscope was reserved for career urologists. There was a policy of resecting prostates of up to, say thirty grams, as estimated by rectal examination, and treating those above this weight by open operation. This was purely a pragmatic decision, based on a balance between the time and skills available. These days open prostatectomies are relatively uncommon.

John Swinney assisted me at my first nephrectomy (surgical removal of a kidney), on a fifteen-year-old girl. After ligating the renal artery with number one black silk, I was about to place a second one when he stopped me.

'A surgeon must be able to trust his knots, David,' he said.

I slept fitfully for about five days afterwards from the anticipatory anxiety of a phone call informing me the girl had suddenly collapsed into shock from blood loss as the vital ligature slipped. If only he had allowed me to place what the late surgeon Lord Moynihan of Leeds referred to as his 'hypnotic stitch' I would have felt much better.

***

There were no housemen in the department and we registrars had to do all the routine ward work, such as blood tests, cross matching, clerking of patients and when on call for the wards, injections for the IVPs. Since an IVP took only fifteen-to-twenty minutes, and there were two x-ray rooms, we were up and down like yo-yos from ward to ground floor all day, being interrupted from clerking patients except for a quiet hour between one and two in the afternoon when the radiographers had lunch. I vividly remember darting around one particularly busy day when a pretty blonde staff nurse, Kath Tyrrell, asked me to come to a cubicle. She looked anxious and I thought a patient had a problem, but on opening the door, it was empty. There, on the bed table, was a tray with a main course and a fruit salad.

'Get that down you,' she said, then she smiled and left.

One night an emergency was transferred from South Shields with retention of urine caused by an enormous prostate. I was allowed to operate on the case and was amazed to feel what seemed like a baby's head on rectal examination. I felt very proud of myself when I enucleated what turned out to weigh 250 grams, which I thought must be a record. JS smiled and brought me down gently by saying he removed one of a kilogram in Egypt during the war! We also had a man of twenty-six who developed retention of urine on a mountain, due to an enlarged prostate. He was the youngest JS had ever seen.

An old man attended for dilatation of his stricture. By coincidence the Prof was passing as I showed the patient into the room for the procedure and he took me aside.

'I'll do this, David,' he said. 'He has a long-standing and particularly difficult stricture. He's a nasty piece of work and would think nothing of suing you if anything went wrong, but he can't sue a Professor of Urology.'

If a stricture is roughly or unskilfully dilated, a so-called false passage can be created. This must have occurred in the past, or he had persistently neglected himself, for he had the multiple scars behind the scrotum of the only 'watering can' perineum I have seen. The Prof managed satisfactorily and then he and the old man got into conversation as he was shown out of the door. The man was profoundly deaf and on account of this had a very loud voice. Outside the room was the outpatient waiting area, which was full to overflowing. Just as we emerged, he called out—in a Yorkshire accent, not Geordie—for all to hear.

'Aa've nivver been the same since that teacher stuck his cock up me arse when aa were eight.'

Swinney gave that little smile of his, but the back of his neck turned red, indicating the widespread embarrassment we all felt.

We occasionally saw the red neck on pre-operative ward rounds. One thing Swinney couldn't stand was when haematuria (blood in the urine) was not taken seriously by GPs. Several times when men with cancer of the bladder were admitted for treatment and asked when their symptoms first appeared, the reply would be a year of more ago, but the doctor had given them some red and black capsules (the antibiotic ampicillin) and the blood had cleared up, only to reappear more recently. JS would smile sweetly, but the neck reddened, indicative of inner fury. Haematuria should always be investigated, especially when painless and total (that is, throughout the stream) and not assumed to be a 'water infection'. The only possible exception is what used to be called 'honeymoon cystitis' in a young woman experiencing sexual activity for the first time. What once was a well-used term is now meaningless, with modern sexual mores. I stressed this point once when Keith Yeates asked me to give a talk to GPs at a weekly postgraduate session. In the front row one of them was lolling about with both arms outstretched on the leather headrests behind him.

'Young man, are you really trying to tell me I should refer every patient of mine with haematuria to you?' he drawled in an overbearing manner.

'Yes,' I replied.

'We would swamp you,' he countered.

Unfortunately, I did not have the presence of mind to react as I should have, by challenging him and his colleagues to indeed swamp us, saying the service would respond accordingly. Too often, GPs felt they should act as gatekeepers and play the lottery with patients, relying on chance and statistics favouring a trivial cause for most symptoms. It was a pity Keith Hodgkin's book was not compulsory reading in those days. It demonstrates the relative frequencies of serious disease in the undifferentiated cases in general practice.

I once saw a young lady who gave a history of a dreadful sore throat followed a few weeks later by a single episode of haematuria. She was only twenty-two and had a raised antistreptococcal titre in the blood. It seemed likely she had a post-streptococcal glomerulonephritis (inflammation of the kidneys). Nevertheless, I proceeded to cystoscopy, and believe it or not she had a small papilloma of the bladder. One would not expect to find a papilloma in one so young, but the lesson is to always carry out the correct investigation.

The senior house officer at the satellite urology unit at Shotley Bridge was a chap called Peter Losev, who was often seconded to our department. Peter was a huge man, probably six-foot-five inches, and broad with it. He had a dark complexion and Brylcreemed black hair. Facially, he looked like a younger version of Silvio Berlusconi, the late former prime minister of Italy, and he was much older than most senior house officers, probably in his early forties. His claim to fame, or so he told us, was that he had played in goal for Czechoslovakia, which was still under communist rule then. At some stage he entered Holland, where his wife still resided, and he obtained Dutch citizenship. He gave away very little else, but I have no reason to doubt his story. Peter was a great character with a wicked sense of humour and was popular with the nurses. During his time at Shotley he was lonely in residence and approached the local amateur football club. The following week, the headline in the sports page of the local newspaper was, 'Consett sign international keeper'. It was quite true, even though he was a man now in his forties!

A month or so before Christmas, John Swinney did a second stage urethroplasty on a boy of about fifteen and the Prof wanted him kept in hospital until he was healed and his catheter removed. This took several weeks. As Christmas approached, the boy was helping the nurses decorate the ward by painting various Disney characters on the windows. I was doing a ward round and after I admired his artistic ability, the staff nurse whispered, out of earshot, that the nurses all thought he was what would now be referred to as gay, because he seemed so effeminate, something that had passed me by. Coincidentally, he called me back and mentioned he was puzzled that since being in hospital he hadn't needed to shave.

The penny dropped and I quickly grabbed his medicine chart to discover he had been taking Stilboestrol for five weeks. This is a synthetic oestrogen and was given routinely for a few days in men having operations on the penis to prevent painful uncontrolled erections postoperatively. In this young man's case we had forgotten to stop it.

The week before Christmas a man was transferred from St George's Hospital, Morpeth, for investigation of haematuria. He was in his mid-sixties and had been a patient in this long-stay institution for the mentally ill since he was a young man. His accompanying notes gave no clue as to the reason for his prolonged stay. Infuriatingly, the only medical, as opposed to nursing, documentation for recent years was an annual recording of ISQ (*in status quo*), that is, unchanged, labelling his 'condition'. To my surprise, I could have a perfectly normal conversation with him (this statement might make some of my more cynical friends smile, but I aim to be serious). He described his symptoms clearly, discussed the news and knew who the prime minister was. In fact, I felt embarrassed asking such questions. I asked if he could play the harmonica that was on his bed table and he entertained the ward with a few carols, in keeping with the festive season. The only sign of any mental aberration I could detect was that when discussing his family history he believed his father was still fighting on the Western Front. Otherwise, nothing. I'm sure in different times and under different conditions this poor man could have led a fulfilling life. By now it was too late—he was totally institutionalised. He seemed content enough, but what a waste.

A few months after I left urology following this first placement, Prof Swinney surprised everyone by retiring at the age of sixty. He was presented with an oil painting of the department by the local ex-pitman artist, Norman Cornish, which was specially commissioned by Keith Yeates. His retirement was prompted by his eldest son's move to farm in Bunbury, Western Australia. Having recently established a renal transplant service with Ross Taylor, upon whom the leadership now fell, he rapidly grew bored in Australia and offered to do the same for Perth. His son's farming venture having either failed or been unsatisfactory in some other respect, both returned to the UK. Prof Swinney finally retired to Banffshire, where he died in 1988. I last saw him in 1984 at the 150th anniversary of the founding of the medical school, when he remembered me, and we had a good chat. He is yet another man whom I think of with affection and gratitude and who had a big influence on me.

***

Although my next job was in general surgery, I returned to urology as a rotating senior registrar for one year from February 1976 and it seems appropriate to continue my experience in this specialty despite being out of chronological sequence. I had been a senior registrar for eighteen months with Dickinson and McNeill, who had a subspecialty interest in vascular surgery. Usually, one was expected to do at least two years as a senior registrar to reach the requirements to offer oneself as a subspecialist in a particular field. However, I had already spent three years on the unit at varying degrees of seniority and the Professor of Surgery, Ivan Johnston, felt I was becoming 'typecast', and suggested a move to urology. I never knew whether the professor's recommendations for my career moves were for my benefit or for that of others, but he was a dominant personality, and I agreed, although Peter Dickinson was not happy.

When I came home on my first day I told Mary I'd made the biggest mistake of my life (I was not referring to my marriage to her, I hasten to add). Even though I had thoroughly enjoyed my time there as a registrar, I was initially depressed at moving from the bright, airy RVI to this cramped old building. In fact, it turned out to be one of the most thrilling years of my training so far.

After his retirement, John Swinney was replaced by Reg Hall, but being the new incumbent he was 'sent' to Shotley Bridge, to await the opening of the brand new, larger unit at the Freeman Hospital in 1978. David Essenhigh moved from Shotley to join Keith Yeates at Newcastle General. His move proved a boon to me because he used the 'hot loop' for prostatic resections. This was a potentially more dangerous instrument than the 'cold punch' but easier to learn to use. With the advent of fibre optics it could have been made even easier by the use of a teaching attachment through which the consultant could see and guide the operator's movements, but it was deemed too expensive. British short-termism as usual.

During my year I was in the operating theatre for two and a half days a week, with two cystoscopy clinics in addition. I carried out more than 1,000 cystoscopies, about 250 open prostatectomies, and the same number of transurethral resections, exactly twenty-five nephrectomies, plus six radical nephrectomies for cancer and six ileal conduits for incontinence, plus an uncounted number of ureterolithotomies for stones. At the end of the year I was a confident and accomplished surgeon (and modest, as always) and was undecided whether to apply for the career senior registrar post vacated by Keith Baxby. But urology was rapidly becoming a specialty in its own right. I enjoyed old-fashioned general surgery and could not foresee vascular surgery becoming a career specialty in the immediate future, so I opted not to apply. Although I did not use a resectoscope again, I have never regretted my urological experience. Later, at Middlesbrough, which was a subregional centre for the specialty, I did several radical nephrectomies for cancer. In the early years, the urologists did not directly admit emergencies and were content for me to do open prostatectomies on patients with retention and ureterolithotomies for stones. The huge operative load I undertook also gave me a confidence boost.

David Essenhigh was an ideal chief. He was quiet, casual and never seemed to be in a hurry. He was clearly upper class (I believe his father was a High Court judge). He spoke in a refined way, was very bright and looked the part, having an extremely high forehead, almost like those of Dan Dare's archenemies, the Mekon, extending up to a bald pate, with residual curly brown hair at the edges. He was no snob, got along well with the nurses, among whom he had his favourites, and he had a good sense of humour. His main attribute from the training was he would let us senior registrars operate on more or less what we liked but never neglected us, either personally assisting us or sitting in the theatre anteroom for help or advice as required. Every now and then he would tell us to have a rest and he would do the next case. He was one of the few consultants who behaved in this way. As registrars we were expected to learn operative surgery by observing the consultant, and operating only under the guidance of the senior registrar. But on acquiring the then hallowed status of senior registrar, we suddenly and mysteriously became competent and were usually left to our own devices when the consultant finished the early cases of the day. Hence the somewhat cynical but widespread surgical maxim of the times, 'See one, do one, teach one.'

Because of its reputation, the department attracted doctors from overseas and else-where. One was Ian Jenkins, who was in the Royal Navy and at the end of his first day asked me to show him the hospital bar—as if we had such a thing! Ian was a protégé of Norman Blacklock, surgeon to HM the Queen, and who was nicknamed 'Hemlock' by the Duke of Edinburgh. Ian rose to the rank of vice admiral and also became well-known to the Queen, accompanying her on various state visits. Sadly, he died suddenly in his sixties in 2009. At the time he held the ancient role of Constable and Governor of Windsor Castle, which includes a residence in the Round Tower. The Queen took the unusual step of ordering the flag of the tower to be lowered to half-mast as a mark of respect. Another was a Libyan who was recalled back home at his government's expense simply to listen to one of Colonel Gaddafi's interminably long speeches being delivered in the open air, after which he could return to us.

Keith Yeates gave a dinner party to welcome another, a Brazilian with an elegant wife. As their home was in Rio, I asked if they took part in the famous Mardi Gras, a question that was received with almost speechless horror, followed by an embarrassed, stuttered reply in the negative, adding that they merely 'observed'. I realised they were very upper-class Brazilians, who watched the peasants cavorting down below from the safety of their apartment balcony, occasionally showing a royal wave of appreciation. It was at this event Keith showed us his Lowry. He also had an early book by Thomas Bewick, which he described as being 'before the bar'. Bewick produced endplates of detailed but tiny rustic scenes at intervals in his books, and this one showed a peasant woman squatting down in a field to have a pee, the urinary stream being visible if one looked carefully. Understandably, this was considered *très risqué* in the eighteenth century and Bewick had to insert a five-barred gate in the next edition, one bar of which now obscured the stream, but not the buttocks. Hence, before the bar.

One morning Keith pounced on me as I entered the department. At this early hour he had been called to see a man in Casualty who insisted on a private consultation. Keith was required in London at the office of the *British Journal of Urology*, of which he was editor, and asked me to deal with the patient. The story was that the man, who came from Belfast, had been apprehended by 'the boys' (the IRA) in a pub, taken to a back alley, knocked unconscious and when he woke up had an excruciating pain in the penis and bladder, made worse by attempted micturition which produced only a few drops of blood. He concluded that something had been rammed up his urethra, presumably as a warning, and took himself off to Belfast Airport to escape, with the first domestic flight available being to Newcastle. Keith did not believe a word of it, concluding that the man had instrumented himself for sexual gratification, perhaps a bizarre thought to the man in the street, but something we occasionally saw. In fact John Swinney kept a tin box containing objects he had removed from urethras or bladders over the years. Indeed, it was amazing that the male urethra appeared to possess the power of deglutition (the process of swallowing) under certain conditions. I once saw a man who had inserted electrical insulating wire up the urethra (I know exactly what any male reader is doing now). As luck would have it, the wire looped and knotted itself within the bladder so that he could not extract it and was forced to come to hospital, to his eternal embarrassment. No wonder the ancient Greeks believed the gods toyed with the lives of earth dwellers. Anyway, Keith said the Irish patient found rectal examination exquisitely painful and a plain x-ray showed a small spring above the pubis, so I was asked to cystoscope him and take things from there.

On doing so I immediately observed a hexagonal cylindrical object impacted in the bed of the prostate. No wonder it was so painful. After washing out some turbid, blood-stained urine, some letters were visible on the object. I gave a running commentary to the theatre staff, spelling out each letter as I could see them—'L...A...D...'—and the anaesthetist yelled out 'Ladbrokes!' Sure enough, it was a ballpoint pen embossed with 'Ladbrokes the Bookmaker'. It proved impossible to disimpact, so I had to resort to opening the bladder from above to retrieve it. A high price to pay for a sexual perversion, but perhaps not if his story was true. We never did find out.

David Essenhigh developed an interest in urinary incontinence, not the most glamorous of subjects, but a most valuable one if steps could be taken to relieve such a distressing condition, which is so common in the elderly. He was involved in the new study of so-called urodynamics, measuring abnormal motility and pressures in the bladder, and consequently received frequent requests from the geriatricians (more prosaically called elderly care doctors these days) to see patients on their wards. One winter's evening he asked me to see one on his behalf. I wandered across the dark grounds and entered the separate geriatric block, brightly lit but temporarily abandoned by staff. It was after the evening meal and not one patient appeared to be awake, most either with chins on chest or open-mouthed with heads tilted back. And yet there were four large television sets, one for each wall, fixed on brackets at a height, all at full volume, showing *University Challenge*, with Bamber Gascoigne yelling, 'Your starter for ten is...'

One Friday afternoon I was chatting to David Essenhigh near the entrance—he, as usual, smoking a cigarette—when one of the general surgeons, John McCollum, appeared with his houseman. McCollum was a somewhat eccentric character, a strict Ulster Protestant, tall and erect, white-haired and formal in both bearing and manner. He had some old-fashioned ideas. For example, he had an aversion to antibiotics and hardly used them (there is, of course, a tendency to overuse them, but his attitude was unrealistic) and he did not acknowledge the existence of Crohn's disease.

'Ah, Mr Essenhigh,' McCollum said, drawing himself to his full height and in his still strong Ulster brogue.

'I'm pleased to have caught you. *We* have done a vasectomy [the *we* accentuated as if it was a joint enterprise of some importance]. However, my young colleague here tells me that before the man can resume, er, conjugal relations with his good lady, his semen must be tested before he can be considered sterile. Is that correct?'

Essenhigh confirmed he was correct in his assumption.

'Ah, then tell me Mr Essenhigh, how do we do this?'

'Well, he submits two specimens, one at six weeks and one at twelve weeks.'

'Yes, I understand, but how does he obtain these specimens, Mr Essenhigh? Does he have relations with his good lady using one of these condom things?'

'Oh no, he can't do that. Condoms contain a spermicidal that would kill off any live sperms.'

'Well, how does he produce them?'

'He brings them to the lab in a glass pot, but they must be fairly fresh, within ninety minutes of producing them.'

'But how does he produce them?'

Essenhigh eventually twigged.

'He masturbates.'

McCollum gave a deep sigh.

'I feared as much. Good day to you, Mr Essenhigh.'

Essenhigh smiled, drew one last puff on his cigarette and flicked it away.

'Just as well I didn't tell him he wanks!'

# Chapter Four

# A Year in Theatre Main

In February 1971 I began my year in general surgery on the rotation. As the registrar, I was attached mostly to Ian McNeill, with the senior registrar Nick Batey working closely with Peter Dickinson, Peter D. Ian was widely read and his main interest outside surgery was collecting scientific instruments and antiques. He introduced me to the Gillies needle holder, an instrument that combined insertion of stitches with cutting of the same, dispensing with the need for an assistant to do the latter. Ian was influenced by Fenton Braithwaite, the senior plastic surgeon in the RVI, who Ian described as 'a wizard with the knife'—a compliment indeed, coming from such a neat, skilful surgeon. He was also artistic and incorporated accurate drawings of his major vascular operations in the medical notes. I well remember his sayings, such as, 'The greatest gift one can give a child is to inculcate the habit of reading.' It is the word 'inculcate' that I like. Or, regarding John Buchan, 'He was a terrible snob, but my goodness, he could tell a tale.' He once said to me, probably referring to my excessive knowledge of trivia, 'Dave, you'll addle your brain one of these days.' It was similar to Peter D's remark of, 'Dave, you're a mine of useless information'—possibly an appropriate title for this memoir.

Ian seemed such a gentle soul that I was surprised to find he sometimes went shooting, and I expressed this view. He replied in a soft voice that on a winter's day, with the sun low in the sky and with a shotgun under the arm, 'man is a born killer'. One Monday he told me he was out of favour with Jane, his only child, explaining that at the weekend his preparation for a lecture had been disturbed by the persistent cooing of a collared dove in the garden and he had gone for his gun.

'You didn't shoot it, did you?' I said, surprised.

'Not only did I shoot it,' he replied, calmly, 'but I plucked it, cooked it, and I ate it.'

Just as when I was a houseman, the unit functioned as a happy family, with Peter D and Mac having joint ward rounds and joshing with one another. Peter D was so confident in his skin that he would often defer jokingly to Mac's superior intellect, referring to himself as a simple surgeon who would fail to get a place at medical school now, as his qualifications would not be good enough. It was like saying Roger Bannister would not make a modern national athletics team. They welcomed students and junior staff and were keen teachers. They were happy days, fondly remembered. Peter D taught the principles of surgery to dental students, mischievously stating that he took the subject seriously because it was the only one that elevated Dentistry to degree level rather than a City and Guilds course!

Mac had been a heavy smoker as a young man, and he continued to struggle against the habit. Amusingly, at coffee breaks he would often sit sucking an empty pipe. He eventually died of lung cancer shortly before his eightieth birthday.

The most dramatic emergency we saw was ruptured abdominal aortic aneurysm (AAA, or, in modern parlance, a triple A). Immediate operation was (and is) necessary to save life, but patients often collapse during induction of anaesthesia, when the abdominal muscles relax. Together with his anaesthetist colleague, Alistair MacKenzie, and a research registrar, Geoff Lewis, Mac was testing a so-called G-suit in which the patient was placed before induction. The suit consisted of a large transparent plastic bag, oblong in shape, inserted behind the patient, wrapped around and fastened in front by Velcro and additional reinforcing straps and inflated to a pressure of thirty-to-forty millimetres of mercury (mmHg). The upper part was at about nipple level and the lower at mid-calf. I never understood the physics, but it seemed that a concentrically applied pressure of only thirty mmHg could suppress bleeding from an aorta at, say, 120 mmHg. Obviously, the suit had to be released at some stage, but the intention was to apply it as soon as the diagnosis was made, buying time to prepare theatre, get blood cross-matched and, more importantly, anaesthesia induced, with the operating team scrubbed up ready to pounce. Blood was never transfused until the patient was either in a G-suit or the aorta clamped, because even modest transfusion could provoke a leak by raising the blood pressure. Applying the aortic clamp was the crucial step, not easy because the already released blood and swelling often spreads throughout the back wall of the peritoneum, making the anatomy difficult to discern. Suffice to say, the G-suit became widely used, but in a somewhat more sophisticated form, with separate abdominal and leg components. As a registrar, the only vascular operations I was allowed to do were the femoral anastomosis in aortofemoral grafts, and embolectomies, either of the brachial or femoral arteries, usually under local anaesthesia, using the ingenious Fogarty catheter, a simple device consisting of a thin tube with an inflatable balloon at the tip with which to extract the embolus. Although simple in conception, it revolutionised the treatment of emboli and took the technology of the plastics industry to manufacture such a delicate, disposable device. Embolectomy was one of the most satisfying operations to do—essentially one was saving a limb—and it seemed more satisfying then than now. A significant number were in relatively young patients with atrial fibrillation caused by mitral stenosis, the narrowing of the valve following rheumatic fever in childhood. Such patients are now all dead and although rheumatic fever is caused by bacterial infection with streptococci and the organism is widespread, causing sore throats etcetera, the condition itself seems to have disappeared. Now, most emboli are seen almost exclusively in elderly, unfit people, whose arteries are already diseased with atheroma, and in whom distal thrombosis rapidly occurs, so that complete extraction is more difficult to achieve, with often a less satisfying result. Atrial fibrillation is an irregularity of the heart in which the upper chambers, or atria, beat out of sequence and more rapidly than the ventricles, or lower chambers, leading to turbidity of flow and hence predisposition to clotting. It occurs in about ten percent of people over the age of seventy.

I was always first on call on reception nights (when we admitted emergencies) and slept in, but I was usually covered by Nick and as time progressed was able to disturb him less. Perforated ulcers were common, and one night we received a woman of about twenty-one with a classical history and findings and with air under the diaphragm on x-ray. However, she looked too well, and despite having short, gasping breaths due to pain, she could smile. Also, there was no history of preceding dyspepsia, which was unusual, but not exclusive. Fortunately for her, despite presumably causing her considerable embarrassment, she avoided surgery by volunteering that the pain had commenced suddenly shortly after having vigorous intercourse with her boyfriend in the knee-chest position from the rear. Presumably, with vaginal dilatation, air had been driven up and passed into the peritoneal cavity via the fallopian tubes. Certainly, her pain and tenderness disappeared overnight with simple analgesics and she could go home. I have not seen a similar case since.

Other common emergencies were for intestinal obstruction, both small bowel, due usually to adhesions following previous surgery, and large bowel, due to cancer. We admitted a Pakistani waiter once who had small bowel obstruction but no previous abdominal surgery. At operation the small bowel was cocooned by multiple adhesions, characteristic of old tuberculosis, and packed from top to bottom with undigested rice. All we had to do to relieve the situation was to painstakingly milk the contents into the large bowel for evacuation.

One of the strangest experiences I ever had occurred on Boxing Day. I was on reception with the senior house officer, a Norwegian called Geir Grotte, later a cardiac surgeon at Manchester Royal Infirmary. I was contacted by a houseman from another firm and asked to complete part two of a cremation certificate. The doctor who signed the death certificate filled in part one, but part two had to be completed by a different doctor who had been on the medical register for a minimum of five years. It was usually someone from the same firm, but I was the only one who could be found on the bank holiday who was qualified to sign. It was a legal requirement to view the body of the deceased, so I wandered off to the mortuary, having obtained the key from the head porter's office. However many dead bodies one has seen, there's still something unnerving about entering a morgue alone. Naturally, to use the obvious cliché, it's as quiet as the grave and stone cold. A large book told me which of the several numbered metal receptacles contained the body I wanted. I withdrew it smoothly along its wheeled, grooved support, unfolded the shroud, checked the identification, and replaced it. I then left the area where the bodies were kept through an arch into the post-mortem room. I must have been looking at the form and I lost my balance and stumbled backwards into an obstruction I hadn't noticed, but my fall was halted by me sitting down on a soft, cold object. When I turned round quickly in surprise, a white sheet was dislodged to reveal the body of a morbidly obese woman sitting in an armchair, whose lap had broken my fall. My immediate reaction was a mixture of disbelief, fear and then amusement, but I quickly replaced the sheet and shot out of the morgue faster than you can say, to use another cliché. I'm not sure whether Geir believed me when I returned, somewhat breathless, unstable, but certainly over the years that I have told this story, I get the same slightly amused look of, 'Yeah, pull the other one!' But it is perfectly true. We only rarely saw the degree of obesity commonplace today and clearly she would not fit in one of the standard containers. The only other person of similar size I recall was a thirty-five stone man with appendicitis, whom we had to provide with a double bed obtained from God knows where.

A sad event concerned a Sudanese doctor who joined us for an attachment, initially as an observer. He claimed to have vast experience back home and resented somewhat the necessity for him to be restricted to the role of observer. One Sunday he approached me in the Accident Room requesting some pethidine for a friend of his, a fellow Sudanese doctor, supposedly suffering from renal colic and flying back home that day. I explained it was out of the question to supply this drug on behalf of a person unknown and offered to see the patient. Despite his persistence I held firm, and he went away disconsolate. Flo James, a sister on the Accident Room, and a friend, overheard the conversation and in private confided that he had been trying to obtain pethidine from someone else the previous week. I had a word with Mac, who contacted the physician acting as a conduit for the young man's sponsor in Sudan. I suspect the physician in question took no action, but shortly afterwards the chap was arrested. He had been purchasing morphine and pethidine from a pharmacy in central Newcastle. Because he could prove his medical qualifications, his written prescriptions were valid, and his initial story of acting as a locum in general practice was plausible, so the pharmacist complied until the frequency of the requests made him suspicious and he informed the police. The doctor received a suspended sentence provided he agreed to receive treatment for drug addiction. He was recalled to Sudan, but he could not bear the shame and committed suicide. With the benefit of hindsight, his frequent short absences from theatre were explained, as were the pinpoint pupils which some maintain they had seen, but I confess I never observed this telltale sign.

# Chapter Five

# Hearts...

In February 1972 I sadly left the RVI and the Dickinson-McNeill firm to embark upon the final stage of the rotation, cardiothoracic surgery at Shotley Bridge, a village in County Durham close to Consett, which had a thriving steel industry. The hospital was a collection of single-storey buildings in attractive grounds maintained by gardeners. The separate cardiothoracic unit had been there since 1941.

The unit had been created and led by George Mason, who in 1950 performed the North-East's first operation for mitral stenosis, a mitral valvotomy, and one of the first in the UK. This was a so-called 'closed' operation (that is, it did not involve bypass on the heart-lung machine, which was first used at Shotley in 1960). The surgeon entered the beating heart through an incision in the left atrium and dilated the valve with a finger. Mason was joined by Selwyn Griffin (Peter Dickinson's brother-in-law) in 1947, and in 1951 by William Corbett Barnsley, who confined himself to thoracic surgery. In 1947 the wonderful Dr (Edith) Joan Millar was appointed as the first full-time cardiovascular anaesthetist.

In his excellent short book *The Story of Cardiology in Newcastle,* Hewan Dewar (who died in 2013, just short of his 100th birthday) writes in his usual pithy but astringent manner about George Mason, and I summarise: 'He had immense drive, gave great attention to detail, and could rely on selfless support from his medical and nursing staff. Yet often he did not see his patients before their operations, his ward rounds were infrequent, and he did not personally follow up his patients afterwards.'

As well as mitral valvotomies, other closed operations were performed for congenital heart disease, such as ligation of patent ductus arteriosus, pulmonary valvotomy and shunt procedures for the Tetralogy of Fallot ('blue babies'). These included the

Blalock-Taussig and Potts' operations, and many such patients survived long enough to undergo total correction of their congenital abnormalities using cardiopulmonary bypass long after Mason's retirement. Nevertheless, his success rate began falling behind others in the UK and, according to Dewar, partly because of this and partly because of a clash of personalities between Mason and his colleagues, who found him increasingly difficult to work with, Seaham Hall was upgraded to enable open-heart surgery and both Griffin and Ray Dobson moved there in 1961. Joan Millar wouldn't hear a word said against Mason, always loyal to the end.

Seaham Hall came into possession of the 3rd Marquess of Londonderry on his marriage to the heiress Lady Frances Vane-Tempest and Lord Byron was married there in 1815. It became a hospital in the Great War and remained so until 1978, when all cardiothoracic surgery moved to the new Freeman Hospital in October 1977. It is now a luxury hotel and spa.

As yet another digression, the same 3rd Marquess commissioned the famous Newcastle architect, John Dobson, to build the town and harbour of Seaham, which up to then had been a tiny village, and eventually three collieries were created, Vane-Tempest, Dawdon and Seaham (all closed by 1992). One of the several Londonderry homes was Wynyard Hall, just north of Stockton-on-Tees. The grandfather of my mother-in-law, Rhoda Lack (nee Umpleby), was a tenant farmer on the Wynyard estate, and Rhoda told Mary and I that one Sunday he was tending his pigs when Lord Londonderry passed by, accompanied by a tall, blond, distinguished-looking gentleman. Granddad Umpleby tipped his forelock in deference to his master, and both stopped to admire the pigs, the Marquess's companion showing a particular interest in them, before they continued their walk. The blond stranger was no other than Joachim von Ribbentrop, the German Ambassador to Great Britain. At the time I thought this was an unlikely tale, but I now know that the 7th Marquess, Charles Vane-Tempest-Stewart, who was Secretary of State for Air between 1936 and 1938, was a well-known Nazi sympathiser who met Hitler and entertained Nazi foreign minister Von Ribbentrop both at Wynyard and his London residence. In fact, I recently read that his nickname during the war was "the Londonderry Herr". His wife apparently had a close relationship with Ramsay Macdonald, who was MP for Seaham. In a delicious irony, the Wynyard Hall and estate were purchased by Sir John Hall, who made his fortune from the Metrocentre near Gateshead and is himself the son of a miner. When Lady Annabel Goldsmith (nee Vane-Tempest-Stewart) a daughter of the 8th Marquess, was asked in an interview if she ever returned to the family home in County

Durham, she replied, 'Oh no, people like Kevin Keegan live there now!' (Part of the estate is now an upmarket gated housing complex where the entrepreneur Duncan Bannatyne also once resided). How the worm has turned!

George Mason retired in 1966, the year I qualified, and I only saw him once, when he gave a lecture. Years later, however, I did meet his widow who had an operation by Peter D when I was his senior registrar. Joan Millar gave the anaesthetic, subsequently taking Mrs Mason back to her own home to convalesce. Her address was the Red House, Wooler, in north Northumberland. George had the custom of telephoning the staff as he was about to set off in his Rolls (apparently he had a private income) and asking them to start opening the chest of the first patient, the distance between the two places being about forty-five miles. Years later, in 1979, when I was a locum consultant in the RVI, I had a patient who was a gamekeeper and whose address was that of the Masons. I mentioned the fact, still being under the impression it had always been the family home, and my surprise at it being so far away from the place of work of a surgeon.

'Well, you know why he lived there don't you?' he said. 'A grateful patient gave it to him!'

This business of the assistant opening and closing the chest for his consultant reminds me of the tale of when King George VI had his thoracotomy for cancer of the lung in 1951. The operating surgeon, Sir Clement Price Thomas, was assisted by his senior registrar, and after completing the procedure apparently told the senior registrar, 'Close,' and turned away from the table.

'But Sir Clement,' protested the senior registrar. 'This is the King of England.'

'Precisely,' replied the Knight of the Realm. 'I haven't closed a chest in twenty-five years and I'm not going to start practising on the King!'

And he left.

Mason was replaced by Ary Blesovsky, a South African of Ashkenazi Jewish background, who qualified at Cape Town. I believe he was in the same year as Christiaan Barnard, who carried out the world's first heart transplant in 1967. 'Bles', as he was always known, was a perfectionist. He was a senior registrar in London at Barts, the National Heart Hospital and the Brompton and worked for Lord Russell Brock. Bles obtained excellent results and attracted the same selfless dedication from the anaesthetists—Joan Millar especially, and also Derek Pearson and the nursing staff—as had George Mason. The team developed their skills with the heart-lung machine by carrying out surgery on dogs, probably to train the perfusionists who operated it. Joan Millar slept in the unit to give the dogs intensive care, arguing there was little point in doing the procedure well unless one carried it through. The nursing staff in both the theatre and the cardiac intensive care unit always impressed me because they all came from the small catchment area close to the hospital and yet were highly skilled and worth their weight in gold. A trip to Newcastle seemed to them almost an adventure, usually reserved for shopping at Christmas.

Bles was very good with relatives. Patients came from all over the North-East and Cumbria, so a Portakabin was provided for relatives to stay overnight, and he kept them fully informed about the progress of their kin. However, from the junior medical staff point of view, he was a nightmare to work for. Whether it was his innate degree of perfectionism or the stress of being a single-handed cardiac surgeon doing pioneering work in what seemed geographically an outback I know not, but every single day he yelled at us in the theatre. When I visited the unit and spoke to people the day before I joined, I was asked whether I was starting on the 'Heart' side or the 'Lung' side (the rotating registrar did three months on each). I replied the former and several people independently said, 'Let it all go above you', with no further explanation. None was necessary because I had already been warned, but it filled me with trepidation. At the first operation the following morning I hoped to be broken in gently, but the permanent registrar had been up all night and did not report on time, so the senior registrar, Bob Lawson, started opening the chest by median sternotomy in preparation for a coronary artery bypass graft (CABG) and asked me to harvest the long saphenous vein in the leg, used as the graft. The dissection was similar to that required for varicose vein surgery, so I was competent to do it satisfactorily, but Bles entered the theatre and started shouting and screaming at me not to damage the vein. It was like this for the next three months. Fortunately, Bob was a pillar of strength. A human dynamo, he was tall, straight, calm, an Edinburgh graduate with the soft accent of his Highlands' birthplace and typical dry Scottish humour. Bles never yelled at him. I followed Bob around like a lapdog and he taught me a lot. He, his wife and four children lived close to the hospital. He ended up as a consultant in Manchester but regrettably, I never saw him again after I left Shotley and he died suddenly of pneumonia in January 2017, just before his seventy-ninth birthday.

Although that first operation was a CABG, we did not do many of these, now the commonest open-heart procedure. There were still plenty of mitral valves to replace, post-rheumatic by causation, as well as aortic valves for calcific stenosis, a condition of unknown cause, usually in elderly men in whom as well as breathlessness it can lead to sudden death. Such operations took most of a morning and we only did the one daily. They were transferred to the six-bedded intensive care unit, routinely on a ventilator for at least twenty-four hours, and the heart was supported by a combination of isoprenaline and an alpha-blocker, phenoxybenzamine, which causes vasodilation and a low blood pressure if the circulation is not adequately filled, the theory being that the heart prefers to pump against a low peripheral resistance than a high one. The other problem with Bles was he had no small talk. He was always calm and softly spoken on ward rounds, but at the end he would simply turn, say, 'Thank you, gentlemen', and leave. He taught on a weekly x-ray session but once again was cold and clinical. And yet not only did I respect him for his skill and dedication, but I also actually liked him. But I hated the shouting. Bob was such a good role model that I flirted with the idea of being a cardiothoracic surgeon, but I don't think I could have worked for any length of time with the sort of atmosphere I experienced. With a few exceptions I gained the impression that whereas everyone else realises that the heart is a very efficient and beautifully designed pump, cardiac surgeons still believe it is the seat of the soul and behave accordingly.

***

We did one night a week on call and one weekend in four. I hated the weekends—Mary drove me and Michael the forty-five-minutes from our home in Wideopen to Shotley on a Saturday morning in our Fiat 600 and picked me up again on Monday night. No elective surgery was done at weekends, so the patients in intensive care unit were usually stable, but there were lots of beds to cover, and one had to be a bit of a cardiologist as well as a surgeon, certainly in terms of management of arrhythmias. There was an Indian cardiac registrar, and a consultant, Ron Gold, an Australian from the Royal Adelaide, but both had onerous on-call duties and one was reluctant to trouble them unless absolutely necessary.

The intensive care unit nurses were excellent. On the weekday on-call, one slept in a room in the short corridor beside the unit. In the event of a cardiac arrest, fortunately infrequent, by the time one pulled on one's trousers and reached the main room, they had usually defibrillated the patient when possible. This was before the time of the so-called 'extended role of the nurse', when nurse specialists were trained up to perform certain tasks usually undertaken by doctors, but they already played this role informally and simply regarded it as part of the job. They did not neglect basic nursing care, to which they paid meticulous attention in every aspect, the sisters always taking part and not confining themselves to delegation and recording of observations.

Joan Millar retained a youthful figure even in her sixties and carried herself with the elegance of a well-bred woman. She brightened up every theatre when she appeared. She spoke with a refined voice, known as received pronunciation (RP), a term virtually unknown today and from a time when elocution lessons were *de rigueur* and once typified by BBC announcers. She referred to Shotley as 'the clinic' and amused me by occasionally asking if I had been 'up to town' recently, by which she meant London. When I once mentioned that even if I could afford it, I wouldn't send my children to boarding school, she announced, 'Nonsense, David. I was sent away at eight and it never did me any harm.' I was shattered when I heard, during my sojourn to the USA in 1978, that she had died suddenly in the Freeman Hospital, where she was still working aged sixty-eight. She was asthmatic and I understand she was found collapsed in a lift. It was concluded she had suffered a cardiac arrest due to overuse of an inhaler. I suspect she was the type of person who would have wished to die in harness, but it is a pity she was denied a lengthy retirement. The selfless devotion of people such as Joan seems increasingly rare in our modern, materialistic society.

The heart valves used for replacement in 1972 were of the Starr-Edwards type. These consisted of metal struts covered with Dacron cloth and either a metal or Silastic ball, movement of which was easily heard with a stethoscope and sometimes even without! They were reliable but patients had to take anticoagulants to prevent the increased risk of thrombosis and a small number developed anaemia because the ball damaged red blood cells, causing them to haemolyse. These valves were later replaced by porcine xenografts (pig skin), but they tended to leak eventually and require renewal ten or more years afterwards, although anticoagulants with their potential complications were avoided.

The unit had a connection with Columbia dating from the time of one of Mason's trainees, a surgeon from that country, together with his wife and baby daughter, arrived one Monday to take up a post. I had been up both the previous two nights, so Bles excused me from theatre and asked me to greet our new colleague, Nelson Giraldo, which proved an interesting experience. Nelson was a short, squat individual, in his early thirties, with the complexion and appearance of an Indigenous South American. His wife, of lighter complexion and jet-black hair, was gorgeous, holding a baby in a lovely long, draping lace shawl—a touching sight. They arrived in the UK only that morning, via Heathrow, train to Durham and taxi to Shotley. Fortunately, they were provided with a decent flat by the hospital. Having previously worked in major centres in the USA, Nelson must have been bemused at this rural setting, with its collection of single-storey buildings. We went into Consett first to register him as an 'alien', a painless procedure carried out by a pleasant police constable who seemed delighted to be performing such an unusual task. Nelson needed provisions but had to obtain some sterling currency first and we entered the nearest bank. When I asked if my new colleague could exchange some US dollars for pounds I was overheard, and Nelson and I became a novel diversion as everyone looked on. It seemed to be an unusual request met with obvious pleasure by the clerk, who enquired as to the amount.

'About fi hunderd dollar,' replied Nelson, which was met with open-mouthed surprise by the onlookers, transformed into amused astonishment when he dramatically hitched up a trouser leg and withdrew a great wad of notes tucked into his sock. Not a frequent sight in Consett! Next, the provisions. Having been used to American supermarkets with their pristine, seemingly identical, almost factory-made fruits and vegetables, here was a mishmash of bruised, irregular produce, with a stained floor that had not been cleaned recently, and a shop assistant who appeared to have made herself up on purpose for today's role—blue eye-shadow, mascara and scarlet lipstick, which, regrettably, was smudged at each corner, making her resemble Jack Nicholson's Joker in the later Batman film. Nelson made no adverse comment, taking it in his stride and probably forgetting, whereas the experience is almost as vivid to me now as it was then.

Nelson settled in well and expressed surprise at the quality of the work produced in such an environment. Shortly after his arrival he accompanied a few of us one Friday evening to the local pub, taking advantage of an unusually quiet period. He had now encountered Bles's shoutiness and expressed the view that as a South African he was colour prejudiced.

'Yes,' Eric Butchart responded, 'he's prejudiced against the whites!' Nelson then re-alised he was simply receiving the same treatment as the rest of us. A year or two later Nelson sent Eric a postcard stating he and his wife were expecting another baby—'made in Niagara Falls'!

***

The main cardiac theatre was closed for a week each year for maintenance, during which the senior registrar and career registrar had to take part of their holiday, leaving only Bles and me. There were still a few patients who did not yet justify valve replacement but would benefit from mitral valvotomy, and they were operated on this week. It would have been enough of an ordeal acting as sole assistant to Bles for the procedure, but he insisted on doing one himself and then assisting me for the second. I presume he regarded this as an act of kindness, but frankly I would have rather done without it. By the end I was a nervous wreck. Still, I can always say I've done one.

Some patients develop an element of brain damage following open-heart surgery, attributed to the heart-lung machine. During bypass the flow is non-pulsatile, and in my day micro-bubbles of air had been detected by ultrasound and it was felt these may be responsible. I do not know the current theory, but such damage was not easily detectable in most patients, being more obvious at the extremes of age, or if an operation was unduly prolonged. For example, a young woman with Fallot's tetralogy came for total correction, having had a palliative shunt procedure as a baby. She was reasonably well but could not run and wanted to be able to do so. At operation the arteriovenous anastomoses in the bronchial arteries were massive and the procedure was technically exacting. I was on the 'lung' side at the time, so was not involved. It took nineteen hours, but she never recovered from a coma and was eventually declared brain dead.

Similarly, a boy under five had a total correction for the same condition. All went well and he was pink and serene postoperatively but remained in a coma for days. His parents, devout Christians, almost apologetically asked if some water obtained from the River Jordan by a friend on holiday in the Holy Land could be placed under his bed. Obviously, there was no objection to such a request, and on the third day the little boy opened his eyes and three weeks later appeared completely normal.

During my months at Shotley I bumped into a chap in the year below me who I had known in the RVI. He was now registrar to a physician who was an alcoholic. It seems unbelievable now, but his consultant was said to be often drunk on ward rounds and on one occasion fell over a patient's bed. All hearsay—I only met the man once. My acquaintance, who I will call Chris, was a slim, fast-talking individual, who was clever, but regrettably, like his boss, overindulged in the demon drink, although only when off-duty. I saw him one Saturday when I was on call and he said he was looking forward to a party in the residence that evening. At 2am I was awakened by my bleep emitting the rapid bird-like notes indicative of a cardiac arrest and on dialling 333 was told it was in Casualty, where I found the permanent staff, including a cardiology registrar, attempting resuscitation on a fully clothed man on the floor. My presence was only required to take turns at external cardiac massage. Suddenly, the male nurse exclaimed, 'It's Chris!' Sure enough it was, but in all the rush I had not noticed. The only visible injury was a cut alongside one ear, but he had crashed his car when he should not have been driving. Resuscitation proved futile, and thus ended the life of a young man who would have had a bright future.

# Chapter Six

# ...and Lungs

It was a relief after three months to move across to the 'Lung' side, with its much more relaxed atmosphere. The consultant was Mr William Corbett Barnsley, a much-loved and almost legendary figure, known always as Corbett. His route to surgery was circuitous. He won the Infectious Diseases prize as a student and hence channelled himself in this direction after qualification. Tuberculosis was the most feared infectious disease, but pre-streptomycin the only treatment offered was rest, fresh air or some form of surgery. Most TB cases affected the lungs, and the commonest surgical procedures were to 'rest' the affected lung either by collapsing the ribs, a so-called thoracoplasty, or temporary paralysis of the diaphragm on one side by crushing the phrenic nerve. These operations have been defunct since the advent of anti-tuberculous drugs, but some cases of bronchiectasis (chronic infection of parts of a lung), as well as the after-effects of pneumonia such as empyema or lung abscess, were treated surgically. By the 1970s, the bulk of the work was composed of cancer of the lung and of the oesophagus (gullet).

Corbett wasn't cut out to be a surgeon, if that doesn't sound too incongruous. In fact, his FRCS was honorary; he never passed the exam. He wasn't manually dextrous and his eyesight was poor, but these drawbacks were counterbalanced by enormous experience and a desire to always do the best for a patient, or 'give him his chance', a frequent expression he used. His family were ships' chandlers in Tyne Dock, a small community just east of Jarrow, and he told me that as a boy, 'I was the only lad in the street wot wore proper boots.' He still retained his broad Geordie accent, was of average height but hunched, balding with grey hair, had thick lenses to his glasses and dressed in a scruffy, baggy suit. He walked with a swift shuffle, his myopia giving him an air of bewilderment as he shifted his gaze. He was a chain-smoker of Capstan cigarettes, going through about sixty a day. His teeth were stained brown, but every Monday they appeared to be paler, presumably as the result of an application of smokers' tooth powder at the weekend, only to return to their usual state as the week progressed, and his nylon shirts were peppered with tiny brown-ringed holes where hot ash had fallen. He smoked wherever he could, the exceptions being on ward rounds and the operating theatre, and even in the latter he usually scrubbed up with a cigarette in his mouth, the procedure concluded by a senior sister plucking the fag end from his mouth before pulling up and tying his mask. In fact, this was the only task I ever saw this sister perform, although she wandered around trying to look occupied. Shotley was conducive to smoking because the cardio block had a long, sloping corridor and the buildings were separated by attractive floral garden plots. One ward at the margin of the hospital was called Woodlands and was occupied by patients with advanced lung cancer who were recovering from surgery, receiving palliative therapy or dying. Naturally, it was a depressing place, but in a pleasant setting. The nursing staff here were permanent, presumably by choice. Magpies were frequent visitors to the grounds and if one was spotted a nurse would groan, 'Oh, we're going to have a death today', from the ancient saying about this bird—'One for sorrow, two for joy'. But, of course, they had a death most days.

Every so often someone would ask Corbett what he thought about the connection between smoking and lung cancer. Quick as a flash he would reply, 'I think asbestos is very important'—end of conversation. In fact, asbestos is implicated as a cause of lung cancer, but was better known as a potent cause of the less common, but much more lethal tumour of mesothelioma, which involves the surrounding coverings of the lungs, the pleura, often involving the ribs and diaphragm as well. Corbett sometimes did the procedure of pleuropneumonectomy on such patients, not because it offered a cure—it didn't—but because it could relieve the intense pain associated with the condition. He once told us about a father and son who worked at the Washington asbestos factory.

'The father got it [meaning mesothelioma], the son got it and then the wife got it, and all she did was wash their overalls.'

Ron Gold, the Australian cardiologist, came into the coffee room one frosty morning and sat down.

'I'm going to have to find an excuse to speak to Corbett about a patient, and I don't know how,' he said.

After waiting for the natural response, he replied he had just bumped into Corbett on his way to Woodlands, who had asked his opinion about a patient and had proceeded to outline the case. As usual Corbett was smoking and, like many habitual smokers, he could manoeuvre a cigarette around his mouth and speak without removing it with his fingers. Unfortunately, Ron became transfixed by a drop of mucus on the end of Corbett's nose, which slowly lengthened as the cigarette shortened. Ron was hoping that if the timing was right, the drop would extinguish the fag with a hiss. Consequently, when this failed to happen and he recovered from his trance-like state, he could not remember a word that had been said.

I am convinced Corbett could have defeated the panel on the old TV show *What's My Line*. Nobody who saw or heard him would ever have guessed he was a consultant thoracic surgeon. He had a perforated eardrum and on the infrequent occasions when he used a stethoscope, he inserted only one earpiece. One new junior, unaware of this, thought the other earpiece had slipped out and twanged it back in, only for Corbett to take off like a rocket from his sitting position.

He had an amazing memory, which was even more remarkable when one considers that almost all his patients suffered from the same condition, but he could usually remember which part of which lung he had removed. He relied on his juniors to convey details to patients, but Bob Lawson had a tactful word with him about informed consent and he agreed to partake personally. At the end of a round he asked what was on the following week's list, studied it, and requested the patients to be sent into the office in turn. The conversation went something like this.

'You know your lung? Well, it's a bit like a railway station. It has all these lines spreading out and one of them's got blocked by a tumour, and we're going to take that bit out. All right? We'll do it on Tuesday. Right, off you go.'

Each spiel was a modification, depending on which part of which lung. Afterwards, we would explain everything in much more detail.

Patients came from all over the North-East and Cumbria. The lung cancers had been diagnosed by x-ray, but microscopic confirmation was required and we had a special theatre for these bronchoscopies, the term used for visual examination of the bronchial tree, under either general or local anaesthesia, in which a biopsy was taken. The broncho-scopes were rigid brass instruments before the invention of fibre optics. The examinations were conducted by two anaesthetists, Robin Sykes and BWT (Tom) Ritchie, both real characters.

Robin was a tall, distinguished-looking man with a military moustache, dressed in tweeds, ate Gentlemen's Relish with his sandwiches and read field sports magazines during operations (he had been master of a beagle pack). He was an Old Etonian, had been a lieutenant colonel in the army and later a colonel in the Royal Army Medical Corps, commanding the Northern Hospital TA unit up to 1963. John Walton, the eminent neurologist, refers to him in his autobiography *The Spice of Life* as owning a 1954 Rolls-Royce Silver Dawn, which he delighted in driving to run-down transport cafes and ordering a bacon butty and coffee. Apparently, when he accompanied Robin in the Rolls to a TA camp and the pair were saluted by a RAMC private guarding the gate, Robin turned to Lord Walton and said, 'I wonder how he knew we were officers?'

I once asked Robin to show me the technique of bronchoscopy. Looking at me, not the patient, he inserted the instrument.

'Now, the one at the back is the beer hole—you don't want that. The one in front's the air hole—that's the one you want and if you look down now I think you'll find it's in the right main bronchus.'

This sounds as if he was showing off, and perhaps he was, but he then went through each step and I found his advice very useful for the rare occasions I needed to do the procedure as an emergency. Bob Lawson's predecessor was a Korean called Chung who had a reputation as a technically very adept surgeon and who had worked in several prestigious cardiac units in the States. He told Bob that Robin was the best bronchoscopist he had seen anywhere.

Tom Ritchie I already knew because he gave anaesthetics for Peter D, and also the latter's private patients at the Nuffield. He was another pukka chap, with an upper-class accent and a somewhat affected swagger, but his speech was blighted by a dreadful stammer that he tried to overcome by the marked accentuation of any letter he could always pronounce. He was a Cambridge graduate but a Kiwi by birth, although there was no remnant of the antipodes in his speech. He volunteered that during his voyage to England to take his place at Cambridge he suffered the anxiety that he might be sent straight back because he hadn't obtained a certain subject at matriculation normally required by the university, and he expressed this concern to his tutor at their first meeting.

'Don't worry yourself on that regard, Ritchie,' came the reassuring reply. 'I played rugby for Scotland with your father.'

Tom was a keen sportsman who played cricket for the Borderers and was seemingly on first-name terms with Australian touring teams. He also claimed to have laid out JFK as a member of a Cambridge fifteen against Harvard when they toured the States to play rugby as opposed to American football. Actually, Tom didn't look as if he could lay out anyone, being of slim build. He was well-liked but could be nastily scathing of a junior left to complete an operation by his consultant if it was taking too long for Tom's comfort, even though at other times he could be pleasant to the same person. Whereas Robin, despite his background, was a man of the people, Tom was a snob, albeit a likeable one.

These two kept one another informed about potentially tricky cases they had bronchoscoped and knew their partner would be asked to anaesthetise. One afternoon Tom collared Robin in the coffee room and warned him about a case destined for surgery the following week. The man had a tumour of one bronchus migrating up into the trachea itself, which Tom deemed inoperable. But knowing Corbett's maxim of 'He's got to have his chance', expected his name to appear on the list, which it did. The planned operation was a pneumonectomy (removal of the whole lung) plus replacement of the trachea with Marlex mesh (a proprietary plastic). Robin rarely, if ever, questioned a case, but just accepted every one and calmly proceeded. On the day, Corbett was scrubbing up and Robin had just brought the anaesthetised patient into the theatre when the sister shouted out, 'What position would you like the patient in, Mr Barnsley?' (Patients were usually placed on one or other side for a chest incision, or sometimes flat.) Before Corbett could reply, Robin called out, 'Flat on his back, sister, both arms outstretched at right angles, and cotton wool up both nostrils', indicating that the patient was a goner. Corbett was not best pleased.

***

Whereas the benefits of doing cardiac surgery as a junior were learning the intensive care, valuable in all specialties, those of thoracic surgery were the ability to feel comfortable opening and closing the chest and assisting and conducting parts of a thoraco-abdominal approach for removal of cancer of the oesophagus.

The simplest chest operation was for recurrent spontaneous pneumothorax. This condition can affect young people, who present with sudden pain and breathlessness due to one lung collapsing. It is caused by rupture of a congenital thin-walled cyst, almost always at the apex of the lung, and is initially treated by insertion of a chest drain under local anaesthesia. The lung expands when the drain is connected to an underwater-sealed drainage bottle, which is usually left in situ for a few days to allow the small leak to close. We used red rubber Malecot catheters, which are irritable, creating adhesions that aid closure, but they have been replaced by modern plastics. Sometimes iodised talc was instilled into the chest cavity to provoke adhesions and create the same effect. But if the condition recurred or the leak wouldn't seal, patients were referred for surgery. The cyst, or bulla as it was called in older people with emphysema as a cause, was easily dealt with using the then newly available stapling guns.

All patients had chest drains inserted at the conclusion of a thoracotomy, and they were removed by a member of the medical staff when the lung was safely expanded, usually a couple of days afterwards. Malecot catheters were considered old-fashioned even then. They had the advantage of not only provoking adhesions, but they also possessed two lugs at the end, making accidental dislodgement unlikely. Unfortunately, the protruding lugs made removal painful and despite giving patients an opiate beforehand, they still broke out in a sweat when they were asked to breathe in and hold it, while the catheter was swiftly removed and the retaining purse-string suture tied to prevent an air leak back into the chest.

I carried out twenty-six thoracotomies, some for recurrent pneumothorax and assisted only by a nurse, and lung lobectomies under supervision. I also drained and decorticated a chronic empyema, an abscess at the base of the lung. Corbett advised draining the cavity with BIPP—bismuth iodoform paraffin paste—an old-fashioned antiseptic. I doubt if it is available now. I did as I was told, but the following day the man was confused, an unusual occurrence in someone not hypoxic, septic or an alcoholic. I happened to mention it to Corbett.

'He hasn't got bismuth toxicity, has he? How much did you put in?'

I had never heard of bismuth toxicity, but I'd placed a generous length of BIPP-impregnated gauze in the cavity, so at his suggestion I withdrew several inches, and his confusion disappeared immediately. In Corbett's younger days BIPP was used routinely, and I dare say he had seen his fair share of such cases.

We also treated those patients with cancer of the oesophagus who were suitable for surgery, but the majority presented either too late or were too unfit for the radical thoracoabdominal approach. Increasingly, such cancers affected the lower end of the oesophagus, where it joins the stomach, requiring an operation via the abdomen to free the stomach from all its attachments so it can be drawn up into the chest, which is also opened. The tumour is removed through the chest and the stomach then joined to the cut end of the oesophagus higher up. Kenneth McKeown, of Darlington, devised his own operation where he performed the anastomosis in the neck, rather than the chest, the theoretical advantages being a more radical procedure and avoiding the potentially lethal complication of a leaking anastomosis in the chest cavity, the problem Professor Harding Rains faced me with in the FRCS exam. McKeown was a master craftsman with a low operative mortality. As with lung cancer, the diagnosis was confirmed by biopsy, using a rigid brass instrument with a terminal 'beak', which could be lethal in the wrong hands, especially when dilating strictures, either inoperable cancers, or benign ones following long-standing reflux oesophagitis. I once witnessed two perforations for attempted dilatation, one after the other, by a senior academic surgeon, both of which were rapidly fatal—not at Shotley, I hasten to add. The invention of fibre optics and hence flexible, narrower instruments was a godsend.

The magazine *Hospital Medicine*, sent free to all hospital doctors, was an excellent publication, containing review articles by acknowledged experts and a regular feature entitled Practical Procedures. A well-known senior thoracic surgeon in London wrote one such article on oesophagoscopy, confining his description to the rigid instrument. The same man continued to do bronchoscopies with the rigid instrument, under local anaesthesia using cocaine injected through the cricothyroid membrane in the front of the neck, a procedure regarded as archaic but at which he was very skilled. In the next edition, a professor of gastroenterology co-wrote a letter with his senior lecturer admonishing the eminent surgeon for omitting to mention the (relatively new) fibre optic scope. The editor commented that the letter had been shown to the contributor, whose reply was printed below. The surgeon accepted that a 'miniscule' biopsy could be obtained through the new instrument but pointed out that if the professor and his senior lecturer would read the heading of the article they would see it was labelled 'Practical Procedures'. He suggested that the next time he sees a patient who has swallowed his false teeth he will send for the professor and his sidekick to come with their 'illuminated piece of spaghetti' and see how they got on. The following month the surgeon wrote to complain vociferously at the radical editing of his letter, so the editor published both versions. The one published ended: 'The fibre optic instrument, however, does have one advantage, it can be passed by virtually anyone.' The unedited version read: 'The fibre optic instrument, however, does have one advantage, it can be passed by any professor of gastroenterology and his senior lecturer.' All good clean fun. However, this was the time when medical gastroenterologists were being appointed in numbers and coincided with the introduction of fibre optic instruments. Most surgeons of my generation embraced them and used them throughout our careers. Those close to retirement understandably never bothered and some were content for medical gastroenterologists to refer patients to them for surgery as they felt indicated. Certainly, the load of stomach and bowel examinations, for screening and symptomatic, has become too great over the years for the surgeons alone to cope with.

***

My three-year rotation was now coming to an end, and it was time for me to consider my next move. Traditionally, for those keen to pursue a career in general and/or university-based academic surgery, now was an opportunity to do some research. This was not necessarily the case with a speciality such as plastics, urology, orthopaedics, neurosurgery or cardiothoracics. Here one would apply for a career registrar job of at least one year's duration, before becoming a senior registrar. In general, and certainly academic surgery, it was regarded as essential to do some research in order to obtain the degree of Master of Surgery (MS) or Doctor of Medicine (MD). There seemed no *good* time to do research. It couldn't feasibly be done after house jobs or primary FRCS, nor just before taking up a consultant post, so it had to be somewhere in between. Having been doing practical surgery for four years, one was just becoming technically adept and gaining experience, only to be taken out of clinical work for a crucial two years. On the other hand, one had to follow the trend; rebels were rarely successful. But in retrospect it was largely a waste of time. The only advantages were a recharging of batteries, a period of improved family life and the time to read widely.

The rotation had served me well. I had passed the FRCS at the first attempt and on reflection I was lucky to do six months each in the specialties of urology and cardiothoracics, which was purely fortuitous, because on a different rotation I would have had to do plastics and neurosurgery. Plastics would also have been useful. We did a small number of both full-thickness and split-skin grafts for trauma during general surgical on-call, but knowledge of the more technical aspects would have been worthwhile, whereas neurosurgery was of no use unless one wished to pursue this speciality. I once made the mistake of telling Feg when I was his senior house officer that I had never seen a brain exposed at operation. He feigned surprise and asked what action I would take if a patient was admitted with an extradural haemorrhage. This occurs after a blow to the temple, such as a fall or a cricket ball, when the middle meningeal artery is torn and bleeds into the potential space between the membranes covering the brain. Classically, the victim is briefly knocked unconscious, recovers, and then slowly falls into a coma over the next few hours, one feature being a dilated pupil on the affected side. I replied I would send it to

Newcastle General, the site of the Regional Neurosurgical Unit, only two miles away. Feg grunted, saying such action was quite unnecessary as it was an easy operation—all one did was create a burr-hole (opening in the skull) and stop the bleeding by compressing the torn artery as it emerges from its bony foramen in the skull by bunging in a sterile matchstick! The trouble with Feg is that you never knew when he was being serious or not.

Oddly enough, the *British Medical Journal* reported a case in one of its Christmas editions, when curiosities or humorous stories provide a seasonal break from the usual heavy stuff, in which such an injury was successfully treated by a flying doctor in the Solomon Islands, using not a matchstick but chewing gum from a local native who was watching the operation from a window!

A less successful outcome was described to me by a friend (X), having occurred during his six months' neurosurgery at Newcastle General. A young man was admitted to another hospital with the usual history, kept under observation, and became comatose, after which he was sent pronto to Newcastle General, where X was waiting for him. During transfer along the corridor from A&E to Neuro he stopped breathing. He was intubated forthwith by the accompanying anaesthetist and X took the difficult decision to create a burr-hole there and evacuate the blood clot and then take him up to theatre and complete the procedure in a more relaxed manner. It was conducted in the far end of the corridor, screens having been quickly erected to provide relative privacy, but all to no avail. The following week, at the conclusion of a ward round, the senior neurosurgeon, Laurie Lassman, asked to see X in his room. Lassman was from an East End Jewish family, retained the Cockney accent and had a penchant for expensive, light-coloured suits and loud ties. With trepidation, X knocked on the door, entered, and sank into a deep-pile carpet. At the far end of a capacious room, sitting behind a large desk, rather like J Edgar Hoover or the President of the United States, sat Lassman, who beckoned him across and very pleasantly asked how he was enjoying neurosurgery, adding that as he had a few minutes to spare he would like to get to know him a little better. After a few more banal remarks, Lassman expressed his pleasure at being able to have a chat and indicated that the interview was over. A somewhat bemused X reached the door, when Lassman delayed his exit.

'Oh, by the way, X' he said. 'Don't open any more 'eads in the corridor, will you? I know you were doin' your best, but don't do it again. Do you know where I found out about it? In the pub, that's where.'

The Prince of Wales pub was beside the hospital on Westgate Road and Lassman occasionally popped in. The tale was told to a receptive audience by one of the hospital porters, popular clients of the pub because of their frequent juicy stories—and this was one of the best.

# Chapter Seven

# Time Out

Until the advent of the NHS in 1948, 'Professor' was a courtesy title given to the senior surgeon or physician in the hospital. After this date academic departments were created, with the professor dividing his time between clinical work, teaching and research. Clearly, research is a good thing because progress in medicine needs to be made on a sound scientific basis. However, not everyone wants to work in an academic department, nor could they all. In our day, however, all potential consultants in general surgery were expected to do research, even though the majority would spend their professional lives in district general hospitals. In the United States, conversely, the only surgical trainees who opt to conduct research are the budding department chiefs in teaching hospitals. Research salaries are low, and by the time an American student qualifies these days he is at least tens of thousands of dollars in debt. As a resident in surgery he is anxious to sit his 'boards' and escape into private practice, even though this was usually achieved at an average age of thirty-two, about six years earlier than the equivalent on this side of the Atlantic. One major obstacle was being expected to create our own project. Without help, this is an almost impossible task, especially if it is laboratory based. Even the keenest, brightest individual will find that his 'original' idea has been done before.

I had always been interested in clinical biochemistry, and with my lean to surgery, this led me to the biochemical and metabolic changes that occur following operations and other forms of trauma. I knew the classical monograph on this subject was *The Metabolic Care of the Surgical Patient* by Francis D Moore, who Ian McNeill had worked for some years previously. Ian said I could almost certainly obtain a research post with Dr Moore in Boston on his recommendation, but guarded against it because there was no guarantee I could get back, having presumably burnt my boats! Normally I would have jumped at the chance, but I was naturally anxious at the speed at which domestic arrangements would have to be made, especially with Mary now pregnant with our second baby. Fortunately, Ian had also done some research with Cecil Flear, senior lecturer in clinical biochemistry, and he put me in touch with him. Most clinical biochemists concentrated on providing a service to clinicians, and their research interests were usually in various proteins or hormones, but Cecil's work was confined to the changes in electrolytes within cells and extracellular fluid following trauma. Following most surgical operations, as well as other forms of trauma, such as fractures, blood loss, severe infections and heart failure, several changes in body chemistry take place. Almost every hormone is stimulated, with concentrations rising in the bloodstream. Protein from skeletal muscle is broken down and the constituent nitrogen is excreted in the urine as urea. Similarly, the main cation (that is, positively charged ion) in the cells, potassium, is excreted in urine in larger than normal amounts, but its partner, sodium, the main cation in blood plasma, is retained, together with chloride, as salt. Despite this retention, the level of sodium in plasma falls—a condition termed hyponatraemia. This decrease is often attributed to dilution because water is also retained under the stimulus of antidiuretic hormone released by the pituitary gland, that tiny structure at the base of the brain, which has been termed 'the conductor of the endocrine orchestra'. But this cannot be the whole explanation, because the total concentration of ions in the blood (osmolality) either remains the same or falls only slightly. Much evidence suggests the changes in the cells and extracellular fluid are due to increased leakiness of cell membranes. Under normal conditions, potassium is retained in cells, and sodium outside, by a 'pump' in the membrane that consumes energy. If the pump is damaged, by lack of oxygen, or 'poisoned' by certain preparations, it fails, and the changes seen in trauma are observed. The condition has been termed the 'sick-cell syndrome'. In most patients these changes are minor and self-correcting. Similarly, the hormone changes and loss of protein are transient. But problems can arise if they are prolonged, as, for example, in cases of severe burns, especially when complicated by infection. The reduction of the patient's skeletal muscle can be considerable and can only be modified, but not abolished, by increased nutrition, either oral or intravenous. The various changes appear obligatory, and their extent and duration seem to mirror the magnitude of the trauma sustained. For many years, such changes have been regarded as evolutionary adaptations that are somehow beneficial to recovery. Everyone has probably experienced the 'fight or flight' response, in which the pupils dilate to increase visual field, the heart races to provide oxygen to the muscles to run fast, the tubes to the lungs dilate to aid respiration and, unconsciously, the blood sugar rises to fuel the muscles and the blood vessels to the skin and viscera constrict to allow those in the muscles to dilate. This is the primal response to trauma, caused by the release of adrenaline and noradrenaline from the adrenal glands, and the immediate advantage of this response, at a primitive level, is obvious. However, although adrenaline can relieve an asthma attack, and stimulate a failing heart, prolonged secretion of these so-called catecholamines can be harmful to the cardiovascular system. It is also difficult to see how the 'blanket' stimulation of so many hormones is advantageous, especially when some normally have opposite actions. Although Cecil's research concentrated on sodium and potassium, a new concept in hormone stimulation, called 'stimulus-secretion coupling', was described, indicating that the proximate stimulus was influx of calcium ions into the target cells. For example, secretion of cortisol from the adrenal cortex is stimulated by adrenocorticotrophin (ACTH) from the pituitary, but it achieves this by allowing calcium ions to enter the cells (this is simplifying it somewhat, but the same process has been observed in all hormones studied). Because it is known that cells possess a calcium pump in addition to the sodium-potassium pump, Cecil postulated that as well as the hyponatraemia associated with the sick-cell syndrome, if cell membranes do become more leaky as a result of hypoxia, etcetera, or influx of calcium ions throughout the body may unselectively lead to generalised increased hormone secretion, and such a response may explain, in part, the blanket stimulation observed. This hypothesis was the basis of my research.

I had seen an article describing a method of collecting cortisol secretion from the adrenal glands of dogs, simultaneously measuring the blood flow, a fortuitous technique relying on the unique anatomy of the animal. Being a paired organ, one adrenal could act as a control, while its partner had its blood supply reduced by snaring the supplying vessels, the intention being to produce hypoxia, increased cell leakiness and, if the hypothesis was correct, an increased cortisol secretion associated with the expected cation shifts in the subsequently analysed glands. Fortunately, the scientific and research committee miraculously acquired some funds, and after an interview I was awarded a salary plus extra money for animals. A group of us now shared facilities in the small separate building within the grounds of the RVI that constituted the department of surgery. Within a few weeks of starting my new job, Mary gave birth to our son, Paul, at the Princess Mary Maternity Hospital, so I took a few days off to look after Michael, now two and a half.

As is usual, my research got off to a slow start. I needed a licence from the Home Office to experiment on animals. Fortunately, because the dogs were 'sacrificed' (to use the accepted term) at the end of each experiment and hence were classed as 'acute', this proved easier than if they were 'chronic', in which the animal is allowed to survive for further study. Using the word 'sacrifice' reminds me of a Surgical Research Society meeting I attended, in which a German was presenting a paper about experiments on rabbits. He had a totally serious face and spoke in the stereotypical accent and monotone that we British parody in wartime comedies such as *'Allo 'Allo!*.

*'At ze end of ze eggsperiments, ze animals ver eggsicuted* [this word prolonged and stressed] *by a blow su the head.'* My dogs were 'executed' by an injection of the barbiturate, Nembutal.

Searching the relevant literature was laborious, as everything had to be done by hand. However, a publication, the *Index Medicus*, updated annually, listed journals alphabetically under subject headings and was very helpful. With the internet, such a search will be made much more quickly today, although in my admittedly limited experience there seems to be a tendency to omit some well-conducted work from the distant past. One of the most important papers for me was published in 1902.

I was disappointed from the outset that my work would have no impact on clinical problems. In retrospect, however, it did act as an experimental model, drawing together aspects of the biochemical, humoral and neurogenic responses to surgery and trauma. *Knowledge* of the response is important, though, and this was often sadly lacking, even in experienced clinicians. The classic example is the hyponatraemia often seen in sick patients, perceived as lack of salt and treated accordingly. In fact, the body is remarkably adept at conserving salt and does so even more after surgery, via the kidney and reducing the salt content of sweat. Treating hyponatraemia with saline solutions compounds the problem by forcing more salt into leaky cells and can induce congestive heart failure in the elderly. I stress the word knowledge because in most patients, the hyponatraemia simply needs to be monitored, not treated.

Reducing the blood flow to one adrenal by the method chosen did increase secretion of cortisol, contrary to the established view that such secretion was solely related to the amount of ACTH provided to the gland; that is, the blood flow. However, the reduction in blood flow in the experiments was probably insufficient to create hypoxia. It did, however, produce changes in cation levels in the gland, but opposite to those predicted. Further experiments showed that the cation changes observed could increase cortisol secretion, but both changes were prevented by blocking the nervous impulses, which prevented cation changes in skeletal muscle after trauma.

The main conclusion was that surgery and trauma led to widespread changes in cation content of cells—sodium, potassium and calcium—which itself can lead to unselective hormone secretion, as well as changes in extracellular fluid, and that such changes occur as a result of sympathetic nerve stimulation, which is the primal response to trauma.

I presented the results at a meeting of the Surgical Research Society in London and in May 1974 at the European Society for Experimental Surgery in Salzburg. My presentation at the latter was on the final afternoon of a four-day meeting. Jeremy was also presenting a paper and Dave Tweedle was a co-author of another. Jeremy had been taught to fly by Mike Gill, an ex-RAF pilot who founded a flying school and small airline at Newcastle Airport, so all four of us flew in Mike's twin-engined Piper Comanche. Mike stayed with us for a little rest and relaxation. His mother was Swedish, and he was tall, blond and blue-eyed and exuded an air of confidence, somewhat dented by his initial announcement to us, in Oxford-accented English.

'Just a quick briefing, chaps,' he said. 'In the unlikely event of us having to ditch in the North Sea, I shall ask one of you to pass me that little black thing at the back—it will send out a signal so that the choppers can pick us up.' I don't think he was joking.
Immediately after take-off I could see Mary waving with the boys, now aged four and two, standing alone on the observation roof (Newcastle was a much smaller airport then). We crossed the coast at Arnhem and could see the white crosses of the cemetery. When we stopped at a small airport in Germany for lunch, a Second World War Junkers, grey with its black Luftwaffe cross on a white background, stood next to the air traffic control tower.

On the last lap of the journey Mike announced we were approaching a West German Airforce airfield and that he had not radioed our presence, which he thought might prove interesting. To me it was more than interesting because we crossed the runway at right-angles and what seemed to me a very low height. So low, in fact, we could see the pilot of an American Lockheed F-104 Starfighter combat aircraft (appropriately nicknamed 'The Widowmaker' after a staggering 110 German pilots died flying it), as he looped below us. I still don't know whether Mike was telling the truth about not informing them of our approach. Suddenly, as we neared our destination, the mountains of the Obersalzberg loomed out of nowhere.

During free time we hired a car to Berchtesgaden to view the Eagle's Nest, Hitler's mountain retreat, a fiftieth birthday present from the Nazi Party. The road was closed due to snow and ice, despite it being the month of May, and we retired disappointed to a café. There we were approached by a man who introduced himself as a Hungarian guide, who offered to show us the site of the Berghof and the underground bunkers. He took us to an alpine inn, where he spoke to an old crone who opened a cellar door, and down we went to an extensive complex of bunkers, obviously designed to be impregnable. Any intruders gaining entry would have been mown down by machine guns placed at strategic points. The stone walls were as thick as those of a medieval castle, and each machine gun had a wide range of fire created by a large, square opening into the wall that funnelled back through the thickness by a series of concentric squares, gradually diminishing to where the muzzle of the gun emerged. At intervals along the main tunnel were cells accessed by wrought-iron portcullis gates, designed to house guard dogs—a nice sadistic touch. One often hears myths about mysterious secret passages, but here was one in reality, and quite unexpected, which added to the thrill. Having done some research on these bunkers, I think the alpine inn was the Platterhof Hotel, which was destroyed in 2000 and replaced by the information centre for what is now a museum.

Our guide then showed us the remains of the Berghof complex, which, apart from Hitler's house, had separate homes for senior party members and SS quarters, plus a kindergarten for their children and Eva Braun's trout pool. He pointed out Hitler's house, the steps to which I thought I recognised from contemporary film of Chamberlain and others visiting, and we could wander around at will. Like the vandal I am, I prised off a white bathroom tile, my excuse being that it was cracked. No-one else was at the site—our guide said it was little known and the authorities did not want knowledge of its existence to spread in case it became a shrine for Nazi sympathisers. We saw remnants of damage from allied bombing at the end of the war, but the Berghof itself, which was obviously the largest house, was intentionally destroyed in 1952 and only the foundations and approach path remain. My tile cannot, therefore, have come from Hitler's bathroom, much to my disappointment, but it could be from either Bormann's or Goering's, which were close by. All the other buildings have been levelled, but Eva's trout pool remains. There is another hotel, beside the site of the Berghof, the Hotel zum Türken, which, interestingly, is still run by descendants of the family who owned it in Hitler's time. Apparently, he became friendly with them long before he built his house, but when they refused to sell the hotel, they were incarcerated in Dachau. Fortunately, they survived.

In the first volume of my memoir I described how my surgical career was influenced by Jeremy's father, George Young Feggetter, known to all as Feg. A tower of strength, he was from another era, having spent six years away during WW2, accumulating enormous experience in the surgery of trauma. He sent Jeremy to Harrow, and his daughter, Amanda, to Roedean. At one point he even had a butler, admittedly hailing from Shiney Row, a Durham pit village. Jeremy and I were in the same year at medical school, and as research fellows went to London together to the annual meeting of the Surgical Research Society. Jeremy wanted some salopettes (a word unfamiliar to me at the time), so we went to Simpsons in The Strand. There, public school-accented sales assistants observed a few chinless wonders as they plodded slowly around, having tried on new skiing boots that were aimed to fit perfectly by the injection of a silicone-rubber compound via a valve in the back. The comical Groucho Marx walk being necessary to mould the setting substance was made more amusing by the admiring comments of girlfriends and mothers. We then had tea in Fortnum & Mason, where Jeremy took the opportunity, this being November, to inquire whether the order for his father's Christmas wine order was to hand (I said Feg was from another era). As we left there was a sky-blue Rolls-Royce outside, parked on double yellow lines, engine running, guarded by a uniformed chauffeur on the lookout for police or traffic wardens. The double doors of the store were swung open by a flunky in tailcoat, allowing a tall, straight-backed, elegant lady of a certain age, resplendent in a suit matching the colour of the limousine. She carried a Fortnum's bag, quite small and quite flat, containing, I suspect, about four ounces of boiled ham. It must have been an expensive ego trip.

***

I did not complete my thesis for the MS (Master of Surgery) until 1976. I was fortunate in that although the working day at urology was long, emergencies only rarely required immediate surgery, so I had time to buckle down and write the blessed thing, which came as a welcome surprise to Prof Johnston when he found it on his desk, because I think he had given up on me. I was awarded the MS with Commendation in summer 1977. During my period of research I kept up with clinical work by doing the odd locum and also attending lectures and meetings. Henry Miller, by now vice-chancellor of the university, was an acquaintance or perhaps friend of T Dan Smith, one-time leader of Newcastle City Council, and invited him to speak at the Medical Society. Smith was the son of a Durham miner who became a painter and decorator and developed a business in this field. He was well known locally because of his ambition to make Newcastle the 'Brasilia' of the north and was the leading light in extensive redevelopment of the city centre, which proved controversial. Certainly, change of some sort was needed—after all, the A1 continued from the Tyne Bridge along Northumberland Street, the city's main shopping thoroughfare, and clearly this was unsustainable. However, some elegant buildings were destroyed in the process. T Dan Smith became notorious nationally when he was embroiled in the Poulson affair. John Poulson, an architect-cum-developer, created a large international business, but bribed several people, including Smith, to obtain public building contracts. Poulson went to prison but claimed to be a victim until his dying day. Smith was on bail awaiting trial after being charged with corruption when he gave his lecture one evening. Bizarrely, he arrived in evening dress, looking haggard because of the stress of the impending trial. I cannot recall any of the lecture. My reaction was one of sympathy for a fellow human being in his distress, and respect for his courage in acceding to Henry's request. He pleaded guilty and in 1974 was sentenced to six years' imprisonment, of which he served three years in Leyhill open prison, which is known—to the tabloid newspapers at least—as the 'Savoy of the Slammers'. On his release he maintained his innocence despite his plea and devoted himself to penal reform. I remembered my landlady in Brighton Grove, Mrs Stuart, saying it was well known in certain circles that T Dan Smith's painters were always in new council house estates before the tenders for the contracts were considered. I suppose there's a temptation for some people who contribute to public life to develop a sense of entitlement and become corrupt.

At one Surgical Research Society meeting in London I was seated next to Prof Johnston when a guest speaker, Walter Ballinger, from St Louis, Missouri, gave a wonderful paper. Ballinger had the looks and bearing of a screen matinee idol, and in his smooth presentation described how a series of white rats in his laboratory were made diabetic using a drug called streptozotocin, which specifically destroys the islets of Langerhans. These islets are not in the Pacific Ocean, as some TV quiz contestants mistakenly guess, but in the pancreas, and they produce insulin in response to a rise in blood sugar. Like the adrenal gland, the pancreas has two components with different functions; the bulk of the gland, which lies behind the stomach and whose 'head' is partly enclosed by the 'C' of the duodenum, secretes three enzymes which help digest proteins, fats and carbohydrates, whereas the islets are microscopic collections of cells scattered throughout the gland. Confirmation that the rats were diabetic was easily demonstrated by sugar in the urine. Islets were then obtained from the glands of donor rats. The difficulty here was separating the precious islets from the bulk of the gland, and a form of chemical digestion was used. They were then injected into the recipient diabetic rats so as to be deposited in the liver, where they miraculously survived and cured the condition, as confirmed by absence of glycosuria and normal blood glucose levels (blood is easily obtained from the tail vein in the rat). Study of the livers post-mortem showed the seeded islets had a normal appearance, microscopically. Apart from the difficult process of harvesting the islets, this was a simple but beautifully designed study demonstrating two fundamental points. Firstly, chemically induced diabetes could be cured in rats by implantation of the islets of Langerhans, and secondly, such islets were not rejected. The latter was crucial, and it was postulated that these hormonal cells might not, for some reason, provoke the usual immunological response, for none could be demonstrated histologically. Unfortunately, the truth was more prosaic, and in retrospect, obvious, but this took some time to be revealed.

At the conclusion of the presentation, Prof Johnston was up like a shot, and bounded across to Ballinger, not only to congratulate him but also to offer him a visiting professorship to Newcastle, which was gratefully accepted. I am sure Ivan's enthusiasm was driven by consideration for his wife, who was a brittle diabetic and also suffered from coeliac disease. He possibly saw a light at the end of a tunnel for a cure for her and others like her, but sadly, it was not to be. It transpired that the reason the rats failed to mount a rejection to the transplanted islets was that being inbred over generations purely for laboratory purposes, they were immunologically almost identical. Since then the technique has been used in humans with type one diabetes, but the combined pitfalls of rejection and limited availability of donor organs has restricted the numbers so treated. In addition, some of the immunosuppressive drugs are ironically toxic to islets, as well as to the kidneys, the latter organ being one of those most affected by diabetes itself. At present, pancreatic transplants for diabetes are usually whole-organ in type, coupled with a renal transplant.

Another visiting professor was George Block, a surgeon from Chicago who, in keeping with that city, combined the healing art with the breeding of cattle. He was a jolly, outspoken man, quite unlike the stereotypical American, certainly the east coast type, anyway. He spent most of his lecture elaborating on the tale I here relate. As a chief resident in surgery (the equivalent of senior registrar in the UK) he worked for Warren Cole, an eminent man. In the late 1950s or early 60s, Cole was approached by a national TV company asking to transmit a major operation live. Over here we had a series on the old black and white medium called *Your Life in Their Hands* that showed some operations, but it was a typically British, tight-sphinctered affair, obviously based in London teaching hospitals, the white-coated clinicians remaining anonymous because anything construed as advertising resulted in the culprit being struck off the medical register. Anyway, Cole called George into his study and asked him what he thought of the proposal, which came with the promise of a significant sum to be deposited in the research fund. He thought it was an excellent idea.

'I'm pleased that you think so, George,' Cole replied. 'Because I want you to do the operation—they want us to do an aneurysm.'

If my chief had addressed me thus I would have passed out, but being an American, seeing this as an opportunity to make his name and having the confidence and lack of self-doubt characteristic of his nation, George accepted. Considering the first elective aortic aneurysm was performed as recently as 1954, this was some challenge. Nevertheless, it was an operation they did regularly. Unfortunately, there was suddenly a dearth of patients. As the scheduled date approached, Dr Cole asked George how arrangements were proceeding and was informed no patient was yet available.

'Well, you'd better find one, George,' Cole reportedly told him. 'Because if not, your job's on the line, and more importantly, so is mine.'

Fortunately, up popped a saviour in the slim form of Solly Urek, fit for his age and with what felt like a nice moderate-sized aneurysm (remember, there were no ultrasound or CT scans then). The operation went well, the occasional subliminal expletive muttered by George under his breath went undetected by the microphone and Solly made an uncomplicated recovery. For a few years afterwards, George treated Solly like a private patient, seeing him more frequently than necessary and for a while exchanging Christmas cards with him. Then, nothing. Until a few years later, the phone rang one evening.

'Doctor Block?' said the unmistakable voice at the other end.

'Solly, great to hear from you. What can I do for you?'

'I'm real sorry we lost touch, Dr Block. We moved to Nebraska and somehow just let things go.'

'Oh, that doesn't matter, Solly. What can I do for you?'

'Well, Dr Block, I've got these haemorrhoids that are troubling me.'

'Solly, no problem. You let me know when you want them treated. I'll waive my fee. Just let me know.'

A short silence followed this kind offer.

'Well, Dr Block, I don't want to sound ungrateful—that plastic artery you gave me has worked real well. But, you understand, this here's my asshole, and I want a specialist!'

I don't recall anything else from the lecture.

# Chapter Eight

# The Go-Between

In September 1974 a vacancy appeared for a senior registrar. I expected to be short-listed, but competition would be tough. This was the most important interview of my life so far. Once appointed to this level, a consultant post was a virtual certainty. Most teaching hospitals were parochial. There were usually enough local candidates of sufficient merit to fill the posts, and some members of the interviewing committee would usually know them, but a trend was emerging to appoint more 'outsiders', which increased stress. Interviews were not structured as they are now, with all candidates asked the same questions, and it was regarded as 'not cricket' to pose clinical problems, so the discourse was much more general, and included the role of management. Hardly anyone took an interest in hospital management, which in those days was called administration, and the poor old administrators kept to themselves, were looked down upon and occasionally mocked in the Christmas concert. In retrospect, not only was it unkind, but it was also wrong, because many of them were just as dedicated to good patient care as the nurses and clinicians. Anyway, they've got their own back, and with interest, because hospital managers now are extremely powerful. Understandably so, when you consider that in 2014 the chief executive of the Newcastle Hospitals NHS Foundation Trust wielded a budget of about £770m! Politicians are addicted to reorganising the NHS. In fact, I believe that between the formation of the NHS in 1948 and 2014 there was only one year, 1967, when there wasn't some sort of reorganisation. My interview coincided with one such, the nature of which escapes me, but because of an increasing tendency to involve clinicians in management as opposed to simply being asked for their advice, presumably to share the blame when things went awry, questions might be asked on such a topic. So I obtained a copy of the relevant government white paper, at not inconsiderable expense,

I might add, and after carefully reading it three times, was no wiser at the end than I was at the beginning. It may be just me, but I don't think so. Most clinicians feel the same. Our brains are not wired to think in abstract terms. We like specifics and cannot grasp what seems to us to be Whitehall gobbledegook. Fortunately, no-one broached the subject. What was said remains a blur, except that the chairman, Sir Michael Straker, became irritated when, after asking if I had any plans, I replied that I might take a year out at a recognised 'centre of excellence'. He thought I was implying that the RVI itself was not such a centre. In fact I was merely employing a term that was frequently used. Depending upon their sub-specialty interest within the field of general surgery, some senior registrars did go to places such as St Mark's in London to improve their skills in colorectal surgery or to St Mary's for vascular work. I liked Sir Michael. I got to know him a little when he was operated on by Ian McNeill. But on this particular afternoon he was red-faced, sweating and clearly drunk, which I thought was disrespectful considering the importance of the event. He had probably expected to come just for the ride, as the chairman usually withheld a vote unless a committee was split. To my relief, I was appointed. I started working once again with my previous mentors, Peter D and Mac. It was wonderful to return to clinical work, but now I was on call almost all the time.

Although busy and tiring, the life of a senior registrar was good, and we were kept going by a combination of adrenaline and a sense of worth engendered by being regarded as the one who 'ran the show'. I have titled this chapter *The Go-Between* because the senior registrar was the intermediary, bridging the gulf between the consultants and the junior doctors and nurses. We were senior enough to deal with most clinical problems, but young enough to be approachable and handle the variety of problems facing juniors, be they clinical, technical or even personal. I knew all the patients (whereas each consultant was familiar only with his own) and had operated on a good proportion of them. In theory, the senior registrar alternated call with the registrar, but Peter D expected his senior registrar to cover the latter. Each generation of medical graduates thinks their successors have had it easy. In the days before the NHS, consultants were honorary (that is, unpaid). Although they gained their reputation in the hospital, they earned their living from private practice. However, they were also, surprisingly, more powerful and expected the hospital staff to be more or less permanently available. The British Medical Association (BMA), which represents doctors' views to the government of the day but was (and may still be) regarded somewhat cynically by many hospital doctors as the 'GPs' trade union'. It did, though, have a junior doctors' division, whose representatives tended to be rabble-rousers, and during the period that I was a senior registrar they succeeded in obtaining 'extra-duty payments', awarded for onerous on-call rotas. These were divided into A and B units, A for being regarded as first on call outside the hospital and likely to be called in, and B for those less likely to be called in but nevertheless constrained to one's abode for either advice or second on call, mobile phones having not yet been invented. I did not resent being permanently on call. Apart from during my holidays, I expected it, I wanted the experience, and, with two small children, I did not expect to be gallivanting, anyway. Nor, indeed, did I expect the extra remuneration—to some extent it came out of the blue, as I had been too preoccupied with work and study to keep abreast of medical politics. However, few people refuse a gift horse. I remember Mary and I buying extra presents for the boys that first Christmas and soon we could afford a higher mortgage to move into a five-bedroomed semi just around the corner, especially as I expected to be a senior registrar for at least five years. The extra payments could prove embarrassing because sometimes senior registrars and even registrars started earning more than their consultants, because the latter had open-ended contracts that did not include 'overtime'. Nevertheless, it grated when undeserving special cases emerged, as they do. For example, at Newcastle General the chief bacteriologist had a grossly inflated view of himself and his speciality. He insisted his senior registrar deserved permanent A units, as he was always on call, but, as everyone knew, bacteriologists are 'never' called out. I apostrophise 'never'—once in a blue moon they were. I once called one out to the RVI in the middle of the night. I was operating on a six-year-old girl for presumed appendicitis. The appendix was normal, but she had a collection of thin pus in the pelvis. There is a condition called primary pneumococcal peritonitis, rare but well-documented, and I was pretty sure this was the diagnosis. If so, old-fashioned penicillin was the best antibiotic treatment, whereas if we treated any infection 'blind' (before bacteriological confirmation), we would usually give a modern broad-spectrum type. I wanted a Gram stain to give a good idea of the causative organism (most abdominal infections are Gram-negative, whereas pneumococci are G-positive). This chap was most reluctant to leave his bed, telling me to use a cephalosporin, but I was persistent and was proved correct. He probably lived on that story for some time, how he was dragged out of his bed to save a child's life.

My experience after nearly forty years in the NHS is that if you want something done, always ask a busy man. He is busy for a reason. My first secretary, a butcher's daughter, complimented me by saying there was always a long queue outside a good butcher's. She didn't appear to consider that I may be disturbed by the analogy. With reference to my churlish remarks about the senior Newcastle General bacteriologist, although he was laboratory-based, he somehow managed to wangle a whole ward, designed to deal with the possibility of rare or difficult-to-treat infectious diseases. He must have been very persuasive or pulled a fast one because with the usual shortage of beds it was difficult to justify. I was introduced to the ward and the sister in charge by Keith Baxby when he and I were senior registrars on urology. She was highly competent and always willing to transfer cases to her care to justify her presence. As most seriously ill patients have some form of infection, it proved easy to persuade her boss to accept them and they were well looked after, partly because of the low occupancy of the ward. She was always referred to as Mrs Robinson, never Sister, possibly because she was an incorrigible flirt, like her namesake in the film *The Graduate*. She was at least ten years older than Keith and me but always gave one that certain look. If she showed you to a patient's bed by walking ahead, her gait was a vision to behold!

We were on reception every Wednesday and a weekend day five weeks out of six, but in addition took vascular calls three weeks out of four. Vascular cases were usually ruptured aortic aneurysms, the remainder being sudden threatened limb loss due to embolus, thrombosis or trauma. One complicated case was a lesson in only doing what is necessary. A lady in her early forties requested a tubal ligation for sterilisation from a Sunderland gynaecologist, her family being complete, and opted to be a private patient. She also had a mild degree of urinary incontinence when coughing or stretching, which she was advised could be treated by an anterior repair, but if she had a vaginal hysterectomy, both problems would be solved without needing an abdominal incision and the repair would be sounder. She agreed, but on the evening of the operation her blood pressure dropped, and lower abdominal swelling indicated internal bleeding. At operation, the gynaecologist found free blood with some active bleeding, and he understandably panicked. In desperation he called for help from a urologist and eventually both were satisfied the bleeding was controlled. And so it was, but so was the circulation to her right leg, as was discovered the next morning. The vascular surgeon at Sunderland thought discretion was the better part of valour and had her transferred to Peter D. The right common, external and internal arteries had been tied, as had the veins. Circulation was restored by releasing the ligatures, no reconstruction being required, but the veins were irreparably damaged, and she developed persistent swelling of the whole limb. Not only that, but days later a discharge from the wound proved to be urine, and an intravenous pyelogram (IVP) showed a leak from the right ureter. Keith Yeates decided the ureter was too wrecked to be salvaged, so she lost her right kidney at another operation. This poor lady had four operations, lost a kidney and had a permanent post-phlebitic leg with swelling and extra weight, making walking burdensome. All because she leaked a few drops of urine when she strained. And would you believe it, she remained cheerful and accepted everything with apparent equanimity—or so it seemed. Her only consolation, I presume, because I never found out, would be several thousand pounds in compensation for clinical negligence. This case was exceptional, and I have never seen anything so disastrous since, certainly not resulting from surgical interference. An army surgeon at the Duchess of Kent Military Hospital in Catterick transferred a patient with 'ischaemic legs', with a request to try to save them. The man arrived promptly but both legs were completely gangrenous to groin level and above. He had sustained thromboses of the abdominal aorta and both iliac arteries, a condition not uncommon in large vascular units. It usually presents resulting from a chronic build-up of clot upon narrowing of the arteries because of atherosclerosis and causes either pain on walking or at rest, the latter a precursor of gangrene. Only rarely does it present as established gangrene. In fact, in nearly forty years, I dealt with many blocked aortas but only saw one other case like this, a woman in her eighties who suddenly became paralysed from the waist down and was initially admitted to the spinal unit. In her case the pelvic organs were also ischaemic, and she was dead from septicaemia within five hours of admission. Ian McNeill and I amputated the man's legs as high as possible, but even the rarely performed hindquarter procedure was impossible, as both buttocks were dead also. We had to leave the wounds open, packed with antiseptic gauze, and wait to see what remained viable, in the vain hope that we could eventually obtain some form of skin cover. The patient knew he had lost his legs, but the full horror of what remained was kept out of his sight by a cradle covered with bedclothes. His frequent dressings were painless. He was nursed in a cubicle, was unfailingly cheerful, reading his paper and picking his horses. The problem was insoluble and only nature or the Almighty could end it. For about three weeks he reported he felt well and pain-free and he ate normally (his rectum, wafting in the breeze, functioned normally) until finally one morning he said he felt a bit queasy. Six hours later he was dead. As Mac said, the Good Lord always solves the insoluble.

A similar apparently insoluble problem was a resident of the long-standing Somali community in South Shields, who presented with an advanced cancer of the rectum. The only possible treatment then was to remove the whole rectum, close off his bottom and bring the large bowel to the skin surface as a colostomy, so his stools would pass into an adhesive disposable plastic bag. But Muslims have strict rules about hygiene and despite all our explanations, pleadings and counselling, he was adamant he would not have the operation. As far as he was concerned it was prohibited by the Quran. He was a tall, slim, elegant man with a dignified bearing. His bald scalp revealed a magnificent long, linear scar starting just above one eyebrow and extending backwards to the downturn of his skull, the sort which a nineteenth-century German university student would be proud of receiving in a staged duel. He said it was caused by a bullet while 'fighting for the British'. He did not possess a dressing gown and wore the standard NHS towelling robe provided, with its brightly coloured stripes like those of Joseph and the Amazing Technicolor Dreamcoat. In this garb, he strode up and down the ward almost continuously, his arms folded and extended out in front of him. Every time one passed him in the course of ward duties he barely paused as he pointed to the left side of his abdomen and declared, 'No shit here,' before continuing on his way. Eventually, all we could offer him was local radiotherapy; on its own, an unsatisfactory treatment.

***

Peter D had a thriving private practice and operated on Tuesday afternoons at the Nuffield Hospital in Jesmond. He insisted on me assisting him, even though Tuesday was the only free afternoon I could otherwise devote to study or writing. This was especially challenging as he expected me to review for publication all his cases of upper-limb ischaemia. He paid me £10 for the session but declared me on his tax return as an assistant! I was fond of him and owed him a lot but did find this a bit galling. After one of Peter's teaching rounds we adjourned to the seminar room for a cup of coffee and a chat. The head of the radiology department, Charles Warwick, put his head round the door to discuss a case. He then changed the subject and asked Peter's opinion about the result of the interview they had both attended the previous day, in which they had appointed a registrar in psychiatry. The successful candidate was the daughter of a consultant member of staff. In the presence of the housemen, a registrar, six students and myself, Peter D replied there was no doubt that the best candidate was the Yorkshireman, but what with his accent, being rough around the edges and with her background, they really had to appoint 'the girl'. Charlie Warwick agreed, but I think he detected a visual element of surprise in his young audience, and said 'Oh, well, Peter, I'd better leave you now, your staff may be worried that we are not able to appoint the right people.' Coincidentally, he looked at me as he opened the door.

'No,' I said, 'I'm just worried about my Yorkshire accent!' Peter D looked suitably embarrassed.

Ian McNeill had a good brain, was artistic, widely read and a technically skilful surgeon, but at this stage in his life he seemed content to simply go through the motions and never seemed as enthusiastic or driven as his colleague. He was quietly diabetic, however, which possibly made him somewhat lethargic. There was a widespread rumour he had been offered the chair in surgery before Prof Lowdon, but I doubt if any single person had this gift in their power and suspect it was simply suggested that his application would be welcomed. He did not apply and after becoming a consultant never produced any further research or publications, although he took an interest in the progress of the G-suit and provided specimens for Cecil Flear, whose work on the 'sick cell syndrome' he admired. He always did his duty, though, and was methodical in everything. Unlike Peter D he had a full-time contract and undertook no private practice. I thought this was because he had a political objection, but a few years later when the rules changed, so did he. The resulting financial rewards enabled him to indulge his passion for antique scientific instruments.I cannot recall whether jogging as a pastime had been popularised by the American Jim Fixx by the mid-1970s, but there have always been a minority of keen athletes among the population. One such young man presented with the interesting story that he had developed bloody diarrhoea after running a half marathon. Investigations revealed no abnormality in either the structure of his large bowel nor the blood supply to the whole gut, and we concluded the bleeding was caused by his gut slopping up and down during running—which begs the question why the problem is not more common. I have only come across one other case since. The young man was none too pleased about the obvious advice given, but I don't know what miraculous solution he expected! Mac once presented a rare case of coeliac artery compression to a teaching meeting. As the aorta passes from thorax to abdomen through a hole in the diaphragm, it immediately gives off a branch, the coeliac artery, which itself branches to supply part of the stomach, liver and spleen. This coeliac trunk can be compressed by tough fibres of tendon encircling the hole. In rare cases, such compression was thought to cause pain, especially after meals, when the blood supply to the gut is normally increased, but opinion whether the condition truly existed was controversial. However, not only did Mac's case show clear localised compression of the artery on a lateral angiogram, but the patient's pain was totally relieved by an operation to divide the constricting band. Despite this, our old friend Mr McCollum, the surgeon who was not keen on antibiotics and did not believe in Crohn's disease, caused a stir.

'Mr McNeill,' he said. 'I think you are misleading these young men—everybody knows you can cure angina by means of a laparotomy.'

The procedure he referred to is an exploratory operation of the abdomen. This apparently outrageous statement provoked muffled laughter but, like many of McCollum's generalisations, there was an element of truth. Any form of treatment, including surgery, can have a placebo effect, and although one would not advise a laparotomy (cut into the abdominal cavity) for angina, it was true that some patients who required abdominal surgery for a genuine reason, but who incidentally had angina, noticed an improvement or even complete relief afterwards. They possibly limited their activities postoperatively and/or lost some weight. Also, now that aortography is much more common than it was then, apparent coeliac compression is not infrequent and appears to be mainly asymptomatic.

Alan Horler, one of my chiefs when I did the medical house job, became a patient of Mac's after discovering a lump in his neck while shaving. He turned out to have cancer of the thyroid, requiring a total thyroidectomy. It's interesting how experienced and knowledgeable clinicians react when they are patients. Although as a physician Dr Horler would not usually treat this condition, he probably knew as much as I did. Yet he continually picked my brains, seeking reassurance, especially when he frequently saw me late at night attending to admissions and expressed surprise at how hard I worked! In fact, the commonest form of thyroid cancer, the papillary type, is one of the 'best' to have, if one could choose. His was of a different type, from which he eventually succumbed, although he survived for several years.

Dr Horler's brother, Ramsay, a GP in Gateshead was a keen cricketer. Ex-housemen of the RVI formed a team called the Victorians and played in one of the local leagues. The team varied, depending on clinical commitments, but were mainly middle-aged. One day their opponents were batting and lost a wicket. The incoming batsman was halfway to the stumps when one of his colleagues shouted.

'Hey, Fred,' he said. 'You've forgotten your box.'

'I don't need a box against this lot,' was the riposte.

What happened next could have been taken from AG Macdonell's description of a cricket match in his famous satire *England Their England*. Although sometimes planned, this scenario never seems to succeed in real life. Ramsay Horler could bowl evil off cutters.

'Right, you so-and-so,' he muttered.

His first ball turned wickedly and rammed into the batsman's gonads. The recipient stood motionless for a moment, before sinking onto both knees and depositing his lunch in an arc down the pitch. The witnesses cherished the image, which was recounted at every subsequent reunion.

***

I was at Sister's desk one day when a nurse emerged from behind some curtains drawn round the bed opposite. With a concerned expression, she asked me to attend the occupant, a skinny man in his sixties. He was staring in horror at several feet of his small bowel, which had emerged from his abdominal wound—created not by me, I hasten to add—and spilled onto the bedclothes beside him.

'Is it serious, doctor?' was his only comment.

I reassured him we would soon put him right. He had endured an exploratory operation for what proved to be inoperable cancer and suffered a burst wound (dehiscence) following a prolonged bout of coughing. This complication is far less common now than it was then. During his recuperation from this second procedure, I was joshing him about his habit of always studying the racing pages, when he told me this tale. He was one of several children, the eldest of whom, a son named Emmanuel, died in infancy. A second son was named in memory of the first. The family's social life revolved around the workingman's club, and one night shortly before the 1960 Grand National, this particular son, now the eldest and a grown man, entered the club and announced that the previous night he had won the race in a vivid dream. He was apparently the life and soul of the party, always cheerful, and friends surrounded him, all asking the name of the horse. He said he didn't know but was certain it was he himself, rather than a horse, which had won. They scrutinised the list of horses for clues but could not agree on any particular one. The winner turned out to be Merryman II! His parents, it transpires, often referred to him as Manny the Second.

An interesting case that could have had a tragic outcome arose when I was called to see a young woman who had been rescued from the Tyne. The Newcastle quayside is now well-developed and lit up, with pubs and clubs and the focal points of the Glasshouse and the winking-eye Millennium Bridge, which constantly attract sightseers and photographers, but in the 1970s it was dark, depressing and down-at-heel. Fortunately, some people heard the cries of a young woman who was in the river and clinging on to a steel ladder. She was rescued by the fire brigade and on arrival at the hospital was cold and dirty, constantly shivering, but also covered in multiple stab wounds. Her story was she had been assaulted by a person unknown, stabbed and thrown in the river. None of the wounds required stitching and she was admitted simply to be cleaned and warmed up and made comfortable and to have her wounds dressed. The next day a detective who had taken her original story telephoned me and asked if the wounds could have been self-inflicted, which had not crossed my mind. On reflection there were no injuries to hands or forearms to indicate an attempt to defend herself. The wounds were all superficial and all on her left side—and she was right-handed. When challenged, she confessed she had indeed stabbed herself and descended the ladder into the river. What motivated this act? Her boyfriend was a merchant seaman. When last on shore leave he had bought furniture for her flat. Unknown to him, not only had she been working as a prostitute, but she had sold the furniture to pay off debts. On his return he discovered this loss and after a row he stormed off and returned to sea. In a fit of pique she had carried out the act of self-harm. The policeman told me the reason he took the matter so seriously was that had she drowned, her boyfriend, now at sea, would have been the prime suspect—especially with the stab wounds and with others knowing about their altercation over the furniture and, he suspected, the prostitution.

My final Christmas Eve on call for the firm[1] was quiet, but in the late evening and during the night we had a huge number of 'patients' who required observation on account of head injuries incurred in drunken fracas or falls. The observation unit in the Accident Room only had six beds, and we eventually had another thirty or so scattered throughout the hospital. The old Nightingale wards sometimes accommodated up to five in so-called centre beds, but this put extra pressure on the nursing staff. Peter D's wife Nancy was shocked when she attended with him on the customary Christmas Day greeting of staff and patients. Instead of seeing a few sweet old ladies and postoperative patients, there was an untidy collection of smelly, sweaty drunks sleeping it off. Peter D had long since been defeated in his mission to preserve old traditions by carving the turkeys, and he soon left the patients to their trays from a heated trolley.

---

1. The now obsolete term used for the medical staff in charge of two wards, male and female, and consisting of two consultants, a senior registrar, registrar and two house officers.

After my eighteen months on the firm, Prof Johnston called and suggested I needed a change. Peter D was not pleased, informing me I needed at least two years with him if I wanted to offer vascular surgery as a sub-specialty. But the issue had been decided. Peter and I got on well, and as he realised I would not work for him again, he invited Mary and I, with the boys, to his large mansion near Corbridge for afternoon tea. At first the boys were shy, but they soon lost their inhibitions and to their parents' embarrassment, started larking around. The Dickinsons had a leather rhinoceros, large enough for a child to ride, and Michael started treating it like a bucking bronco. I was sure he would cause irreparable damage to what was clearly an expensive item, and it was a relief to get away. Peter D died in the summer of 2013, in his ninety-first year, and at the reception after his funeral I met his eldest son and mentioned the rhino. He said it was still in the family. It had lost an ear but was otherwise intact thirty-seven years later.

# Chapter Nine

# A Flash in the Pan

In February 1977, I was transferred back to my old hunting ground, Pavilion 1, site of my house job eleven years previously, but now occupied by Leslie Brian Fleming and Frederick Denis Hindmarsh. Of the four general surgical units in the RVI, this was the least popular with trainees, for reasons that will become clear. Brian Fleming had been a loyal and hardworking first assistant to Prof Lowdon and was blessed with manual dexterity that made him a quick, skilful surgeon. In the 1960s he was known as 'Flash' Fleming, probably referring to a combination of operative speed and his style of dress. Being a bachelor and living with his mother, he obviously had no-one else to spend his income on, as evidenced by his fashionable clothes and cars. He appeared in no hurry to be appointed a consultant and hung around until Feg retired, when presumably he was a shoo-in. He was a complex character. His rapid speech was like that of the late TV personality Larry Grayson, whose act relied on his effeminacy. Everything about Brian was hyperactive—his walk, his camp hand movements, his general impatience. He was fuelled by a large intake of black coffee, accompanied by almost as many cigarettes as Corbett Barnsley. Between cases he sat in the surgeons' rest room with a large flask, holding a cigarette and tapping the ash in an exaggerated manner, peering over his half-moon spectacles as he made a show of rapidly completing the *Daily Telegraph* crossword for all to see. Despite the almost universally held view about his sexuality by those who knew him, there was never any evidence of a relationship and my own opinion, as an amateur Freud, is that he was an asexual narcissist. Everything and everybody had to revolve around him, and I suspect the presence of another impinging on his life was unthinkable. His one concession was to take one of the paediatric sisters, an unpopular spinster, to the annual Nurses' Ball.

He was appointed academic sub-dean, a position he was unsuited for, but being single, I suppose it was thought he had the time to devote to it. He did seem to take some interest in students but could be unkindly rigid in his interpretation of the 'rules'. One boy was allowed only three days' leave following the death of a parent, and another who, due to no fault of his own, arrived three days late after a three-month elective in South America, was made to repeat the whole month of his next assignment instead of having free time to study.

Flash was a sitting duck for the annual Christmas concert. I was the first to portray him, as 'Crazy Legs' Fleming, a Red Indian brave in a sketch based on High Noon, but all I did was exaggerate his walk and the manner of his smoking. Subsequent portrayals were apparently unnecessarily cruel, but he insisted on attending with his mother in tow, to demonstrate he could take it. Despite his apparent but unproven predilections, he always seemed to have female house staff. The choice would be his, of course, and I don't think they applied specifically for his post—we applied to the hospital and went where we were sent. The nursing sisters were loyal to him, although they were the strangest I ever came across in the RVI. The saving grace was the staff nurses being a jolly, sensible bunch. The house staff told me they and the sisters were often asked, 'What are they saying about me?', referring to me and the registrar.

Brian had to have total control and could be petty. He never delegated and changed virtually all decisions, even trivial ones, made by me or the registrar. He did most of the elective surgery, and even when he left some simple cases, such as hernias or varicose veins, he had to peep over one's shoulder and suggest some minor change in technique to copy him. It was a hopeless place to be a trainee, would not have survived modern governance and was regarded as a penance one had to pay. Brian, of course, thought he was wonderful. It's interesting that most of the moaning about him came from men. Women seemed protective of him and treated him (subconsciously, I suspect) as one of their own. I wonder how he would have responded to a female trainee.

I already knew the other consultant, Denis Hindmarsh, as Feg's colleague. He was now approaching retirement and we saw less of him than Brian because half his contract was at South Shields. Old photographs showed Denis was strikingly handsome as a young man and was apparently regarded as a 'bright young thing', but at some stage he suffered a nervous breakdown, the nature of which was never discussed by those of his generation. The only hint of some problem was uttered by Feg who, when he went on holiday, said to 'keep an eye on Mr Hindmarsh', but did not enlighten us. His uncle, TA Hindmarsh, had been a surgeon in the RVI, well-known for his skill at thyroidectomies, which he passed on to Denis, who had an original mind, inventing his own operation for inguinal (groin) hernia, termed the 'contractile' repair. But he had a limited repertoire, which is a polite way of saying he was good at what he was good at. He was laid back and I always marvelled at how his knots held. He tied them so adroitly that it looked careless. One of his disarming habits was the production at thirty-second intervals of a sudden and fleeting Gordon Brown smile—his face transforming from a cheerful, tooth-baring grin into a blank expression in less than a second. He strolled with a lethargic swagger and every movement, such as the mannered stance at the end of the bed, or a turn in someone's direction on hearing them speak, was slow and deliberate. He was a keen golfer and if he wore brown suedes and a navy-blue blazer for a Saturday morning ward round, we knew he was bound for Foxton in north Northumberland for a round. He was a terrible snob, but I liked him because there was no malice about him. He didn't seem to have much empathy for his patients, however.

One of his eccentricities was believing intravenous fluids should not be given unless absolutely necessary. A patient who would not take oral fluids for a couple of days after an abdominal procedure would receive tap water in a milk bottle erected on a drip stand, and instilled via a red rubber tube up the rectum, instead of IV saline! In fact, this is a perfectly safe and cheap way of administering fluid for a short time, but it was regarded as quaint and obsolete even then.

Denis could frequently be unintentionally amusing. His first words one morning were, 'I see the bloody car workers have gone on strike again!' He then began a rant about the working classes. It was this extension of his argument from the car workers to the working classes in general that irritated me, and to my own surprise I leapt to their defence, saying that most of our patients were working class and by and large were reasonable, civilised individuals who weren't out to destroy society. He thought for a while before replying.

'I suppose you're right, Clarke,' he said. 'I know the working classes well. I've worked with them during the war. We had the most wonderful swimming off Tobruk. If it had not been for that bugger Hitler we could have had a whale of a time.'

Between theatre cases he often pinched the nurses' *Daily Mirror* in the rest room and sank as low as he could in his seat. One article made him harrumph—was when Marlborough College began admitting girls to the sixth form and the opinion was expressed that it might discourage homosexuality in an otherwise all boys' school. Denis exclaimed in theatre that it was a load of rubbish. He had been to a boarding school and seen no evidence of homosexuality. The anaesthetist, John Inkster, a tiny man, highly intelligent and with trenchant views, retorted, 'Well, maybe nobody fancied you.' Denis took this as a personal affront and refused to speak to him for the rest of the list.

In his outpatient clinic I tended to see the return cases. Most were follow-ups after surgery, but some were still under investigation of their presenting condition, and I soon learned that Denis nearly always requested the wrong test first. I got on the wrong end of one of his mistakes when I was called into his consulting room, where a lady radiologist was holding up the first film taken during a barium meal requested for abdominal discomfort and swelling. On the screen was the trickle of barium progressing through the oesophagus, but lower down was the skeleton of a foetus, approaching a twenty-eight-week size. Denis merely chuckled and said he was sure Mr Clarke would be delighted to give the lady the good news. She was called and escorted into my adjoining room by a nurse, who placed her on a couch curtained off from her seated, burly, lorry-driver husband. In the flurried interval between, I somehow smelled a rat and when I sat down next to my new patient she had a curious expression on her face—a mixture of sadness, apprehension and even a little smile.

'Do you know what the x-ray has shown?' I whispered as quietly as I could. When she demurred, I said, 'Surely you must know you're going to have a baby?'

At this a tear ran down her cheek and, despite my attempt to preserve privacy, a deep voice boomed from beyond the curtain.

'Well, that's very strange because I've had the operation,' clearly meaning a vasectomy.

Quickly trying to defuse what could have been an embarrassing confrontation, I explained that unfortunately a few vasectomies failed, and we had better get him checked. It was obvious, however, that the poor woman had been in denial and must have had an affair while he was away working. I have no idea how long he was placated by my delaying tactic of suggesting he might no longer be infertile, but I telephoned the GP to put him in the picture. Like most experienced family doctors he had seen it all before and was unfazed by being left to deal with it.

When operating, Denis wore an all-in-one romper suit instead of separate shirt and trousers, and he stood on a mat. On the rare occasions when he was called out for an emergency to a different theatre, the mat had to be sent for. He was once discussing his friendship with the well-known London surgeon Arthur Dickson Wright, then reputed to be the best after-dinner speaker in the capital, but now better known as the reviled, violent and alcoholic father (or so she claimed) of his now deceased daughter, Clarissa, of *Two Fat Ladies* TV fame.

'I learned a lot from Dickie Wright,' said Denis.

After waiting expectantly for some technical tip of operative surgery, I was amused to hear that one should always use a padded mat to relieve one's feet. Insistence on such accoutrements, even at emergencies, might seem childish, but I once had to call Peter D out to help with a traumatic tear of a femoral artery associated with a fractured femur, and he was initially reluctant to come because he wouldn't be able to wear his usual shoes. Fortunately, he relented.

Each theatre closed for a week or so for maintenance, and on one occasion we had to use the professorial theatre. There was always an element of rivalry between firms, and Denis and I were in the changing room getting ready for the first case when a bookcase caught his eye. It contained all the expensive, large volumes of Rob and Smith's *Operative Surgery*, which were available for on-the-spot reference, and to deter borrowing were each held captive by a chain attaching them to the wall.

'That tells me two things about this firm,' said Denis. 'First, they don't know their work, and secondly, you can't trust the buggers.'

Denis was almost the last of the RVI's old breed who could request special items such as his romper suit and mat. His gloves came from a different supplier from all others, and he had an obsession with white silk, rather than the standard black, as a ligature. He was the only surgeon who used it. Whether his insistence was because he thought it emerged from the silkworm's bum that colour, I never knew. He once asked for Brompton's cocktail for a terminal patient, only to be informed, to his fury, that it was obsolete and no longer available. As the name implies, this preparation was developed at the Royal Brompton Hospital in London in the 1920s, initially for those dying from TB, but it entered widespread use for any terminal illness and was a mixture of heroin, cocaine, chloroform water, an alcohol base of brandy or gin, sometimes chlorpromazine (Largactil) as an antiemetic and sedative, and honey to counter the bitterness. Sounds wonderful! The pharmacy no longer provided Brompton's cocktail or some other long-established substances such as Mercurochrome. This red liquid was the best astringent antiseptic going, but because it was nephrotoxic (adversely affecting kidney function) in large doses—that is, if you covered a quarter of the body in it—the so-called 'academic' nurses were flexing their muscles with their newly acquired status and attempting to ban this and certain others. It was being replaced by convenience products, usually expensive and American, which simply macerated wounds. Contrary to their proclamations, these substances made them more prone to infection, whereas Mercurochrome dried out the area, which could then be left exposed to the air, visible for inspection and without the necessity for other than a simple dressing.

***

A man in his twenties was admitted with abdominal discomfort and swelling. He appeared to have an eighteen-week pregnancy and his scrotum was empty of testes. He came from an old-fashioned, deeply religious family, his siblings being sisters, and it seems he had not missed his testes. He had an inoperable malignant teratoma of one or other of his abdominal testes (undescended testes are pre-malignant) and was treated with chemotherapy. One of the agents used, bleomycin, causes severe oral ulceration, making eating normally impossible for some time. He was fed intravenously via a central line in the subclavian vein in the neck, the tip of which was almost in the heart. It was Easter Monday, we were on call, and the registrar and I were at the sister's desk when we heard a panicked cry from the single cubicle behind us, where our patient was situated. As we entered he was shouting, 'I've gone blind, I've gone blind!' In the confusion it took a few seconds to notice his feeding catheter had dislodged and was dripping white fat emulsion, Intralipid, into the bed, but also we could hear without a stethoscope the so-called waterwheel murmur caused by air in the heart. This settled and his general condition remained good, but he was blind, and examination of the optic fundi revealed white segments in the blood vessels indicative of air. This was unexpected, because any air sucked into the vein with respiration on disconnection of the drip should have gone to the lungs, not to the arterial side of the circulation, so one had to postulate the presence of a small residual congenital patent foramen ovale between right and left atria (that is, a small 'hole in the heart'). Sophisticated modern cardiac ultrasound has shown that this anatomical abnormality is more common than previously thought. The registrar, Peter Veitch, had the bright idea of contacting Prof Denis Walder with a view to treatment in the hyperbaric chamber used mainly for compression sickness. Walder was enthusiastic and rapidly mobilised his assistant to set it up and sat with the patient while he was treated with hyperbaric oxygen to about two-to-three atmospheres. Unfortunately, there was no improvement, which the prof said should have occurred if it was going to succeed. However, on the morning of the second day after the event I visited him, and as I walked round to one side of his bed his head followed me. I thought he was reacting to my footsteps, but he said, 'I can see you, doctor!' All was well. Unsurprisingly, though, he did succumb to his advanced malignancy months later.

A Glaswegian in his twenties was admitted with abdominal pain. He had an upper midline scar suggestive of previous ulcer surgery, but from his history we got the impression that things were more complicated and requested his old notes from Stobhill Hospital. He seemed to be a drifter, but when I arranged to gastroscope him in the endoscopy unit, there to give him moral support was a tanned, muscular young man with a blond bouffant hairstyle and a V-necked sweater that exposed a large gold medallion. He put his fingers to his mouth in the manner of Frank Spencer, as portrayed by Michael Crawford in the 1970s' English sitcom, Some Mothers Do 'Ave 'Em.

'Ooh, what are you going to do to him?' he cooed, showing almost maternal concern. The examination showed no abnormality. When his medical notes arrived they revealed he was the only child of well-to-do Victorian parents who had produced him relatively late in life. To their horror, when he was sixteen they discovered he was offering himself as a male prostitute to finance his alcohol habit. Largely ignorant about homosexuality but certainly believing it to be a disease, they took him to see a psychiatrist privately. Peter Veitch and I perused his notes in the seminar room, and one sentence written by the psychiatrist to the family's GP stood out as unique and startling. We had never heard anything like it before, nor have I since. Before revealing it, I should point out that, probably as a result of his chain-smoking, Brian Fleming had a parchment-sallow complexion accompanied by fullish lips.

'He has the sallow complexion and the thick lips of the constitutional homosexual,' read the sentence describing our patient.

On reading this we roared with laughter, both obviously on the same wavelength, and we were still laughing when the door was flung open by Brian.

'What are you laughing at?' he repeated in a staccato, with a hint of paranoia. Trying to keep a straight face, I explained we had received the notes about our puzzling patient (who had been lying through his teeth about his past history) and came across the following statement, which I solemnly read out to him. Brian compressed his lips and inverted them into his mouth.

'Wem, I'b nebber hermed ob dat bepore,' he said, with difficulty, and he flounced out.

About this time, Sam McKelvey, Prof Johnston's first assistant, obtained a consultant post in his home city of Belfast. Both men were built like Ian Paisley and just as loud and brash—it must be something in the diet. I knew the favourite to replace him was Johnny Farndon, despite his being four years junior to me, because he had declared his wish to become an academic, but I also knew the post would provide a large clinical load and responsibility, which I was not currently getting, and felt my application might demonstrate this. I did Brian the courtesy of asking his advice, but he was non-committal. He couldn't really deter me on the grounds of the wish to pursue an academic career or not as he had held the post himself, and despite his title of academic sub-dean, in no way could he be described as an academic. Anyway, I applied, and Johnny and I were interviewed. As we chatted beforehand Johnny was clearly nervous, but I was unusually bullish, feeling I had nothing to lose. The Prof was away, but no way would he have allowed his colleagues to appoint other than his choice, so the interview was a formality. I was asked why I had applied when I was already a senior registrar. I replied that I needed more operative surgery than I was getting. As expected, Johnny got the job, but judging by what transpired, my comments probably hit the spot.

I had submitted my MS thesis a few months earlier and knew the result would be announced one Friday in August and expected a call from the Prof's office. Having not heard by five o'clock, and expecting the worst, I called Joan, the Prof's secretary, whom I had known since I was a student. She sounded flustered, which worried me even more, and said she would try to find him. With bated breath I heard her footsteps trotting along the corridor and, in the distance, the booming voice of the prof.

'Good news, David,' he said suddenly. 'You've been awarded the MS with commendation. Well done, congratulations. Now, I've been meaning to speak to you. As the *senior* senior registrar, I wonder if you would like to join my unit, with Johnny Farndon.'

When I next saw Brian after the weekend he was in a coolly furious mood, accusing me of plotting to leave his unit without discussing it with him first. What really riled him was that previous senior registrars had expressed their displeasure at the lack of 'training' under his supervision. I protested that it was the Prof's suggestion that I move and assumed it had been mentioned as a matter of courtesy, but to no avail. Brian believed what he wanted to and that was that. He knew I hadn't initiated the move but didn't have the balls to confront the big Ulsterman. Anyway, in theory, being the trainee, the position was supposed to be for my benefit, not his, but this was not the attitude taken—unlike today, when things have turned full circle and trainees rule the roost.

One other point, just to stick the stiletto in a little further. When Mary and I attended a North of England Surgical Society dinner, she was placed to Brian's left, the lady to his right being already of his acquaintance. He didn't say a single word to Mary all evening. That just about sums him up. A skilful technician, hardworking, but a seriously flawed personality whose defects sadly overshadowed his gifts.

# Chapter Ten

# An Absence of Professors

And so, with a mixture of relief and slight apprehension, I transferred to the professorial unit in September 1977. Professor Johnston was a formidable figure. His nickname derived from his initials, IDAJ, 'I decide all jobs', and was pretty accurate. One didn't relax in his presence, everyone keen to show enthusiasm and to impress. Fortunately, he fitted the collective noun we used for men in his position—an 'absence' of professors—and was often away at visits, conferences and examinations, allowing Johnny Farndon and I to get along with much of the work. I knew Johnny and I would gel. There was no rivalry. We were both easy going and with me being four years older, I could sometimes assist him and even take him through procedures he hadn't performed before. Also, the Prof's two consultant colleagues, Ross Taylor and the senior lecturer, kept to themselves. Ross had been in the RVI since he was a senior house officer. He worked ferociously hard and had not appeared in a hurry to climb the ladder of promotion. He was eventually rewarded with an NHS consultant post, having been a senior lecturer which, although of consultant status, is academic in nature, with a limited contract, and so appointees are expected to move on to professorial chairs in due course. He took up renal transplantation after John Swinney pioneered the procedure in Newcastle and also took part in the vascular rota. He undertook private practice and now he was no longer beholden to the Professor, worked very much on a sessional basis and did not 'hang around' as much as he used to. An American visitor came once and, unused to the working practices of the NHS, asked Ross if he could shadow him for a day. The day proved not exactly typical, but the timing was perfect. In the morning Ross did a leisurely business round with the juniors, followed by formal teaching at the bedside with medical students. After a light lunch, he did an aortofemoral graft on his vascular list, finishing at about five o'clock. He happened to be on both vascular and transplant call. No sooner had he completed the graft than a ruptured aortic aneurysm was phoned in. As he was closing the abdomen of the latter, another triple A (abdominal aortic aneurysm) came in, and in the middle of the night a cadaver kidney became available and was duly transplanted. Almost twenty-four hours had elapsed. The American was ecstatic.

'That was great, Ross, really great,' he said. 'Now, how much do you reckon you've just earned?'

Ross thought for a while. 'Oh, about fifty quid,' he said.

'Gee, back in the good ol' US of A, you'd have just collected 20,000 bucks!'

At least there was only one professor, one senior lecturer and one lecturer in each department in those days. Soon, distinguished long-standing individuals were rewarded with a personal chair, and then Americanisation set in, so that nearly every Tom, Dick and Harry became a 'Professor', even in district general hospitals. Thus, over the years, the collective noun switched from 'absence' to 'proliferation' of professors. In the USA, the head of an academic department has the title of professor, often named after the donor of the funds to create the chair, and this title appears on official publications, but he is never addressed as such—always simply as 'Doctor X'. I'm sure this is because so many others may also call themselves 'professor', including assistant and associate professors, who are often relatively junior, until the original sense of the title becomes demeaned.

The endoscopy unit was then fairly new and in a side-room off a ward. It was run with the coolest efficiency by a slim, dark, quiet-as-a-mouse SEN or state enrolled nurse, who do two years training instead of three, were often considered 'inferior' and now no longer existing, having been replaced by 'auxiliaries'. She was marvellous. Everyone in the NHS knows people like her, who give years of devoted, efficient duty for scant reward and no prospect of promotion for lack of the 'right' qualifications, but whose absence on holiday causes the place to temporarily collapse. I soon became proficient at upper gastrointestinal endoscopy. Most older general surgeons never learned the technique (which is easy to acquire), and simply referred patients to us. Colonoscopy is more difficult and was still in its infancy then.

One of my most memorable cases was a fisherman in his early twenties from Peterhead, whose boat was docked in South Shields. By some miracle, he was found at the bottom of a dry dock, into which he had either fallen or been pushed. God knows how he survived. His only injuries were concussion, a fractured pelvis and a huge retroperitoneal haematoma (bleeding into the tissues behind the abdominal contents and surrounding the kidneys). He was discovered after dawn and had almost certainly been in the dock overnight. The consequent loss of blood and hypotension led to kidney failure, and he was transferred to the RVI for dialysis. His renal function was improving when blood suddenly started pouring from his rectum. On recovery from severe blood loss of whatever cause, one can, rarely, develop ischaemic colitis, in which the reduction in blood supply to the colon damages the lining, which bleeds. However, this condition is not only usually self-limiting but is even rarer in one so young. He needed a transfusion of several units, but the bleeding persisted and was clearly not going to stop spontaneously. Without removing the whole colon 'blind', so to speak, the only way to identify the bleeding point was a mesenteric arteriogram, a procedure conducted only rarely then. We managed to get one, which had to be terminated due to his unstable condition shortly after extravasation of injected dye was seen at the hepatic flexure (where the colon turns below the liver). I proceeded to do a right hemicolectomy, thus removing the source of bleeding, which ceased. One week later he re-bled torrentially and I did a blind left hemicolectomy, once again stopping the bleeding. Ischaemic colitis in the rectum is even more uncommon, and usually mild, but exactly one week later he bled again, so there was no alternative but to remove the rectum and create an ileostomy, that is, a permanent anus in which the end of the small bowel, the ileum, is formed into a spout and brought out to the surface of the abdominal wall. As you can imagine, following a combination of severe injury, kidney failure and the addition of three major operations in two weeks, he sustained extensive weight loss and muscular weakness, and although he made a full recovery, it was prolonged. I once saw him virtually suspended between two female physiotherapists when they were 'mobilising' him, and he reminded me of the late Rod Hull's Emu, both weak, skinny legs just swinging in the breeze. I always maintained his life was saved by Tennent's Lager because he had almost no appetite and it was all he would ask for and willingly drink. I was tempted to write to the company with this recommendation. Very ill patients often lose their sense of taste for a while, and it can take months to regain their preoperative weight. His appetite may also have been reduced by the presence of the ileostomy—it tends to work shortly after eating and in hospital transparent bags are preferred, meaning the effluent can be observed, and this may have put him off his food. At home patients use opaque bags. I once saw a man who mentally rejected his ileostomy for this reason. Once again it had been done as an emergency without the chance to prepare himself, and he simply refused to eat because he associated it with the production of what he regarded as an offensive effluent. Fortunately, a psychiatrist cured him using suggestion therapy under sedation.

I was called out of my bed one night by no less a person than the Professor of Anaesthesia himself, Ed Cooper, requesting my presence to do a tracheostomy. A lady needed an emergency hysterectomy but suffered from ankylosing spondylitis (a fused spine due to a rheumatoid-like condition) and he was unable to intubate her. The latter was necessary because her abdominal muscles needed to be paralysed to allow the surgeon sufficient muscle relaxation to perform the procedure. The drug used to paralyse them also acts on the muscles of respiration, so that ventilation was required for the operation, after which the drug is reversed by a specific agent. The smell of ether as I entered the hospital would have guided me to the theatre had I not known which one to seek. Ether was almost obsolete then, having been superseded by newer agents, but it was safe, even though it irritated the lungs and was flammable. Prof Cooper was sitting with a mask clamped on the patient's face, and her chin was almost on her chest. My immediate reaction was to exclaim, 'How on earth am I going to do a tracheostomy on her?'

'David,' he said, calmly. 'I am not going to call you out in the middle of the night to ask you to do something easy.'

It was almost impossible to extend the neck to access the trachea and I still don't remember how I did it, but I did. Ed Cooper's response stayed with me, and I have used it myself.

Prof Johnston had an interest in endocrine surgery and we often did parathyroidectomies. The four parathyroid glands lie behind and close to the thyroid in the neck, each one normally being about the size of a pea. Their function is to regulate the calcium level in the blood, which becomes raised if one is the source of a benign tumour (adenoma), or if all four become enlarged for reasons unknown (hyperplasia). The raised calcium can cause kidney stones, thinning of the bones and general symptoms such as dyspepsia, constipation and depression. In the seventies our usual source of patients was those with stones whose serum calcium had been measured. Others were picked up when a raised calcium was a chance finding, but this was much less common then. Today, a routine biochemical screen includes a calcium screening together with a multitude of other chemicals, but back then a calcium had to be specifically requested with a good reason. These days many subjects are discovered before they are symptomatic. The old surgical textbooks show photographs of patients with advanced bone disease, virtually unknown today, but I do remember one man who was transferred to us from the old Yugoslavia, and whose bone disease was so bad that he sustained a pathological fracture of the femur simply as he was moved from trolley to operating table.

The routine was for the Prof to remain working in his office while his first assistant or the senior registrar opened the neck and displayed the thyroid. He was then summoned via an intercom between office and theatre and boomed back in his Belfast-mid-Atlantic accent that he was on his way. Shortly afterwards, a door slammed, followed by the furious splashing sound of the Prof scrubbing up. He then appeared, all fingers and thumbs, as star of the show in his daydream at least. Meanwhile, the anaesthetist, surgeon, assistant and nursing staff waited patiently. He then took over, searching for the parathyroids. Even if a single adenoma was easily found, it was still subjected to microscopic inspection by frozen section, a technique in which a piece of tissue is quickly frozen so that a thin section can be cut by an instrument called a microtome and examined unstained by a pathologist. Each gland was treated similarly, in turn. This was quite a performance, prolonging the operation considerably, but did not perturb the Prof because it was the only one on the list in which he participated. Each frozen section took about twenty minutes. The prof's anaesthetist, Guy Horton, an older man with Edwardian sideburns and frequent facial tics, was occasionally irritated by it all, especially the palaver with the intercom, which was generally viewed as a professorial conceit. Once I opened the neck and was encouraged by Guy to delay notifying the great man until the last minute. As luck would have it, I found all four parathyroids very easily, and one was the seat of an obvious adenoma. Guy could not disguise his delight and was almost hopping with joy. Soon, I had the affected gland totally mobilised and attached only by its tiny blood supply, before the Prof was contacted. As usual, he stormed in like a hurricane into a sea of tranquillity and was quite deflated to find that there was virtually nothing left to do. He did, however, have the good-humoured grace to admit he had 'stolen' the case.

The senior house officer was an interesting chap called Jan Stanek, a citizen of the former Czechoslovakia when it was under communist rule. He was on a school trip to the UK in 1968 when the Russian tanks moved in, in response to the Prague Spring, Alexander Dubček's policies of liberalisation. At least that's the story he told me, but in 1968 he was twenty, a bit old to be still at school. Anyway, apparently he claimed political asylum, which was granted but presumably severed him from his family until the Velvet Revolution of 1989 that ended Soviet domination. By means never explained, but I assume the British taxpayer, he got to Oxford and graduated in medicine in 1975. He was house surgeon at the old Westminster Hospital to Professor Harold Ellis, whose influence no doubt persuaded IDAJ to take him on as a senior house officer. Jan was a friendly chap and liked the British because of our 'filthy sense of humour', but there was an element of mystery about him. He told me he was in class at school when news was delivered in a sonorous voice over the Tannoy that the hero of the Soviet Union and first man in space, Yuri Gagarin, had been killed in a helicopter crash. The whole class erupted in cheers and foot stamping, much to the horror of the schoolmaster, who feared possible reprisals if such unalloyed joy in his pupils was perceived by the superintendent as indicating he was teaching anti-Soviet propaganda. During the first few weeks I knew him, Jan often talked about restaurants and wine, and once even about polo. This set me thinking.

'You know, Stanek,' I said quite boldly, admittedly in a jocular tone, when we were scrubbing up for an operation. 'You've only been earning a salary for a couple of years, you drive an Alfa Romeo sports car, you know everything about wine and fine dining and you've even played polo, which must be expensive even if you don't own your ponies. How can you afford it? You must be a KGB agent!'

He roared with laughter but never gave any explanation of how he could afford his lifestyle, and I still don't know. It was obviously a hint of things to come, though. After that, whenever he needed to call me in from home, I would pick up the phone to hear, 'KGB here!', in a deep voice, followed by a laugh.

He later returned to the Westminster Hospital, where Professor Ellis must have taken him under his wing again, as they co-wrote a book describing the history of surgical instruments. I didn't hear of him again until a few years ago when I saw him as the resident expert plastic surgeon on a Channel 4 programme. He has a thriving private practice in aesthetic surgery in London and left the NHS entirely in 1984, just nine years after qualifying, to devote himself to full-time private work. Without wishing to sound envious, what a good return for the British taxpayer, eh?

On Christmas Eve 1977, I was on call for emergencies. A few days earlier I admitted a man with intermittent total haematuria (blood in urine), cystoscoped him and detected blood issuing from the left ureteric orifice. After inserting a fine catheter up the ureter, an x-ray revealed a cancer in the renal pelvis, so he needed a nephroureterectomy, removal of the kidney plus its ureter down to the bladder, an operation involving two incisions. I started at nine in the morning and continued with other emergencies right through until four on Christmas Day morning without a break, except for a short hiatus when my friend and ex-colleague Eric Butchart arrived with Ray Dobson, one of the cardiac surgeons at Seaham Hall, to carry out a pericardiectomy on a child, a rarely performed operation that I was interested to observe. My final operation was on a skinny, middle-aged man with a perforated duodenal ulcer. The operation was straightforward, but he had chronic bronchitis, and the anaesthetist wanted to keep him ventilated on the ITU, so he needed a urinary catheter, which usually took a minute or two. Until now, no-one had seen his penis, but to our dismay, it was the seat of what looked like a small cauliflower. At first sight this appeared to be a cancer, but it was, fortunately, a florid bunch of condylomata, or benign warts. Catheterisation by the usual route was impossible. In fact, we were amazed he could pee, and he needed a suprapubic catheter directly into the bladder. This only took another thirty minutes or so, but it felt like the straw that broke the camel's back, being an unexpected addition to what had been a marathon session. Despite the fatigue, there is nothing like that self-righteous feeling one gets when driving home after such a day, especially when everything has gone well. Within a few hours, however, I was expected to bring the boys into the hospital for the traditional Christmas Day visit and check up on all the emergencies.

# Chapter Eleven

# A Cut Above

My long-standing interest in the metabolic and hormonal response to trauma was further inspired by hearing Francis D Moore speak and reading his publications. I now faced a dilemma. On the one hand, I already had my Master of Surgery and further research experience was not required. I had no plans to follow a career in academic surgery and if I was to take a year out it would be better to go to a clinical centre, preferably in vascular surgery. Some colleagues went to St Mark's in London to do colorectal surgery, but others did an additional year of research—George Bone in Edmonton, Alberta, in cancer research, and Peter Wright and Ian Miller in Boston with Dr Moore. Consultant jobs in those days were still advertised in general surgery, usually with a subspecialty interest, and although I had experience in vascular surgery, it had chosen me rather than I choosing it. I had worked for two excellent surgeons who happened to be interested in that field and also flirted with offering urology as an interest. As I had no clinical centre in mind, and no-one offered me constructive advice, I felt I would regret not following my instincts to go to Dr Moore's department in Boston, where I was accepted after a letter of introduction from Prof Johnston.

Looking back four decades at the arrangements to be made while I was still in a busy job makes me feel exhausted. We were luckier than most, however, because months earlier Mary and I met my old classmate Gerry McLoughlin and his wife Liz, who were now settled in Liverpool but also planned to spend a year in Boston, several months before us. They offered to find a house for us to rent in the same street as them in the small town of Needham, eight miles west of Boston. All the houses were owned by the same Italian American landlord and occupied mainly by itinerants. We had to go as a family to Edinburgh to obtain J1 non-resident alien visas directly from the American consul. Paul, aged five, told his primary school teacher we were going for a 'freezer', which puzzled her, thinking 120 miles was a long way to drive for a bargain. We could stay for a year and a day without paying UK tax on my US salary. After that we were no longer entitled to work there nor return to do so within two years. President Jimmy Carter was apparently alarmed at the influx of foreigners applying for jobs in competition with US graduates, and he overreacted by making such limitations.

I sold the car, rented our house to a New Zealand family and flew out a week ahead of Mary and the boys so I could set up the new home. Monday April 17th 1978 was the big day. Aged thirty-five but still wet behind the ears, never having seen a Boeing 747 before, I was seated beside a Bostonian mother and her grown-up daughter, who were interested that I was going to a Harvard teaching hospital but totally ignored my excited observation that Concorde was gated close by.

I did not realise Logan International Airport was on an island off Boston and thought we were landing perilously close to the sea. Gerry was kindly there to meet me, in his green VW saloon, disappointingly a European car when they were still relatively uncommon in the States. Maple Street, Needham, was a quiet *cul-de-sac* with semi-detached clapboard houses and communal 'backyards' (their term for lawns), with the railroad running behind our house.

Furnished accommodation seemed to be unknown, and the next day Gerry took me to the warehouse where he had rented his furniture. It proved expensive, but we persevered. Some people acquired furniture at 'garage sales', a practice and term that only crossed the Atlantic thirty or more years later. Despite being a consumerist society, the Americans tried to sell anything they no longer needed, instead of either giving things away or simply disposing of what could be perceived as rubbish.

Gerry had the day well planned. He took me across the Charles River to register at the Harvard University office and showed me the statue of John Harvard, surrounded by college dormitories in the eponymously named yard. Harvard founded the college only sixteen years after the Pilgrim Fathers arrived in the *Mayflower*. He also showed me the famous newspaper kiosk in Harvard Square where one could buy newspapers from around the world, including Britain, the day after publication. Being of Irish descent and a good Catholic, Gerry was amused to tell me how he once saw a chap reading the *Sligo Champion* in the kiosk. Once settled in I made a trip every Monday to buy the *Sunday Times*, but soon went native and took the Sunday edition of the *New York Times*, which was over an inch thick.

Francis D Moore (known as Franny or FDM) was now aged sixty-six and had relinquished the position of Moseley Professorship of Surgery and head of department to John Mannick, a vascular surgeon, and Gerry's research chief. Franny moved out of the Peter Bent Brigham Hospital (PBBH, or simply 'the Brigham'), and into the Good Samaritan building close by.

The Brigham was built in 1912, and during my year its multi-storey replacement took shape and was visible from our laboratory. When I arrived there was a large crater in the ground, and when I left there was a building of fourteen octagonal-shaped storeys that had just been 'topped out'. It was clumsily renamed the Brigham and Women's Hospital, because it was now an amalgam of the old Brigham and the Boston Lying-in Hospital, the Children's Center and the small Robert Bent Brigham. The whole area between Huntington Avenue and Brookline Avenue was a huge medical complex—the Brigham, Harvard Medical School, the Children's Center, the Countway Library, Harvard School of Public Health, the Sidney Farber Cancer Center, the New England Deaconess Hospital and the Beth Israel Hospital, all nearby.

FDM now held the Elliott Carr Cutler Chair in surgery and had an office in the Countway Library, the largest in the world devoted solely to medicine. Now in the twilight of his career he no longer operated but still saw patients who he farmed out to young attending surgeons in the Brigham if they required surgery. His research budget was much diminished compared to at his peak, but still large by British standards. He was also involved in raising funds for the new hospital.

Franny was a modern Renaissance man, whose constellation of talents was staggering. He had a privileged upbringing near Chicago, spending summers at the family ranch in Wyoming, and was educated at a small private school founded by the affluent local community, including his parents. The quality of the education is evidenced by four scholars from his year of about thirty pupils attending Harvard. A fellow pupil was Laura Bartlett, his childhood sweetheart. They married while he was still a medical student and raised five children together. Even when I knew him, he still referred to his beloved Laura as 'my bride'. He was a talented musician who could play the piano, clarinet and accordion and he took part in and wrote musical sketches and plays. At Harvard he was president of the university magazine, the *Harvard Lampoon*, and joined the Hasty Pudding Club, the equivalent of the Cambridge Footlights in the UK. In 1934 he wrote the club's annual show entitled 'Hades, the Ladies', which imagined what was unthinkable, Harvard as a co-educational institution, which, of course, it inevitably became. The director of the

1934 show was a certain Alistair Cooke, who held a Commonwealth Fund Fellowship at the time and became a lifelong friend of FDM's. The show was such a success that it went on a road trip, which included a performance before President and Mrs Roosevelt in the White House. The president had himself been a member of the Hasty Pudding Club in 1903. Cooke was born in Salford in 1908, educated in Blackpool and Cambridge and became a US citizen in the 1930s. He became well known in the States for introducing *Masterpiece Theater*, a US TV programme that showed the cream of British TV drama and ran from 1971 to 1992. Each episode began with him seated in a winged armchair and saying, 'Good evening, I'm Alistair Cooke', and in 1984 some of the show was reprised for a fifty-year reunion. The curtain opened to reveal the great man seated in his usual pose and mouthing the same introduction. This scene alone made the show worthwhile for the audience. Cooke was also known in the States for his TV series *America*, made for British viewers, the accompanying book proving successful in both Britain and America. But, of course, his real claim to fame in the UK was his weekly fifteen-minute radio programme *Letter from America*, which ran from 1946 until a month before his death, at ninety-five, in 2004—2,869 episodes.

Francis Moore's principal contribution to surgical knowledge was his research into the composition of the body and the metabolic, hormonal and nutritional consequences of trauma, including surgery and subsequent convalescence. Body composition means the amount of water in the body, the blood volume, the extracellular space, body cell mass and so on. Before such compartments were measured, replacement of blood and fluids following major injuries sustained in battle, burns or surgery was largely empirical, dictated by a 'seat-of-the-pants' policy. FDM's research enabled resuscitation to be conducted on a more scientific basis. His introduction to the subject was inspired by Fuller Albright, an endocrinologist at the Massachusetts General, where FDM did his surgical residency. Albright researched aspects of metabolism, biochemistry and nutrition, and under his tutelage FDM took a year out to learn basic research methods, including a course in nuclear physics. This latter proved invaluable to his later work with a variety of the newly available stable and radioactive isotopes after the war. Measurement of total body water, for example, was theoretically simple. A known quantity of 'heavy water', or $D_2O$, D being deuterium, a stable isotope of hydrogen, is injected into the experimental animal or human subject, the dilution measured by mass spectrography and the calculation easily made. $D_2O$ behaves the same as $H_2O$ and, being non-radioactive, is measured by its tiny difference in mass from $H_2O$, rather than using a Geiger counter. Other isotopes, both stable and radioactive, were used to measure further body compartments and chemical constituents, such as sodium, potassium and calcium, a process Franny termed 'a chemical dissection of the body by isotope dilution'. Separate components of a co-ordinated, long-term research programme were conducted by research fellows such as myself, passing through for a year or so, and a large number of scientific papers was published. They were combined in two textbooks which have become classics—*Metabolic Care of the Surgical Patient* (1959), a 1,100-page tome, and *The Body Cell Mass and its Supporting Environment* (1963). Franny's interest in burns was prompted by the tragic Coconut Grove fire in Boston in November 1942, in which almost 500 people died. At the time he was an on-call resident at Massachusetts General and witnessed not only skin burns but the effect on the lungs and subsequent kidney failure.

Most of the work described above followed his appointment as Moseley Professor and Chief of Surgery at the Brigham when he was barely thirty-five. He left the Massachusetts General, with its 850 beds, for the Brigham, with only 250. Although it already had a good reputation, mainly due to the brilliant, innovative neurosurgeon Harvey Cushing, who held the chair from 1912 to 1932, it lacked cardiothoracic, ophthalmic and gynaecological surgeons. In his autobiography, *A Miracle and a Privilege*, published in 1995, Franny describes the challenges he faced in developing a thriving clinical and research department. One of the many qualities I admired in him is unconsciously demonstrated in his book but something I noticed within a short time of meeting him. Without arrogance, he had sufficient confidence in his own intellect and ability to seek out and appoint colleagues of stature and promise. He did not, as some leaders do, surround himself with mediocrity so they stand out themselves. In addition, he was soon joined by a brilliant physician, George Thorn, a pioneer endocrinologist, and the pair got on well. Of the 250 beds, the majority were occupied by surgical patients. Despite its size, the Brigham was described, with the usual Bostonian modesty, as 'this little place, with only 284 beds, has made more contributions to progress than any other hospital in the world'—the quote of an anonymous surgeon. Another said, 'We write all the textbooks.'

Franny was also an excellent communicator, able to reduce complicated subjects to simplicity in brief sentences. He was an inspirational speaker—it was his lecture on the background to the first successful kidney transplant performed in his department, which I heard him deliver in 1968 in Newcastle, that inspired me to work for him, even though I had no particular interest in transplantation. Nick Tilney (of whom more later) said if he entered Dr Moore's office feeling depressed about the progress of his research, he would leave a few minutes later expecting to win a Nobel Prize!

I doubt if Dr Moore was ever truly idle. His life and work were compartmentalised. When one met him to discuss research he opened a battered suitcase and extracted a sheet of A4 paper on which he had roughly sketched out the days of the week, divided into AM and PM. On it his programme was written out, with deletions and alterations, and which viewed from across a desk looked an indecipherable mess. But he knew what he was about and preferred it to a book diary. This compartmentalisation even extended to his leisure time. When he first invited our family at short notice one Sunday to his country home in Marion, on the coast at Buzzard's Bay, fifty miles south of Boston, I had to decline. We had not yet bought a car and there was no public transport from Needham that day. He was most persistent until he finally realised it was impossible. When we eventually went at a later date there was another guest, a violinist called Bruno. At the outset Franny explained his house was ours for the day to do what we wanted, but he was going to spend the first hour accompanying Bruno on the piano. The pair would then go sailing for an hour and he would then return to join us for lunch and a swim. Everything proceeded just as he had planned.

'People say I'm a workaholic,' he would say. 'I reply that I'm an *enjoyaholic.*'

And it was true. Incidentally, when we went through the gate at Marion we were greeted by a large sign in the garden, on which was written, 'Raccoons verboten!' The house was procured in 1947 and gradually added to as the family enlarged, so that all could be accommodated for special occasions. As with most Americans who owned a second home, a Stars and Stripes fluttered from a tall white flagpole and the lawn extended to a personal jetty jutting out into the water, which, being south and protected from the Labrador current, made for swimming in what felt like soup. Our boys were fascinated by this jolly man who unexpectedly (for we had warned them he was Dad's boss and to be on their best behaviour) taught them how to spit out the seeds from a watermelon. Mrs Moore was a quiet, kind lady, interested in children (she had five of her own), but who spent most of the sunny afternoon after lunch watching the Red Sox on television.

The department's major claim to fame from the public's viewpoint was the first successful kidney transplant in 1954, the donor and recipient being identical twins. Several other transplants between identical twins took place in the intervening seven years or so, but they were fortuitous, and it was 1962 before one was performed between two unrelated people. By this time a drug, azathioprine, could suppress the recipient's natural immunity, the so-called rejection phenomenon. All these operations at the Brigham were carried out by Joe Murray, primarily a plastic surgeon, oddly enough. Roy Calne, of Cambridge, England, had used a drug called 6-mercaptopurine to suppress rejection of kidneys in dogs and in 1960 he came to the Brigham, where he and Joe Murray worked together to seek the best of several drugs tested on dogs after kidney transplants and settled on azathioprine.

After returning to Cambridge, Calne's interest switched to liver transplantation and in collaboration with Roger Williams of King's College Hospital, London, he created the largest British series of liver transplants. In 1990, Joe Murray was belatedly awarded the Nobel Prize for Medicine. Of course, other people, most of them dead by this time, made significant contributions, and Joe referred to them in his Nobellian address. They included Franny, whose enthusiasm and collaboration played no small part in the success. In fact, Franny himself performed the Brigham's first liver transplant in 1963, but the programme was discontinued within a few years. A portrait of FDM adorned the front cover of *Time* magazine in 1963, the issue devoting a large section to recent advances in surgery and featuring his department. This understandably ignited jealousies, especially in a speciality such as surgery, with big egos jostling for position, and he soon discovered who his real friends were.

Having crossed the Atlantic and committed myself to a year with Dr Moore, he took the wind out of my sails somewhat on our first serious meeting when he remarked I would be wasting my time if I did not aim to be an academic surgeon. Having no ambitions to be a professor of surgery it was already too late for that, as I had few publications, but I did nurture a faint hope of a post in the RVI, a place I loved. He told me that using a novel method, I was to continue ongoing research into measuring protein turnover, synthesis and breakdown in normal volunteers initially, followed by patients. Fortunately for me, a fellow Briton, Brian Sugden, had been engaged in this work for nine months as a Glasgow-Harvard exchange fellow. Although he was returning home shortly, there was sufficient time for him to brief me fully on the project. Brian was younger than me and hailed from Sunderland but qualified at Glasgow. The Glasgow-Harvard exchange had been active for several years and was useful to both sides—the Americans in Glasgow obtained far more operative experience than they would ever receive at home and the Glasgow boys became involved in well-funded research projects. Brian and I did exactly the same work and were paid the same salary of $17,000. By some legal quirk that I never understood, however, he paid no tax, whereas I paid the going rate of a non-resident alien of a straight thirty per cent, with no deductions allowed.

A few years earlier Nick Tilney had held such a post and had also worked in Oxford. Unusually for an American he was a great admirer of the NHS and was apparently sorely tempted when offered the post of Professor of Surgery at Edinburgh after Michael Woodruff's retirement. Eventually he said he couldn't afford to, as he had just got divorced. It did mean, however, that Nick reserved a special affection for the British fellows and sought us out. Only a few days after I arrived in April, when it was still cold in Boston, and when I had only met him once, I bumped into him and he exclaimed, 'Good morning, David, and how are you dealing with the rigours of the New World?'—an amusingly quaint expression.

Later he invited me as his guest to a lecture and dinner at the Harvard Club. It was a swish affair and he sat me in the red-leather armchair President Kennedy had used at some university honours ceremony. Nick was a vascular and transplant surgeon and part of his research involved studying the rejection phenomenon of heart transplants in rats. A donor rat was sacrificed and its heart transplanted into the recipient by stitching it to the aorta and cava in the abdomen, so that this rat now had two hearts. The technique was easy to acquire after some practice. The recipient was anaesthetised with ether delivered via a cardboard cone over its snout and shortly after the operation it came round, staggered a bit, and then went straight to its bowl of chow.

'The rat is the king of beasts,' declared Nick.

The heart could easily be checked by a crude ECG and when it was rejected and stopped beating, the animal was killed and the transplanted organ removed to study the stages of the rejection process microscopically.

# Chapter Twelve

# A Brit in Boston

My research for the next year centred around measuring the total nitrogen turnover, protein synthesis and breakdown using an amino acid—glycine—labelled with the stable isotope of nitrogen—N15—the measurements being made in normal volunteers receiving a variety of intravenous feeding regimens, together with a series of patients with different clinical conditions. This sounds complicated and technical, but I will keep my summary simple. The many proteins in the body all contain, in varying numbers and arrangements, up to twenty amino acids, all of which contain the element nitrogen. Nitrogen can be treated as a proxy for protein. There is a turnover of protein in the body that amounts to about four times the daily intake, so clearly, most is recycled. This process is not 100 per cent efficient and so a certain amount of protein is lost, almost all as nitrogenous products in the urine, mainly urea. All body proteins have a function, and in healthy individuals with a normal diet are not used as fuel, but they can be in situations of starvation and illness. If one measures the amount of nitrogen in the diet (that is, protein), and the amount excreted in the urine, allowing a small figure for losses from the skin and faeces, the difference is termed the nitrogen balance—positive if the subject is manufacturing or conserving more protein than they are losing and negative if more is being excreted than the intake. In starvation, with no intake, nitrogen balance is negative, but as time passes it falls to a half or third of what it was initially. Certain tissues, such as the brain, blood cells and parts of the kidney and nerves, can only use glucose as fuel, amounting to about 150 grams per day, equivalent to 600 calories. In starvation, with no fuel intake, they must use a substitute for glucose, because stores as glycogen (a form of starch) are limited to a few hours. Fat, which forms the main store of calories, cannot be converted to glucose, but protein can, although after a week or two the brain learns to use ketones (but not fatty acids) from the breakdown of fat. The largest source of protein in the body is skeletal muscle, and this explains why starving subjects lose muscle. This loss of muscle is larger and more dramatic after trauma such as operative surgery, soft tissue trauma and fractures and especially severe burns, and is prolonged or magnified by infection and fever. In the severest cases, the reduction of the body's muscle can amount to thirty per cent, at which level death may supervene due to weakened respiratory muscles and immunosuppression. The response to trauma is more pronounced than starvation, due to complex changes in biochemistry and hormones. Whereas the process in starvation is easily reversed, that following the severest cases of trauma can merely be obtunded (partially reversed), until the persisting causes, for example infection, are dealt with. Severe illness is naturally accompanied by starvation, especially in most patients in intensive care units who cannot take food by mouth, and nutrition has to be supplied by other means, often intravenously. Because such solutions have a high osmolality, that is they are concentrated compared to blood, they irritate vein walls and have to be administered via large veins close to the heart, by means of a central line, which itself can cause problems in both its placement and subsequent possible infection.

A negative nitrogen balance can be caused by decreased synthesis of protein, increased breakdown or a combination of both, and at the time of my research it was not known which. This was not just of academic interest, for if it was purely one or the other, it might aim further therapeutic advances in the correct direction. Also, there was still argument about the precise roles of glucose and fat as calorie sources coupled with amino acids to synthesise protein. Glucose was used almost universally and especially in the USA. Although a fat emulsion made from soya had been available in Europe since the 1960s, it had only been accepted for use in the USA in 1975. The theoretical advantage of fat is that it has a high calorie-volume ratio of about 1:1 (one gram of fat equals nine calories), but more importantly it is of the same osmotic concentration as blood, and can therefore be given via peripheral veins in the forearm, the usual site of a drip.

The lab had been led by Margaret (Peggy) Ball for more than thirty years, ever since FDM was appointed. Peggy was a Radcliffe graduate (the female equivalent of Harvard), a spinster, and a co-author of Franny's huge tome, *The Metabolic Care of the Surgical Patient*. She had a broad, muscular frame, with similarly broad facial features and long, dark hair. She ran a tight ship, with high standards and a somewhat dual personality. Whereas most of the time she was pleasant and could show great kindness, if something or someone annoyed her, her mood suddenly blackened, her voice became even deeper than usual and her features ferocious. She growled with anger, the place went quiet and staff scurried away if they were not the object of her ire. Peggy frequently visited Ireland, where I presume she had relatives. She was also a *cordon bleu* cook who had attended courses in France. Her apartment was close to the lab, but the family home was in Great Barrington, west of Boston in the Berkshire Hills, where she often went at weekends. She had a staff of three technicians, all graduates, one gofer-bottle washer, and a male secretary-typist, Arthur, who was cultured, widely read and obviously gay, although this term was not used then. Like Peggy and so many Bostonians he was a devout Catholic with Irish ancestry and would often call out to me in jest, 'Free my people!' In my ignorance it took me quite some time to detect his meaning. He was a private individual who rarely mentioned his life outside work, but during my time there his widowed mother died of lung cancer. He continued to work but mentioned to Peggy that in her final days he had slept in the same bed as his mother to keep her warm, which struck me as both strange yet a touching act of love and devotion. There was a wake the night before the funeral by her open coffin, another custom unknown to me, which was attended by most of the staff as an act of respect for Arthur. Like many gay men he had a sense for the aesthetic, so I was surprised one Monday when he returned from being driven by friends to a weekend in New Hampshire and moaned that there was 'nothing but trees, and more trees—I got tired of trees'.

One day the film star Lauren Bacall, widow of Humphrey Bogart, opened a store across the Charles River, so Arthur and I took the T subway train (short for MBTA, the Massachusetts Bay Transport Authority) to see her. Some people were standing and I was just on the point of rising to offer my seat to an elderly lady when Arthur pulled me back.

'Don't,' he said. 'She'll think you're getting fresh. She won't be grateful.'

I'm sorry to say this is yet another curse that has crossed the Atlantic, along with grey squirrels and Disney princesses. Anyway, I can always say I have seen a Hollywood film star of the old school.

One of the technicians was Lourdes Hojelko, a refugee from Castro's Cuba. She was always elegantly dressed, had lustrous black hair, was tastefully made up with mascara and striking red lipstick and spoke heavily accented English with precision. She came from a privileged background but left the island after Castro's takeover.

'Tha' bastar' Fidel,' she used to say. 'He even take my shoe off me on de quayside!'

One of the other girls, a science graduate, asked me in the 'fall' why I was so taken with the colours of the trees, and did we not have deciduous trees in England?

This lab and that of the Brigham were assaying hormones such as insulin and glucagon as a routine, procedures still only available in the UK in research institutions. Franny had been far-sighted in that blood specimens from several of his earlier projects had been frozen and stored, so assays for hormones unavailable at the time of collection could be conducted when they were developed, the perfect example being glucagon, a hormone secreted by specialised cells in the pancreas and small intestine, which raises blood glucose by converting it from amino acids. For the studies, the dietetic department of the Brigham created oral diets containing specifically requested amounts of protein, carbohydrate and fat, and the pharmacy did the same with the solutions of amino acids, glucose and fat emulsion. N15 in the urine samples was measured by mass at the Massachusetts Institute of Technology (MIT), situated on the north bank of the Charles River in Cambridge. I enjoyed going there because much of the building appeared dated, and yet within were the laboratories and offices of several Nobel Prize winners. One had, for a fleeting thrill, a vicarious connection with scientific genius.

Our studies in normal volunteers were conducted in The Clinical Center (TCC), developed for the pioneering endocrinologist George Thorn, Dr Moore's colleague. It was a hospital ward staffed by trained nurses who were familiar with the importance of accurate and timed collection of specimens. Some patients were also housed there, especially those requiring strict aseptic barrier nursing. I recall one in particular, a young man who had received a bone marrow transplant for leukaemia but developed graft-versus-host disease, a form of reverse rejection in which the grafted stem cells reject the host, rather than the usual way round. This was in the early days of such a procedure. The poor man was confined to a glass cubicle that was sealed (apart from the air change). Visible from the outside he sadly resembled a plucked chicken, hairless, a nose like a beak, skinny and with scaly, flaking skin. He eventually died, causing upset among the nurses, who had cared for him for months.

Our volunteers were paid $150 for a six-day study in the unit. Those on an oral diet received four meals a day, to which they had to adhere strictly, and the rest on intravenous regimens were inconvenienced by a drip, inserted by an IV nurse, whose sole job was to perform such a task throughout the hospital (lucky interns!). If it was a central line, however, with the tip placed close to the heart in the superior vena cava, it had to be sited by a resident, although it was always fed up via a vein in the forearm, not in the potentially risky subclavian vein in the neck, the usual site for long-term feeding. The other inconvenience was they were requested to pass urine every three hours, so they never got a full night's sleep. Apart from this they were free to lounge on their beds, watch TV, smoke and drink water *ad libitum*, but nothing else by mouth. They could also potter about for exercise as long as they pushed their drip stand with them. We advertised for them in the *Boston Phoenix*, a weekly alternative magazine popular with students and hippies because of its stimulating reviews on music and local entertainments. Our advert was placed among the section containing an extensive personal column of offers and requests for a bizarre, to me at any rate, range of sexual practices, and I was fortunate to have Brian to translate for me. For example, WHBM stood for 'well hung black male', 'golden showers' were requested by people who derived pleasure from being urinated upon, and one request I particularly remember was for 'female amputee required—must have well-rounded stump'. Every time I went to MIT I looked up at the block of flats next to it and wondered which one was the source of, 'How's about some daytime dalliance in my Cambridge high rise?'

The volunteers were all of a type, probably because of the nature of the readership. Naturally, they were unemployed, but most seemed bright and articulate—I can recall only one who was clearly poor, with an address to match. The others were often bearded and more like hippies. They were always screened beforehand, especially for hepatitis B. Obviously, we didn't want any drug addicts; the nature of the study precluded this anyway, but one cannot be too careful when money is involved. We always paid them $30 for the screening exam and blood test and never saw some of them again. Word must have got around. Unlike in the UK, where there has long been an enviable record of public service in the voluntary offering of blood donation, American donors are paid. Understandably, people such as drug addicts, desperate for cash, are attracted, or should I say, were. Before AIDS, going back to the sixties when there were no tests for hepatitis B carriers, and indeed hepatitis C and even rarer types that had not yet been described, a significant percentage of patients undergoing open-heart surgery, in which the heart-lung machine was primed with several pints of donor blood, suffered postoperative jaundice, some of which would prove fatal. At the time of my studies, AIDS had not yet reared its ugly head.

***

When we first moved, I took the 6.25am train from Needham to Back Bay Station in Boston, and then the above-ground T down Huntington Avenue to Brigham Circle, just opposite the main entrance to the Brigham. The Americans generally practise the aphorism 'early to bed, early to rise'. The train was mainly occupied by white men reading the *Wall Street Journal* and there was little or no conversation.

It is almost impossible to function in the States without a car, but it was two months before I bought one. Two Newcastle chaps who had already been to Boston recommended a car dealer in Needham Heights who they reckoned was trustworthy. I was there waiting to be taken for a sucker, as they say, but the Ford LTD Country Squire I bought for $1,000 served us pretty well, except for needing a new transmission when our time was almost up. It was a lime green, half metal, half 'wood' shooting brake, as we would have called it in the UK, almost long enough for a plane to land on. The engine capacity was in cubic inches, but if my maths proved correct, it was equivalent to five and a half litres. I was slightly put off by the mileage of 72,000 but the salesman said it was 'just run in'. The power steering was still the best I have encountered, even now—you could turn the car in full lock with one finger. The proprietor remembered all the Brigham boys from Britain and seemed to have an affection for the old country, even though, as he said, 'Trust me to be in the only damned battle that we lost—I was dropped at Arnhem!'

Mary settled in almost immediately, as did the boys, who were registered at High Rock school, which was accessed through a cut only a couple of streets away. We had taken some of their schoolwork from England to show the headmaster so he could choose the correct class, because children in the States do not start school until they are six. They soon learned the pledge made by every child at assembly every day, with a hand placed over the heart—'I pledge allegiance to the flag of the United States of America, and to the Republic for which it stands, one nation under God, indivisible, with Liberty and Justice for all'—flag pronounced *flayeg*. They also picked up the local slang—'retard', 'faggot' and 'gross'. A little stream nearby was the 'creek' and a small copse of trees was a 'thicket'.

Within hours of arriving, Michael and Paul were playing with the local children. The lawns surrounding the houses had no separating boundaries, so the playing area was communal and Maple Street was a cul-de-sac, so it was safe.

A few days later Paul maintained he had seen a beaver as he jumped the creek.

'Don't be silly, Paul. Beavers are extinct,' replied Michael, mistakenly.

'It did stink, Michael,' said Paul, so we knew he was telling the truth.

To obtain a telephone, all one did was to visit the Bell Company office, pay $5, take the offered handset and hook it up. At home in the 1970s a phone took six-to-twelve weeks to be installed, although fortunately doctors on call were treated as special cases. Mary thought one of Michael's friends was being cheeky when he just picked up the phone to call his mom, only to discover that local calls were free. This explained why in the winter, when it could be bone-chillingly cold, kids who lived opposite one another could spend an entire Saturday morning on the phone to their friends without incurring any charges. Supermarkets were a revelation compared to ours. Fruit appeared to be manufactured to size and colour rather than a product of nature. Apples were huge and red, but we soon found them to be tasteless. The stores were massive, however, and spotlessly clean. Barcoding and swiping at the till were routine, taking another decade to become commonplace at home. The checkout person passed purchased items to an assistant of pensionable age, who placed them in large brown paper bags—never plastic.

I loved hearing the trains pass on the track behind our house from Needham Heights to Needham Station, with their plaintive whistle characteristic of America and reminiscent of films seen as a child. We bought a small black-and-white TV, which was all we could afford. The boys loved *Gilligan's Island*, a long-running serial about a bunch of castaways, but I was intensely irritated by the plethora of banal adverts for cereals, usually announced in a high-pitched voice at breakneck speed, and especially with the local ads featuring dodgy-looking car dealers with cheesy grins and bad suits. We were lucky in that Boston is one of the most liveable-in of American cities. It is among the few possessing some history and old buildings, being the cradle of the American Revolution, and is of modest population (about 650,000 then), with a pleasant climate. One could guarantee hot summers and, despite freezing winters, the sun shone and the sky remained blue, unlike the low, leaden overhanging cloudy skies and the damp atmosphere in Britain. The state of Massachusetts had been Democratic for years, the senator being Edward Kennedy, and so tended to be more liberal and civilised (my term) than some of the far right-wing 'redneck' states. Two examples—free public libraries, strict gun laws. I witnessed little overt racism, but most poor blacks were confined to one area, Roxbury. Franny did once tell me that, 'to my shame, we only appointed our first black resident a couple of years ago'.
Boston was a city of education, with nine universities plus about fifty colleges, and at least nine hospitals, all with teaching and research commitments. One did not witness the gross obesity that plagued the country even then, more to the south and mid-west, the mainly educated young people seeming to take care of their bodies—and, of course, jogging was almost endemic.

A transition was taking place in the American love affair with the automobile. Although gasoline was still only approaching a dollar a gallon, the average American complained about the rise in price and, probably coupled with the minority but nevertheless vociferous environmentalists, there was a new tendency to purchase smaller, more economic models than the big, brash gas-guzzlers. Sales of Toyotas were rising but with plenty of veterans of the war with Japan in the Pacific still alive, such cars were often the objects of vandalism. Better-off Americans did not regard their cars as status symbols, unlike in Britain. Franny drove a battered, dusty station wagon, with a set of oars perched on the roof, presumably for use at Marion. John Mannick drove a BMW, a marque rarely seen then, but a neurologist called Morgan broke my generalisation by driving a white model made by the British company of his name and with the registration plate *NEURONE*.

The Governor of Massachusetts, Michael Dukakis, travelled to Boston City Hall on the T, presumably to make himself appear 'one of the people'. One day I recognised him as he approached, and greasily greeted him with a, 'Good morning, Governor', to receive a, 'Good morning, how are ya?' Ten years later, in 1988, he was the Democratic candidate for president, opposing George Bush Senior. Although I felt the latter to be a more serious contender, I rooted for Dukakis, solely because if he won I could always say I had spoken to the President of the United States. He was, of course, soundly defeated.

Dukakis was guilty of a psychological misjudgement of his fellow countrymen in the winter of 1978-79, which could have been prevented had he asked my advice. The winter before, Boston had suffered a severe blizzard in which lives were lost. Despite severely cold winters being the norm, apparently the blizzard came unexpectedly. We experienced an extremely cold one, without the usual snowfalls although at one point some was forecast. Anxious to avoid the catastrophe of the previous year, the governor broadcast that in the next twenty-four hours, only people whose jobs were deemed essential should attend work. I could have told him what to expect—there was a 90 per cent turnout. Never hint to an American that his job might not be important. I dare say that if the same had applied in Britain (certainly in the 1970s) hardly anyone would have turned up, but I concede the same would probably not apply now.

During the winter of 1978-79 we witnessed the Dickensian images of our own country's troubles through American eyes, via the medium of television. We experienced mixed feelings of embarrassment, depression and anger at the Winter of Discontent, with homes illuminated by candles, piles and piles of uncollected rubbish, the dead unburied and the ubiquitous braziers warming the hands of the strikers. Far from gloating, the usual response to the plight of a foreign country in trouble, American reporters seemed bewildered that such a normally respected ally could be brought so low by its own people and reacted with sadness. Within a few weeks of our return, a Conservative government was elected under the leadership of Margaret Thatcher, and even hardened socialists were hoping and praying for a new beginning.

# Chapter Thirteen

# Living the Dream

Franny suggested that as an act of courtesy I should make an appointment to meet John Mannick, who had succeeded him as Moseley Professor, and was now overall Chief of Surgery. I found Mannick an intimidating figure. He had a stern, expressionless face, his facial skin appearing stretched, as if he had undergone plastic surgery (he hadn't), and with his short silver blond hair I could imagine him in a stormtrooper's uniform. His office and the entire floor of the department appeared unchanged since the days of Harvey Cushing in the early 1930s, and I was told this was a deliberate act, in homage to the great pioneer of brain surgery. The walls were of panelled mahogany and the lamps had those old-fashioned green shades one sees in films of the 1940s and 50s. The décor was out of character from the contemporary research and clinical work being done, just as MIT's had been.

Mannick was a vascular surgeon and over the years after my return to the UK I saw him at roughly annual intervals at international vascular meetings, but only spoke to him once, when in 1994 I introduced myself, really to enquire after Dr Moore. He recognised me, said he had dined with Franny only the previous week and that the latter had just published his autobiography. Over succeeding years I was sorry to see Mannick become increasingly disabled by a marked kyphosis of the spine, presumably because of late-onset ankylosing spondylitis, which caused him to bend forwards to an alarming degree. He was at his peak, however, in 1978, and conducted the Thursday evening Morbidity and Mortality (M&M) and Saturday morning 'grand rounds' with authority. He did have a sense of humour, but it was restrained, as he showed once when a resident had the temerity to add some levity to the proceedings from the back row of the tiered amphitheatre.

'The jokes come only from the front row in this institution,' he said.

I always sat in the back row at grand rounds and was amused every week to witness the same scenario. As soon as the lights were dimmed for the first slide, the back light revealed the silhouettes of the residents in the rows in front of me. Within seconds heads would loll to the side as these overtired young men and women keeled over involuntarily to snatch a few moments of delicious sleep, only to jerk up again when the lights sprang into life at the end of the projection.

The M&Ms were weekly affairs, regarded as compulsory, although no formal record was taken. They were attended by the surgical chiefs, other 'attending' surgeons (that is, consultants) and residents. The Chief Resident chalked up the names of the various 'services' and tabulated deaths during the previous week, plus the perceived complications. Each was then presented by a resident, followed by an often forthright and robust discussion, the whole purpose being to improve quality. Deaths were judged as preventable or not, and I was amazed that if the post-mortem results were discussed by a pathologist, the microscope slides were always ready to be shown by projector. At home they would have taken a lot longer.

American hospitals are largely competitive, relying on finance from insured patients. The Harvard teaching hospitals had enviably large endowments from philanthropy but were still motivated to achieve success and hence the practice of regular surgical audit was considered obligatory. It was also of educational value and with the proximity of several other hospitals, attracted cross-attendance from other residents. At home, we did have weekly meetings, usually case presentations, and any form of M&M was informal, but we have now caught up with the Americans and formal, obligatory sessions under the umbrella term of 'clinical governance' are now the norm.

The term 'grand rounds' was an anachronism, as it had nothing to do with a ward round but was a presentation from one department or a lecture from a distinguished visitor. The one I remember best occurred not long after my arrival, on the morning of the day of our colleague Nick Tilney's second marriage, to which Gerry had been invited. The visiting speaker was a fellow Briton, Lord Smith of Marlow, formerly Sir Rodney Smith, and a former president of the Royal College of Surgeons of England. Lord Smith was a friend of Dr Moore's and a fellow polymath, who could have succeeded as a professional violinist as well as a surgeon and had played cricket for Surrey's second XI as a young man. His surgical reputation was based on his co-editorship with Charles Rob of the fourteen-volume *Operative Surgery* textbooks, profusely illustrated, and referred to in the profession as *Rob and Smith*, together with enormous experience in the repair or reconstruction of damaged bile ducts.

Gallstones are common, affecting up to about ten per cent of the population, and although not always symptomatic, they cause trouble often enough to make removal of the gallbladder (cholecystectomy) one of the most frequent elective abdominal operations. The gallbladder, the shape and size of a small pear, lies beneath the liver in the right upper abdomen, and its function is to concentrate the bile, manufactured in the liver, which drips down from that organ in the bile duct, a tube about a centimetre in diameter. The gallbladder enters the bile duct about halfway along its length via its own short duct, and bile is usually diverted into it because the small nipple at the end of the bile duct where it enters the duodenum remains closed by means of a small muscle. In response to a meal, especially a fatty one, the gallbladder contracts due to the effects of a hormone, and simultaneously the nipple muscle relaxes, allowing concentrated bile to enter the duodenum and help emulsify the fat in the diet. If stones are present, this action can cause intense colicky pain, only relieved when the organ relaxes again. If prolonged, or a stone gets trapped, inflammation and infection may supervene, making the victim acutely ill. Mothers will tell you that gallstone colic is worse than labour. The effect of fat explains why patients with mild symptoms or a single attack who wish to defer surgery are advised to avoid fried foods.

Removal of the gallbladder is usually a straightforward procedure, but complications can occur for two main reasons. Firstly, anatomical variants are common, and secondly, previous inflammation from attacks of colic can distort the anatomy and create a difficult dissection because of scarring. Normally, the cystic duct leading from the gallbladder to the main bile duct is divided and tied, as is the artery to the organ, leaving the intact bile duct. If, due to one or other of these potential problems, the cystic duct is mistaken for the bile duct, or the latter clamped inadvertently if bleeding occurs, the structure may be cut across or tied, and sometimes the damage may remain undetected until the patient either becomes jaundiced or leaks bile from the wound. Such misadventures are rare but can be devastating and repair of the bile duct, especially if damaged high up near the liver, can tax the most accomplished surgeon. Few have developed the techniques to deal with the problem and Lord Smith was the main one in the UK. Richard Cattell, of the Lahey Clinic near Boston, had been the expert in the USA, but he died in 1964. Cattell became internationally famous for operating on Sir Anthony Eden, whose bile duct was damaged by an eminent London surgeon in the 1950s. Eden's recurrent attacks of ascending cholangitis, comprising fever, shivers and jaundice, have been blamed by some for his poor judgement during the Suez crisis, when he was prime minister. Fortunately for Eden, Cattell succeeded in relieving this potentially fatal condition. Despite its rarity, most cases were passed to a handful of surgeons who could build up a huge series. In his lecture to us, before a packed auditorium, Lord Smith's first slide brought an audible gasp when he showed a series of 350 cases. The lecture was beautifully delivered and he described his innovative method of dealing with high strictures of the duct as it emerges from the liver. Finally, he described a most difficult case. A rich Irishman, married with a young family, developed a total pancreato-biliary fistula following gallbladder surgery in the Republic, and was flown to London for Sir Rodney (as he was then) to deal with. Smith described the technique that allowed him to solve an otherwise lethal condition. After a hospital stay of some months, the man was ready to be discharged, by which time he was ambulant but hampered by a troublesome foot-drop (the inability to lift the front of the foot) caused by pressure on the lateral popliteal nerve behind one knee, sustained as a result of immobility and profound muscle-wasting during the earlier part of the illness. This foot-drop was helped by a splint and a walking stick. As he stood on the steps of the hospital, and after pouring out his thanks, he bade farewell with the following statement.

'You know, Sir Rodney, when I was flown across from Dublin with me brother the priest on one side, and me other brother the lawyer on the other, I knew I was a very sick man,' he said. 'I prayed to the Lord—please Lord, I have a wife and a young family, please don't let me die, please save me for me family—take an arm or a leg, but don't let me die.'

And then, tapping his leg with his walking stick, he added, 'You know, I wish I'd never said anything about arms or legs!'

I seemed to be one of the few attendees who found this hilarious, a typical example of the Irish sense of humour. But this was Boston, home of one of the largest populations of Irish Americans in the US and where, unlike the Irish themselves, any reference to them by an Englishman will be perceived as a slight or insult if it possibly can. At question time, an Irish-American surgeon aggressively prefaced his question with, 'Well, it's pleasing to see at least one Englishman doing an Irishman a good turn...' Poor Lord Smith tried to maintain a smile, but it was forced, a mixture of hurt and bewilderment.

Gerry reported that during the wedding reception that afternoon, several people present at the lecture expressed dismay at how Smith had misjudged his audience and insulted the Irish, but they were wrong. It has long been said that the English tell jokes against the Irish to mock a perceived lack of intelligence in the same way the Americans do, or did, tell Polack jokes about the Polish. But the only Irish jokes I hear now come from those claiming an Irish heritage, however tenuous. What the complainants seemed to have missed was that the source of the jest was the Irishman. In similar vein, an Englishwoman wrote to a newspaper about her driving holiday in Ireland. She and her companions called at a rural pub one sunny Sunday morning and requested coffee for four to be served outside in the sun, and this was duly presented. When the lady went to settle the bill she was told there would be no charge. Surprised, she asked why.

'Well, firstly,' said the lady proprietor, 'we're not open. And secondly, we don't serve coffee.' There's no answer to that.

***

We befriended a couple in Maple Street who were Catholics from Northern Ireland. Kathy had the green eyes and black hair of the Emerald Isle and was friendly and effusive. They had three boys, the eldest just older than Michael, and all five played together. The couple ended up in the USA because they were unmarried when Kathy became pregnant and they had been ostracised by both families, except for Kathy's grandmother. This was a shame because they were a lovely family, rent apart by the intolerant attitude of so-called Christians. As David Jenkins, the controversial Bishop of Durham, once said, 'The reason why most people are not Christians is because of the behaviour of some Christians.' However, both became successful due to hard work and could move from rented accommodation to their own home in Minnesota the following year. They kindly invited us to their home to spend Christmas Day afternoon and evening with them, knowing we would be separated from our families. Kathy once asked Mary to accompany her to a ceilidh, neither of us at the time knowing what one was, and was embarrassed at the end when a collection was made 'for the boys'—it was going to the American organisation NORAID, which raised funds for the IRA.

When the building of the new hospital got underway, I saw flags flying one day for the topping out ceremony. Alongside the Stars and Stripes was the Maple Leaf and I commented to one of our lab technicians that some of the builders must be Canadians. He looked at me as if I was a dolt and when I repeated it said, 'It's the Red Indians.' When I looked puzzled he explained that many steeplejacks are Red Indians, as we used to call them, or as they are now labelled, Native Americans in the USA or First Nation people in

Canada. Apparently, it was believed that a feature of their race is a lack of fear of heights, although this now appears to have been a myth.

Franny was raising money for the new hospital and on several occasions when we were discussing our research, his secretary put through calls from his fellow fundraiser, Noah Herndon. I usually rose from my chair to leave but he always indicated to me to resume my seat. During one such call Franny spoke in a deep mournful voice.

'Bad news, Noah, bad news,' he said. 'I went to Marblehead yesterday, to lunch with the Coolidge family. I think they must have hit hard times. Missus would only promise a hundred thousand and the boys only fifty thousand each. I was expecting half a million!'

*Only*! It reminds me of the quote describing the actress Sarah Bernhardt's performance in *Antony and Cleopatra*: 'How different, how very different, from the home life of our own dear Queen.'

Franny's contemporary, the endocrinologist George Thorn, was acquainted with the Coolidge family and I assume this was the origin of the connection. I also assume that 'Missus' was the daughter or daughter-in-law of Calvin Coolidge, president in the 1920s. Known as 'Silent Cal', after being informed of his death, the satirist Dorothy Parker famously said, 'How can they tell?'

At the other extreme, but in keeping with the Bernhardt quote, one day he was cock-a-hoop because 'a Hollywood film director wants to give us eight million dollars'. I wonder if this was Charles Haas, who I had never heard of, but who was a film director and is referred to in FDM's autobiography as a lifelong friend from their schooldays and as Harvard undergraduates, and who died in 2011, aged ninety-eight.

The Brigham had eleven operating rooms and about thirty operations were carried out daily, excluding emergencies. Unlike in the UK, where each consultant has defined operating lists, in the US the lists were created by a scheduler, responding to demand and arranged accordingly, and not necessarily by speciality. A surgeon might do one operation early in the morning and another at noon in a different room, although most of those at the Brigham were vacated by just after midday, unlike at home where our lists rarely finished on time because we tried to pack in as many cases as possible.

***

In the USA, Medicine is a four-year course, as opposed to our five, but it is a postgraduate degree, starting at age twenty-one after completion of a BA or BS degree. For example,

Franny took anthropology as a first degree. Hence, a US surgeon will start his residency at twenty-five, but within seven years can become board-certified and enter independent practice as an attending surgeon, whereas I and most of my peers were close to thirty-eight when we were appointed consultants. The so-called Modernising Medical Careers plan now aims to produce NHS consultants at a similar age to the Americans, but whereas over there the residents still work long hours (recently reduced to about eighty from close to a hundred!), the EU Working Time Directive (currently unchanged despite Brexit) limits British trainees to an average of only forty-eight. The Royal College of Surgeons estimates that newly appointed consultants will have experienced about 6,000 hours of operating, compared with five times that by my generation. Dramatic though this appears, my colleagues and I developed vast experience in an unstructured way, learning from the registrar when a senior house officer and from the senior registrar when a registrar, and only rarely assisted by the consultant. If modern trainees are shown how to do a procedure properly, and personally assisted by an expert, I am sure it is possible to produce soundly trained surgeons in the shorter timescale.

We were fortunate to have our education provided free, a great boon, even though our salaries were low in the early years. Some Americans start out in practice in debt by over $200,000 and now British students have to pay up to £9,250 per annum in tuition fees, plus living costs. When we were in Boston, Harvard raised its fees for undergraduates to $8,000 pa (I presume those for medical school would be even higher). The TV cameras went to Harvard Square to gauge the reaction. One student was asked if he thought the education at Harvard was worth $8,000 a year.

'The education ain't but the degree sure is,' he bravely replied. I wonder what his tutors thought!

In the RVI, doctors carried a 'bleep' controlled by the switchboard. When bleeped, one dialled a four-digit number, which was answered almost immediately by an operator, who gave the source of the message. To me, the word 'page' meant a boy in a Shakespearean play or a pantomime who brought messages. I had not met it as a verb, nor the word 'pager' as a noun, but at the Brigham a Tannoy system continually paged doctors and other members of staff, the message reaching all corners of the hospital. For example, 'Paging Dr X, wanted in the OR immediately.' In time we learned to use the verb over here and to rename the bleep a pager, but we did not adopt the Tannoy system. I'm not sure which was preferable. It was difficult to ignore a bleep, especially in company. The Tannoy was easier to ignore, because the quality of the sound was variable. One of life's rules was, and maybe still is, that if one wanted to go to the toilet to use a cubicle, so to speak, one's bleep would sound, and more often than not it was the rapid bird-like chirrup of an emergency call.

At some stage Gerry and I met, by chance, Andy Duncan, another graduate of '66, who was now an attending radiologist in Boston, having previously worked in New York. He specialised in interventional radiology, mainly arteriograms. What interested me was that when on call he was not at the end of a phone, but more or less working continuously, reading CT scans, routine x-rays and doing various interventions. This, of course, is the way it should be—there is little point in possessing expensive pieces of kit such as CT scanners if they are not fully utilised, both for routine and emergency cases. But the department was so well-staffed that the on-call rota was not onerous.

Gerry told me a story that clearly had elements of truth in it, but some details seemed implausible. Perhaps they had become muddled up with the retelling, as so often happens. It concerned a senior colleague of Gerry's in Liverpool, John McFarland, who had taken a year out at the University of Mississippi. He had somehow met Lee Harvey Oswald, President Kennedy's assassin, not long before the event. The true facts were revealed in 2013 when John died, aged eighty-three. Although he passed away in October, the *Daily Telegraph* delayed printing his obituary until November 22nd, being the 50th anniversary of Kennedy's death. With due respect to John, the only justification for publication of his obituary in a national daily was his tenuous connection with Oswald. In September 1963, John and his wife boarded a Greyhound bus from Jackson, Mississippi, bound for Mexico City. Three days later when they changed buses at Houston, Texas, they met Oswald, who told them he had come from New Orleans, where he was secretary of a branch of the Fair Play for Cuba Organisation and was travelling to Cuba hoping to meet Fidel Castro. Because it was illegal to travel to Cuba from the US, he was going via Mexico City. After the assassination, the McFarlands recognised Oswald from newspaper photographs and informed the authorities. However, it seems John was occasionally contacted by FBI agents at intervals following his return to Liverpool, suggesting they still harboured some suspicions about him.

***

A few weeks before Christmas there was a symposium about intravenous feeding and metabolism at the New England Deaconess Hospital, across the street from the Brigham.

Sir David Cuthbertson was a guest lecturer. He was then in his late seventies (he died aged eighty-nine in 1989) and was a household name in the field of metabolic research because he had described the biochemical response to trauma using the experimental model of fractured femur in rats. He was a medically qualified biochemist who directed a research laboratory for twenty years. He used the terms 'ebb' and 'flow' for the acute response followed by the convalescent phase, respectively, of the response to trauma. Franny held a dinner in his honour at his home in the suburb of Brookline, and Mary and I were invited together with about a dozen other guests. I was placed next to a middle-aged, red-headed lady who was glamorous and elegantly dressed. She was the wife of George Cahill, head of the Joslin Diabetic Center based at the Deaconess, and an expert in the physiology of starvation and diabetes. Looking at this clearly well-to-do lady with her trim figure, it was difficult to believe she was the mother of six children. She initiated and maintained our conversation, asking questions about myself and my family and seemed genuinely interested, as women often are. She appeared to have travelled worldwide and I eventually felt slightly embarrassed as I continually replied in the negative to her questions about various places she assumed I must have visited. Nevertheless, she seemed a nice, genuine person and I felt comfortable in her company and could have happily spent the rest of the evening in conversation with her. At the end of the meal, when guests were circulating, Franny, with a gleam in his eye, said, 'You seemed to get on very well with Mrs Cahill, David.'

'Yes,' I replied. 'She's a really interesting lady.'

'Do you know what her maiden name was?' he asked, before continuing without waiting for a reply, 'DuPont!'

He left a few seconds for it to sink in and then added, 'They only own most of Chesapeake Bay!'

Even I, in my relative ignorance, knew DuPont was the company that had invented nylon and manufactured a vast variety of products. It was founded in the early nineteenth century by a French Huguenot family and originally made gunpowder. I had assumed that with six children and the surname Cahill they were Irish American Catholics. Mrs Cahill was formally named Sarah, but nicknamed Sally, presumably after one of her ancestors who had the same nickname. She was born in Wilmington, Delaware, the site of the company's headquarters. Her husband, George Cahill, was an expert witness for the prosecution in Danish-born British socialite Claus von Bülow's 1982 trial for the attempted murder of his wife, Sunny, by injecting an overdose of insulin. The accused was found guilty, but the conviction overturned on appeal three years later. The defence had found eight medical experts, none of whom implicated insulin as a cause of Mrs von Bülow's coma, from which she never recovered. She died aged seventy-six in 2008, having been comatose for twenty-eight years. These experts attributed her state to a combination of prescription drugs and alcohol. Dr Cahill, however, persisted in his opinion that the only possible cause of her well-documented hypoglycaemia could be insulin, illustrating his argument by lining up sugar cubes along the witness box. Sunny's blood insulin was measured on one occasion (she underwent two comas, recovering from the first), and was 'out of the ballpark', according to Dr Cahill. The validity of the analysis was challenged by the defence. At one point Dr Cahill muttered, 'It is so difficult for me to answer inane questions.' There is no doubt he felt justice had not been served by the successful appeal. Six months into our stay, Gerry and family returned to Liverpool and were replaced from that city by Andrew and Kathy Wu, a Hong Kong Chinese couple, who took over both the rental of the house and Gerry's VW. They considered the furniture rental to be excessive and cancelled the contract, which enabled them to demonstrate their practical skills at an early stage. Irish Kathy kindly gave them a three-piece suite no longer required—in fact, it had been virtually destroyed by their three boys. Andrew called me over one weekend to show what they had done. They bought some hessian, or sackcloth, in Boston, and covered the suite like professional upholsterers. A few weeks later, just to rub it in, Andrew asked if I had any spare cardboard boxes and I gave him several from our basement (this space, which seems to be an integral part of every American house, is an absolute boon). Later that day he invited me to pop across to see the result of his labours—a Wendy house with several storeys, chimneys, doors and windows. I returned home feeling more than a little inadequate.

Andrew qualified in Sydney, Australia, and did his house jobs in Launceston, Tasmania. I thought this must have been wonderful, but he grumbled that they were all inbred in Tasmania and the climate and scenery did not compensate for the people. Aged sixteen he won the Sydney Young Musician of the Year award, playing the piano, which he regarded as his second instrument, the first being the flute. His father was apparently cross when he came to the UK, regarding Britain as 'finished', and advised Canada instead. But Andrew loved Liverpool, praising both the people and the culture, and indeed when he returned he took up a post as a liver surgeon, a new speciality. This was after spending some time with the French surgeon, Henri Bismuth, the most eminent specialist in the field in Europe. Naturally, Andrew learned conversational French in three months before departing.

***

In October 1978 the American College of Surgeons held its annual meeting in San Francisco, a city that frequently hosts the gathering because even America has few cities with sufficient hotel facilities to accommodate its 20,000 delegates. I was told the air traffic controllers dread this event because so many of the surgeons pilot their own planes—not always, presumably, very well. I went with Liam McKean, Brian's replacement as the Glasgow-Harvard exchange fellow, the Brigham Research Fund paying for our flights and registration. Liam and I were only given permission to go at the last minute and were forced to stay at the airport hotel. This was accessed across a road from the arrivals' terminal, and it must have taken fifteen minutes before we found a sufficient gap to perilously tackle the four-lane highway. Only after doing so did we discover it was illegal and we should have phoned for a courtesy bus.

We met up with Franny, who took me and Dan and Mary Finn, an Irish couple, on a cable car and then for a drink at the Top of the Mark, the bar on the nineteenth floor of the famous Mark Hopkins Hotel on Nob Hill. We were invited and transported to a party in a house owned by an admiral in Sausalito, the town at the northern end of the Golden Gate Bridge, whose mayor at the time was said to be the madam of a local brothel. Here I met a flamboyant Texan with auburn hair and a large, waxed moustache. He was aptly nicknamed Red Duke and was said to have been a resident in the emergency department of Parkwood Memorial Hospital, to which President Kennedy was taken after the shooting. The president was given a tracheostomy, a strange procedure in a man who had lost half his skull and underlying brain.

The trade exhibition was enormous. Company representatives, all smartly dressed and with cosmetically enhanced dentistry, beamed and greeted, only to switch off abruptly when they recognised the British accent and realised there was nothing to be gained financially from any further contact. This was a popular social and educational occasion, and although Americans are known for their casual dress, here the senior surgeons were turned out like 1950s' film stars, immaculate and, to our amusement, often accompanied by much younger wives—number two or even three. I suppose surgeons are high earners with social status and hence attractive to women, but they also have to work so hard that they see less of their wife than she expects or desires, a rift develops and often the cycle repeats itself. Franny was an exception in so many ways, not least of which was his and

Laurie's devotion to one another for so long. One of the best things about the trip was flying from coast to coast by day. It was like having a map of the USA laid out before us and showed how sparsely populated and boring the great plains are. A silo, a flat green expanse, thirty seconds later, another silo, and so on.

Our local baseball team, the Boston Red Sox, played at Fenway Park in the city centre, the ground with the smallest capacity in the country, at just over 20,000. Tickets in the 'bleachers' could be obtained for as little as $2, so at first it amazed me that the club could afford to pay their star hitter, Jim Rice, five million bucks. The answer was, of course, TV. Baseball is a perfect game for commercial television. There are 162 games in a season, each one televised and lasting about three hours. Every time a hitter is out an advert appears until the next man is in and settled. This seemed to average about one every seven minutes. The population of Massachusetts was then around five million and the game was also beamed to the catchment area of the opposition. Naturally, with a three-hour game, everyone was seated, and I initially thought this might be why I witnessed no hooliganism, which we were used to in football in those days. While it probably contributed, the true reason was the absence of support for the opposition, other than the club directors and management. The distances were too great. The closest to Boston was New York, home of their long-standing rivals, the Yankees, at 200 miles.

After leaving a game, no-one seemed to talk about it—it was already history—whereas after a football match at home, the regulars back in the pub seem to have mentally record-ed every incident and precisely when it occurred, like a sports' reporter, and animatedly recapitulate the whole proceedings.

On summer weekends, Mary and the boys came to the games with me. One hot day there was a double-header—two games for the price of one. The opponents were the Kansas City Royals and we were lucky to witness a grand slam when a hitter struck a home run with the other three bases loaded, so that all four players trotted in, leisurely and triumphantly, to the cheers of the spectators and the bass chords of the electric organ. Baseball, like cricket, is a complex game and can be addictive, much more so to me than American football. The latter was big business, even for amateur teams. The professional team, the New England Patriots, played well out of town, and tickets were both difficult to obtain and expensive. Even Boston College, an amateur team, charged $8 a game, although I did once read they spent $50,000 a season on Elastoplast alone! The annual grudge match between Harvard and Yale seemed to have lost its cachet, probably because scholarships were no longer available for sporting prowess alone at these two Ivy League leaders. Students were judged on academic ability, which meant the players were only average or below. Our family had all looked forward to Independence Day, but unfortunately continuous torrential rain washed out all the parades and celebrations. Generous contributions from the Brigham's Friends' Association kindly offered itinerants such as us tickets to the Boston Symphony Orchestra, conducted by their now long-standing musical director, Seiji Ozawa. It was the first time we had witnessed a performance by such distinguished musicians.

# Chapter Fourteen

# So Long to the States

Both our mothers came to stay for several weeks, overlapping for a short time. Mrs Lack arrived first and we all went to Niagara Falls, a five-hundred-mile drive. When I was discussing our proposed trip with Chris Zook, a graduate economist preparing a PhD thesis about the costs of surgery, a subject of great interest to Franny, I was surprised to find him embarrassed and defensive about our proposed destination as he cautioned us not to expect too much. Chris was a highly intelligent, cultured Harvard graduate, who also had an MA from Oxford, where he had been a Rhodes scholar. It was only on returning from Niagara that I discovered it was not the spectacle of the Falls that concerned him but because, like Las Vegas, it was one of the most popular honeymoon resorts in the States, especially with the poorer section of the population, and had all the associated kitsch one would expect, like Blackpool in the UK. This sounds terribly snobbish, and although some motels did appear downmarket, in terms of their dress and behaviour, the tourists did not. The visit was an eye-opener in many ways. For example, the last section in the approach from the south, the American side, became increasingly industrialised and something of an eyesore as we passed the inappropriately named Love Canal, which had recently featured in the national press as a deposit for cadmium, mercury and other toxic elements. The Falls comprise two components, the American Falls, more or less running in line with the Niagara River, and the more famous Horseshoe Falls, which extend across both banks, at right angles to the American Falls, and have to be approached by crossing the Rainbow Bridge into Canada. American citizens can cross unheeded, but as British citizens we had to stop at the central booth and show our passports, although the occupants seemed both surprised and embarrassed that we had bothered to declare ourselves. Once we reached the Canadian side everything was much tidier, with trimmed lawns and pretty flower beds just as in British public parks. There was even a statue of King George VI. Many Americans failed to venture onto this side, despite access to better views, and the *Maid of the Mist*, the boat that approaches the foot of the Falls. We did not take the boat, but did don sou'westers, boots and mackintoshes to walk directly behind the torrent. We also took the cable car further up the river to view the whirlpool and then inspected the various barrels and other such vessels in which usually desperately poor daredevils had risked their lives in attempts, successful and otherwise, to drop the 180 feet over the precipice. Finally, we stood at the point where Captain Webb, the first man to swim the English Channel, attempted to cross the river at the rapids. He must have been persuaded by a large financial incentive, felt himself indestructible or been stupid, because one look can tell any reasonable person the feat is quite impossible, as it so proved, when the poor man's body was recovered days later, well downriver.

On my return to the lab, Chris seemed relieved to hear we had enjoyed ourselves. Incidentally, Chris analysed the records of several thousand patients from a variety of hospitals and showed that about forty percent of national medical costs were spent on patients who survived less than two years. I dare say this figure is larger now, with an ageing population suffering multiple chronic conditions such as diabetes, asthma, heart failure and stroke and in whom more interventions are possible to prolong what is often a miserable existence. A topical subject for all sections of society to address. Chris is now an author and advisor to business, having written several books analysing what makes successful companies remain so (as one might intuitively guess, it is those that retain their initial core interests and do not attempt to diversify into sectors of which they have little expertise) but he shows this by careful study. His books have been praised by *The Economist* and *The Times*, so he has predictably made great strides since his time with Dr Moore. When my mother arrived, we all went to New York for a weekend. I was apprehensive about driving and so did my homework, and all went well until the final hurdle. We passed the Triboro Bridge, all well signposted, and headed for Manhattan. It was almost as if the locals had done it on purpose—I suddenly saw, low down at about waist height, a small rectangular sign saying, 'Manhattan, turn right 100ft' (one hundred feet!) and, naturally, no sooner had I seen it than I was beyond it. About 100 yards further on was a toll booth and I asked the attendant if I was OK for Manhattan.

'Just missed it,' he seemed pleased to say, and so on we went until we managed a turn right at the southern tip, near the Battery (as the song goes, 'The Bronx is up, and the Battery's down').

With relief I pulled onto FDR Drive, which extends the full length of the east side of Manhattan, but could I find a left turn? No. At the very top I succeeded, but to my horror found we were now in Harlem, which in those days was still regarded as unsafe, certainly for white people, but we arrived early on a Saturday afternoon and the streets were quiet. Rumours abounded, such as not to stop at a red light, but I did. In the lane beside me was a black man in an open-topped car. I wound down the window and asked if he could direct me to 10th Avenue, where our hotel was located (on the edge of Hell's Kitchen) and he rattled off instructions before the lights changed. If one hesitates for more than a second or two in the States, one provokes a cacophony of blaring horns, so we both set off, but he slowed down, sounded his horn and tucked in behind me. I thought we were going to be held up at gunpoint, but at the next set of lights he drew alongside.

'I've just thought of a quicker route,' he said, so we thanked him profusely and found our destination with no further ado.

At one point my mother, sitting in the back with Mrs Lack, was hugging her handbag close to her chest and pleading with me to turn around and go back home! We were all able to have a good laugh afterwards and I felt guilty feeling afraid of a black man doing his best to help. Years later, when I read Tom Wolfe's fat novel *Bonfire of the Vanities*, I identified somewhat with the main character, a successful banker, who drove to JFK Airport to collect his mistress, got lost in Harlem on returning to Manhattan and in doing so made a driving error that led to his downfall. So it could even happen to a resident.

After cleaning up, and before we went out to explore the city for the first time, I opened a window to look into the street below just as a car drew up with a screech alongside a fire hydrant. The driver got out, removed a large spanner from the boot, unscrewed the top of the hydrant and proceeded to give his car a good wash. Only in New York!

My mother-in-law seemed excited at walking down 42nd Street, thinking of the old film of the musical, but oblivious to the fact that it no longer had a glamorous image and was now a haunt of streetwalkers. Mary knew but did not spoil her mother's little fantasy. I pointed out the Radio City Music Hall to my mother, home to several generations of the famous Rockettes, a long line of chorus girls. Among her memorabilia from my father was a programme for a show he had attended when his ship docked in 1941. She reacted negatively, obviously not wanting a painful reminder of a short, blighted married life, and I took the hint.

We did the usual touristy activities, such as visiting the top of the Empire State Building, and both ladies enjoyed the experience, taking all the noise and people rushing around in their stride. Mary and I were somewhat protective, treating them like old ladies, even though they were only in their early sixties then. We also drove to the White Mountains in New Hampshire to see the splendour of the fall, for which the six states of New England are renowned. The kaleidoscopic scenery results from a combination of climate and species of deciduous trees. With a sudden drop in temperature, especially at night, the sap is cut off from the leaves and the green chlorophyll broken down into different coloured products. Whereas at home there are usually various shades of yellow-brown, east of the Appalachians the different species of maples give rise to reds, gold, orange and yellow, with the gold of birch, purple of dogwood and the bronze of hickory. All these are offset by a normally bright blue sky with cold but sunny days, rust-coloured barns and white-steepled, colonial-style churches. We drove along the Kancamagus Highway, which follows the Snake River, and stayed at a motel in New Hampshire.

Another must was Concord, twenty-five miles from Boston and home of Louisa M Alcott, Emerson and Thoreau. I was taken with Sleepy Hollow Cemetery, which contained several graves of Unionist victims of the Civil War, some of which still had original photographs behind glass of young men in uniform. Especially moving to me was the grave of a recently deceased medical student who succumbed to Hodgkin's disease and whom I had met in the Clinical Center when he was receiving chemotherapy under sterile conditions.

I also took my mother to JFK's birthplace at 83 Beals Street in Brookline. He lived in this small house until he was three, when his increasingly successful father moved the family to a twelve-roomed house close by. The house is now a museum and we were the only visitors. Rose Kennedy, the matriarch of the family, gave a commentary about each room, which could be played by pressing a button. Her descriptions were clear and composed, but when she described the room in which the future president was born in 1917 there was just a little catch in her voice that brought tears to one's eyes, especially when one reflected on the tragedy she had experienced during her life. Out of her nine children, three sons were dead (two assassinated and the eldest killed in action in World War II), the youngest son was soon to be disgraced, one daughter was confined to a mental institution and one killed in an air crash. And yet she retained her Christian faith until the end of her long life.

Towards the end of my research I did some studies on severely ill patients. These had no impact on their treatment. They were already receiving total intravenous nutrition and we just added some N15 glycine and collected urine. One young man had the worst complication following appendicectomy I have ever seen. He was transferred from Rhode Island hospital where he had undergone an apparently uncomplicated appendix removal, but some days later developed signs of intra-abdominal sepsis. At re-operation, some loops of small bowel were adherent to one another (a common finding, but such adhesions are usually loose and can easily be separated if required). Unfortunately, the mesentery containing the blood vessels was inadvertently torn in separating them, thus depriving a segment of small bowel of its supply. Hence the segment was removed and the severed ends sewn together in the usual manner. The surgeon must have anticipated trouble because he then created a feeding gastrostomy by inserting a catheter into the stomach, which was brought out to the surface to provide nutrition postoperatively. One can only conclude that subsequent events proceeded because of poor technique because not only did the small bowel join break down but so did the stomach at the site of the gastrostomy. When the poor man was transferred, virtually the whole of his abdominal wall was open, revealing much of his stomach lining and discharging both gastric and small bowel contents, which are extremely corrosive to skin. In these circumstances, if the patient can be kept alive for long enough, small fistulae will close by healing and those too large to do so can be closed surgically when the time is right. I do not know the outcome. When I left he was still in the ITU, stable, but weeks away from further surgical intervention. If he did survive it could not have been possible without the support of intravenous feeding. By the way, the ITU was called the Bartlett Unit, named after Laurie Moore's family, who had originally financed its creation.

One day I was in the unit when I heard a sweet female voice.

'Say hello to Doctor Clarke,' it said.

I turned round to face a most unexpected, horrific sight. A young man, clad only in a white hospital gown and cardboard slippers, was standing rigid, both exposed arms and legs scarred so badly they were in fixed positions. He had two holes for a nose, eyes within red, hairless lids and bared teeth but no lips. He was held upright by a female physiotherapist on one side and the source of the voice, a pretty dietician with whom I worked, on the other. He and his girlfriend, both aged about nineteen, lived with their newborn baby in a trailer. By some mishap a gas bottle, the source of their heating, had exploded. Fortunately, only the lad was at home. He sustained about ninety per cent burns, theoretically not survivable, but by some miracle (plus, of course, excellent care from the Burns Unit), he had. I could see no future for him, as there was no healthy skin to use for grafting, and felt it was a pity he had survived at all. And then he developed further problems. Due to prolonged nutrition via a central line, an infection led to an acute endocarditis, destroying a heart valve, which was successfully replaced surgically. Amazingly, he actually returned home. Only a couple of weeks later, however, his death was announced at an M&M. He had aspirated a mouthful of food and asphyxiated. The clinical staff involved in his care were devastated but I was relieved, both for his sake and that of his partner and child.

***

Before coming home I took the last two weeks off so we could take the boys to Disney World in Florida. We were given a small farewell party by the laboratory staff, attended by Franny and, touchingly, by Mrs Moore. And then on Sunday April 1st 1979, our twelfth wedding anniversary, we set off west on the Massachusetts Turnpike to Sturbridge Village, before turning onto Route 86 via Hartford, New Haven (home of Yale University), Stanford and White Plains and crossed the Hudson River by the Tappan Zee Bridge, viewing the Pocantico Hills to the right and the skyscrapers of Manhattan in the distance on our left. Then onto the Garden State Parkway and the New Jersey Turnpike, across the Delaware and Susquehanna rivers to the dirty, sprawling, industrialised outskirts of Baltimore, and finally, after about eleven hours, reached Washington DC and our first stopover, the Best Western Motor Inn.

The following morning a short walk took us to the White House at Lafayette Square, which we bypassed to go to the Washington Monument, where we took the lift (ten cents) to the top, unfortunately shrouded in mist. Then we walked along the reflecting pool to the Lincoln Memorial, followed by the Jefferson Memorial, viewed across the tidal basin. Finally, to the Smithsonian Museum and the Air and Space Museum, the obvious main attractions being the command module of the first moon landing, the flying machine of the Wright brothers (1903), Charles Lindbergh's *Spirit of St Louis* and *Enola Gay*, the plane that dropped the atomic bomb on Hiroshima.

The next day we did the tour of the White House, entering by the East Wing, in which were portraits of various first ladies, the small library used by the President for TV addresses and the Jacqueline Kennedy Garden. We continued via a series of rooms named after colours to the central section, with the seal of the US as a mosaic on the floor, where the president receives heads of state, exiting at the Lafayette Square access. In the afternoon we visited the FBI building where we saw J Edgar Hoover's enormous desk and sawn-off shotguns and Thompson submachine guns of gangsters, ending with a demonstration of shooting of handguns and submachine guns by an FBI officer. Finally, to the National Archives, where, in addition to two unconscious alcoholics lying in the rain, we viewed a fading Declaration of Independence.

On day four we left Washington to visit my Newcastle colleague John Farndon, his wife Chris and their three children. John was a research fellow at Duke University in North Carolina and they had invited us to stay both on our way south and on the return journey. Virginia we found surprisingly boring and Richmond, apart from a few central skyscrapers, was a low-level, sprawling, industrialised mess, with the enormous Marlboro cigarette factory on its southern outskirts. North Carolina produced the biggest change since leaving Boston, the trees and vegetation being a lusher green, and the earth almost red. The Farndons rented an isolated house in a rural area near Durham, home of Duke University, a prestigious institution endowed by tobacco magnates. On this first visit we only stayed overnight, departing the next day for Savannah, Georgia.

The weather was now much improved and although the countryside was flat the gardens were lovely, with blazing red azaleas contrasting with white houses, green fields and a 'Carolina blue' sky. South Carolina appeared fairly nondescript—flat, sparsely populated and boring—but we bypassed Charleston, which appears beautiful and charming in postcards. In these southern states the roadside food stops were mainly Stuckey's—each one identical and all scrupulously clean, selling pecan log rolls, Divinity (a type of candy), bags of pecan nuts, souvenir junk and food. We reached Savannah at dusk. Here the trees changed in character, and many hosted the parasite Spanish moss, which hung from them in characteristic fashion seen in the movies, and palm trees revealed themselves for the first time. Another lovely day found us heading for our final destination of Orlando, Florida. Running out of ready cash prompted a move off Interstate 95 for any small town to find a bank to cash travellers' cheques. I was apprehensive about this, having probably taken too literally the *New York Times*' warning that one should not stop in Georgia unless really necessary if one's car bore a northern state licence plate. Apparently, the state police would always find an excuse to prosecute. Once we entered a rural gas station and the proprietor, the spitting image of Billy Carter, the embarrassing brother of the president, was sitting on a wall chewing a blade of grass. As I got out of the car he jumped down and approached.

'Well, I never, fourth goddamn Yankee in a row,' he politely explained, referring to my Massachusetts plate.

'No, I'm from England,' I said.

'London?'

'No,' I replied.

And that was the end of the conversation.

We stopped at Brunswick, almost on the coast, and a centre for those visiting the small offshore islands. It was a pretty, clean town, with many lovely bushes from which emanated a sickly-sweet smell, the nature of which we had never before encountered. We noticed it again on our return journey, in Savannah, but I still do not know the name of the species. We withdrew $200 from a bank without too much trouble, other than having to produce about three different forms of identification, which I thought travellers' cheques aimed to avoid, but never mind, at least the state policeman on his motorised tricycle didn't run us in.

Many cars overtaking us bore Pennsylvania licence plates and we wondered whether the recent accident at the Three Mile Island nuclear plant near Harrisburg, PA, had prompted families to take a spring vacation in Florida. Through a very busy Jacksonville, bypassing Daytona Beach, we left I 95 for US-4 and a short drive on the Florida Turnpike to Orange Blossom Trail, and our destination, Ramada Inn South. The latter road was misleadingly named, for it was a typically busy American one, with roadside cafes, motels and gas stations, but close by there were some orange groves. Our motel was off-road, built into a square surrounding a swimming pool, with palms and flowering shrubs, and was conveniently placed opposite a McDonald's!

A free bus took us to Walt Disney World about eight miles away on a beautiful morning, eighty-five degrees and a cloudless sky. Our two-day tickets cost $56, a huge sum then, and we entered the Magic Kingdom on a monorail, which traversed the hotel of the Contemporary Resort. After entering Main Street we were immediately greeted by Mickey Mouse for photographs and at the end of the street was Cinderella's castle. The efficiency and cleanliness of everything was impressive. Each book of tickets contained those for A, B, C, D or E attractions, E being the best, or most expensive, if purchased separately. On this first day we visited the Haunted Mansion, with its dancing ghosts and singing figures. Then it was on to the Hall of Presidents, with incredibly lifelike models of all thirty-seven presidents, acting as real ones would. Washington was giving an address, during which others would fidget, place a hand in a pocket or scratch their noses. After that we took the 20,000 Leagues Under the Sea submarine voyage, Space Mountain and the Mickey Mouse Revue. To our eyes, the technology involved was mind-boggling. On the second day we experienced the Country Bear Jamboree, Jungle Cruise, Riverboat, Carousel, the Circlarama of *America the Beautiful* and the Disney Parade, complete with all the characters.

We pondered remaining a third day but kept to our planned schedule when clouds started moving in and the wind rose. Heading back north we soon met black clouds and heavy rain, the sort we rarely experience at home. Even at full speed the windscreen wipers could barely cope, reducing the traffic to a virtual crawl, but at last we reached the Quality Inn, Savannah. As I drove in I thought the place was undergoing renovation. At reception I asked if there were vacancies.

'Yes, sir, but no electricity,' came the reply. 'We had a twister through this morning.'

The tornado had whipped past the motel, uprooted several trees and destroyed the children's playground. We were given candles with our room key, but fortunately power was restored at dusk. We arrived at the Farndons the next day and enjoyed their hospitality for three days, including a tour of the campus of Duke University, which was beautifully kept, with cherry blossom and dogwoods. With no further plans other than getting home, we drove as far as possible and stopped after dark at a Ramada Inn in a dirty, depressing industrial estate in Runnymede, NJ. The menu was expensive, so I ventured out to seek takeaways and found a deserted street with a burger bar. I must have been the first customer of the evening, for I seemed to surprise the owner, a very hirsute Italian American, but on receiving my order he scrubbed up like a surgeon in front of me, before preparing it. I was impressed. The following day, our last on the road, we discovered we had an almost severed fanbelt, which was changed at great expense, and then the car started to stall when idling. Fortunately, though, we reached home.

***

I sold the car at substantial loss to an apologetic proprietor of the garage at Needham Heights from whom it was purchased, but it needed a new transmission. On our last night we slept restlessly at an overcrowded Wu household, as we had to vacate 180 Maple Street. We were then picked up by Liam McKean for Logan Airport, and home.

Was it all worth it? As far as my career was concerned, taking a year out at the late age of thirty-six, in a craft such as surgery, was not the best move. In one respect, I would have been better off honing my operative skills at some highly specialised so-called centre of excellence. However, as an experience of life, I would not have missed it. Nor, thank goodness, would Mary and the boys.

Franny Moore was a giant in surgical research, and I regard it as a great honour and privilege to have been associated with him, in however small a capacity. I only hope some of his qualities influenced me. After returning home, we only met him and Mrs Moore once more, when they called at Newcastle on their way to Denmark, where he was receiving yet another honorary degree. Prof Johnston kindly invited Mary and I and Peter and Ilva Wright to have dinner with the Moores the evening before their departure. In his usual thoughtful way, Franny presented me with a Brigham tie, together with both red and blue Harvard ones, which I still proudly wear from time to time.

Tragically, after fifty-three years of marriage, Laurie Moore was killed in a car accident while driving alone during a sudden and terrible New England thunderstorm in 1988, nine years after I left. It seemed to be the only setback in an otherwise long and successful life. Franny married a long-standing family friend, widow Katharyn Saltonstall. They remained together until November 2001, when, aged eighty-eight, and burdened by chronic heart failure, he ended his life two days after Thanksgiving. His obituary stated he had been awarded more honorary degrees than he had grandchildren—and at the time of his death there were seventeen of those!

# Chapter Fifteen

# From Tyne to Tees

I was back at work within a week of arriving home and needed a car. I was often asked why I bought a Fiat—well, our first new car was a Fiat 600, which was all we could afford, and it served us well mechanically despite being a rust bucket. It was followed by a Fiat 128, which never let us down and was sold when we left for the States. I preferred a change, but in 1979 one had to wait three months for a Ford, and unless one had mechanical expertise, buying a second-hand car was almost a lottery. So it was a Fiat Mirafiori, obtained within days.

As luck would have it, I ended up back with Brian Fleming and Denis Hindmarsh, despite Brian telling his registrar that, 'Dave Clarke left under a cloud', a reference to the time he refused to believe I had not undermined him by requesting a transfer from his unit—although if I had possessed any cojones, I should have. I was now in my fifth year as a senior registrar and the time had come to apply for consultant posts. The senior registrar contract was renewed annually, usually a formality, but after five years, some pressure might be exerted to apply for every vacancy in the country. Providing one did this and was considered to be of the 'right stuff', it was unlikely one's contract would be terminated until promotion was obtained, but one heard stories of 'time-expired' senior registrars who were landed in limbo and ended up in unsatisfactory posts, emigrated or, even at this late stage, entered general practice. During this second stint with Brian, I had to organise the surgical cases for the Finals. This was a chore even when it went well and could be an organisational nightmare. Until relatively recently, surgical cases had been examined solely by surgeons, but now someone had the bright idea to select straightforward cases that any qualified medical practitioner should be able to recognise, as the examination was supposed to be testing general, rather than specialised, knowledge. My job was to pick cases from outpatients during the weeks before the examination or persuade ones already on the waiting list to take part.

I had to clear half a ward, not always easy with unpredictable numbers of emergencies, get the patients there on time and organise the setup, including cribs for the examiners. Candidates were examined at specific times at different locations throughout the hospital, so strict timekeeping was essential, and although this had been stressed to all concerned, did it have any effect? No, is the answer, and sometimes I wondered how some examiners had succeeded in life. I had everything shipshape—a quiet ward, patients all ready, typewritten summaries of patients' details—and planned to briefly show the examiners round, but the first obstacle was a professor of surgery from London, a cold, thin-lipped, humourless man and obviously a control freak who wanted to change everything around to suit himself. I was not best pleased and years later was delighted to see him featured on a TV programme, showing him in consultation with a clergyman who had varicose veins and repairing the hernia of a retired army officer under local anaesthesia in a community hospital. I can think of more profitable ways for a professor of surgery to occupy their time. Not that I bear grudges, you must understand.

Peter Wright succeeded Taffy Jones on his retirement as senior lecturer, joining me in Pavilion 1. I was offered the position of locum consultant, a move that could be frowned upon by the training authorities, such as they were in those days, because one is practising independently without official supervision, but I had to accept. I was entitled to use the consultants' dining room, which I did occasionally, just to show my face. Professor Johnston, no doubt aware of my somewhat shy nature, told me it was time for me 'to throw your weight around a bit'. I had returned from the States a much more confident and assertive person, but this change in personality persisted for six weeks at the most. When a job came up at St Richard's Hospital in Chichester, I thought the description must have been written especially for me. They wanted a general surgeon with urological experience who could also build up a vascular service. Who else would fit the bill, particularly the ability to use the resectoscope? I travelled the long distance to view the situation, arriving at about lunchtime to find a group of loud, confident senior registrars from London discussing the merits of various skiing resorts with the retiring surgeon. I was introduced to him and thought he was presenting me with a wet fish as a gift, but found it to be a flaccid, moist handshake accompanied by—and I shall never forget it—'Newcastle, eh? How nice to see you northern chaps coming to look at our southern jobs.' I glanced at my watch to see how long I would have to wait before the next train home. His colleague, however, who showed us round, was a friendly, approachable fellow. At one point we came across a young, handsome, blond man in a short white jacket, who stood more or less to attention and gave a respectful nod as we passed him in the corridor. The surgeon acknowledged him, smiled, and when out of earshot explained he was a member of the Weston family who was embarrassed by his wealth and worked unpaid as a porter. This meant nothing to me, but I later discovered that Garfield Weston, of Canadian origin, had founded the firm that owned, among other things, the Mother's Pride bakery, and his descendants are billionaires.

I was not shortlisted for the post and none of the metropolitan chaps I encountered got it either, but I met the successful candidate, a good man, at vascular meetings. He set up a screening service for aortic aneurysms long before anyone else in this country, and not only did he confirm the Weston family story, but when I last saw him, the porter was still working at St Richard's. If I had got the job we would probably have had to live in a council house because we couldn't have afforded to live within the proximity of the hospital. I was not shortlisted for Bath either, and looked at a job in Tynemouth, which was too close to Newcastle to attract anything more than routine cases. Finally, I heard that Sam Mottershead was retiring in Middlesbrough. Mottershead had a reputation as a 'character' and the Middlesbrough *Evening Gazette* devoted two whole pages over consecutive nights to mark his retirement and his achievements, giving examples of his surgical anecdotes and aphorisms, none of which were original.

I was shown around Middlesbrough General Hospital by Mike Cooke, a St Mary's man. The new appointee was to work with Mike, whose former colleague was moving to the old North Ormesby Hospital, soon to be replaced by the brand-new South Cleveland Hospital. Mike was interested in upper gastrointestinal surgery, which then still consisted mainly of treatment for peptic ulcers and had founded an endoscopy unit via charitable donations. I was interested to see that he possessed the full range of the relatively recently developed stapling instruments, with bespoke disposable attachments, whereas in the RVI we had only a crude 'Russian gun', suitable for one type of anastomosis and which required a tiresome manual loading of each individual staple.

The post was advertised as that of a general surgeon, with no specific interest requested, and I offered vascular surgery as such. This was accepted informally, with some reservations, as I later learned—apparently Sam requested arteriograms for many patients but operated on hardly any. In those days general surgery included upper gastrointestinal, colorectal, breast and endocrine, most of urology, vascular and general paediatrics. Mike took me across to North Ormesby to meet Alan Tooley and after some chat they both agreed they had told me everything they could.

On the eve of the interview, a Sunday, four of us were asked to attend for 'trial by sherry', a term we used for what appeared to be an informal gathering with a few drinks, but was really an interview by some potential future colleagues. I nearly didn't bother showing up, thinking the procedure uncalled for, but I decided such behaviour would be construed as either overconfidence or bad manners. The next day I was relaxed and somewhat indifferent about the outcome. My love for Newcastle and the RVI had led to me acting like Mr Micawber and expecting something to turn up there. I knew I had a good reputation in the hospital, and Denis Hindmarsh's replacement had not yet been advertised after his retirement. However, it became clear the Prof was intent on expanding the academic complement and did not, correctly, perceive me as an academic surgeon.

I felt no sense of joy or relief on being told I was the successful candidate and did not celebrate. Mary did not betray her feelings, appearing, like myself, somewhat non-committal, but she must secretly have been pleased to be moving to within a few miles of her birthplace, where her mother and younger brother still lived, as well as her married sister and family.

When I told Ian McNeill about my appointment he was not impressed.

'Well, Dave,' he said. 'I don't know what advice I can give you, but most of your colleagues will be shits.'

I was so taken aback that I failed to ascertain his precise meaning. Did he mean my new colleagues were already shits, using the future tense to indicate that I would soon discover this for myself or was it a statement about consultant colleagues in general? I can reveal that one colleague in particular was one, but he glad-handed and greased his way through life, back-stabbing on his way. I initially thought his saturnine appearance was misleading because of small acts of apparent kindness, but his true character was ultimately revealed.

***

The dreaded day arrived when I said goodbye to the RVI. At a small farewell party, I was presented with two pictures of Tyneside to remind me of some of the happiest years of my life. As I traipsed up the corridor I steeled myself not to look back, even though I knew I would often return, but from now on I would somehow be an intruder rather than playing an active role in a long-running play. I now had three weeks of reflection before starting a new life, on June 1st 1980. The first step was to find a place to live and schools for the boys. NHS regulations stated consultants must reside within ten miles of their main hospital, although some discretion was allowed if on call was not onerous and access by road was swift. Few colleagues lived in Middlesbrough itself, preferring small towns and villages such as Guisborough, Hutton Rudby, Stokesley and Yarm.

Although Middlesbrough encompassed some of the poorest local authority wards in the country, these semi-rural communities possessed the highest concentration of science PhDs, a remarkable fact due mainly to the presence on Teesside of the chemical conglomerate ICI, which at its peak employed 30,000 people. Sadly, this is no longer the case since the fairly sudden demise of this fine British company. ICI periodically moved its chemists around, seemingly on a whim, and we therefore had difficulty finding a house within our price range, usually being gazumped by an ICI family. Hence, from June 1980 until February 1981 I commuted from Newcastle, dropping Michael off at school in Yarm and picking him up afterwards. This was possible because it takes time for a new surgeon to build up a busy practice and Mike Cooke agreed to do the on call, initially one day a week (there being seven surgeons *in toto*), although when he took his summer holiday in August I slept in extremely basic hospital accommodation. Fortunately, Mary's Uncle Herb was living with his sister, Mary's mother, in her house in Bishopton. Despite being a shy, retiring sort, he willingly helped out by picking Michael up if I could not make it in time.

It was a relief to find the detached house in Yarm where Mary and I still live. The rear garden backs onto woodland, which soon drops steeply to the River Tees fifty yards beyond. The mortgage rate was fifteen percent but we were charged seventeen at first, and initially, together with school fees, cost about half my salary. That's why we obtained our new three-piece suite on hire-purchase. My mother would have had a fit had she known!

***

Middlesbrough had a population of 145,000 in 1980, with a history of shipbuilding, the steel industry (the second largest blast furnace in Europe at Redcar, ten miles east) and ICI. It was christened 'an infant Hercules' by Gladstone after the discovery in the mid-nineteenth century of ironstone in the Cleveland Hills just to the south, and the rapidly burgeoning steel industry which followed created a town from almost nothing, with a large proportion of the population composed of migrants from Ireland and

South Wales, as well as indigenous Yorkshire folk. About thirty per cent of the present inhabitants are Roman Catholic and the town has a Catholic cathedral and a bishopric that extends as far south as my home city, Hull. It took me a while to latch on, being initially puzzled why so many nurses were called Teresa and Bernadette and why they pronounced the letter 'h' as 'haitch' instead of 'aitch'. They often said their families came from 'the land of saints and scholars'. Although only of modest size, because the town is at the extreme southern end of the Regional Health Authority, it is a subregional centre for certain specialties, such as neurology and neurosurgery, radiotherapy, dermatology, urology, rheumatology, plastic surgery and burns, renal medicine, ENT, ophthalmology, maxillofacial surgery and intensive care. The catchment population of these specialties must be at least 600,000.

Our service was provided by an administrative nightmare of fourteen hospitals. The general hospitals, with medical and surgical beds, were Middlesbrough General and North Ormesby (dating from 1861), which were both replaced in 1981, soon after my arrival, by South Cleveland, built beside St Luke's psychiatric hospital, plus Eston and Hemlington.

Of the original five general hospitals, only Middlesbrough General had an A&E department, and is also had most of paediatrics, both of which impacted on the workload of the two general surgeons, Mike Cooke and myself. Of the other five surgeons, three were at South Cleveland and two at Hemlington, including Frank Walker, former Reader in Surgery in the RVI.

My base, Middlesbrough General, was a workhouse in 1878, with an infirmary attached. It was sited close to what had been the poorest part of town, surrounded on two sides by streets of terraced houses and on the other two by Linthorpe Cemetery and Ayresome Park, home of Middlesbrough AFC. Like so many of our older hospitals, the site comprised several separate buildings, only a minor inconvenience for staff but a nuisance for patients and their porters, wheeling them for x-rays in the wind and rain.

Our block of two storeys contained four wards of thirty beds each, each ward bisected by a corridor, male surgical on the ground floor, female above, with the same arrangement for the medical wards at the other end. An extension housed two operating theatres, offices, a small dermatology ward and the endoscopy unit. Outpatients and x-ray were in a separate central single-storey block and there was a separate paediatric block and a small, modern doctors' residence and dining room. The 'new' block, as it was referred to, dated from the 1950s and contained A&E, orthopaedics, plastics, neurosciences and intensive care. The latter was in unsatisfactory premises, but soon moved to the new South Cleveland. Ancillary buildings included pathology, the mortuary and, last but not least, the VD department, soon to be renamed STD (sexually transmitted diseases), with its separate male and female entrances. I recall being amused but also touched when I saw a young couple stop outside, give a little kiss and a hug and part towards their different entrances.

The old buildings were constructed using the narrow bricks of the Victorian era, and the wards were much narrower than I was used to. Also, other than a sluice for the cleaning and sterilisation of bedpans and suchlike, and sister's office, there were no ancillary rooms. Only three of the thirty beds on each ward were cubicles.

Each ward had two sisters. The senior sister on the male ward was an attractive, middle-aged woman who, despite (or perhaps, because of) having borne five children, was flirtatious, forever giving one the eye. She was meticulous in her appearance and had a professional demeanour, but her surgical knowledge was pretty thin. The junior sister was much more efficient and quietly got on with her job. Both were supported by excellent, hardworking, cheerful staff nurses, who were genuinely dedicated to their craft. The female ward sisters had a higher turnover because of marriage and childbirth, but I never had concerns about the ability or reliability of the nursing staff, a major plus.

On the afternoon of my very first day, an outpatient clinic was arranged at North Ormesby. I soon wondered what I had come to, for on entering the room to see the first patient I found a rivulet of liquid faeces trickling from a height of three feet down one wall, with an apologetic man simply stating, 'I couldn't help it, doctor.' But three feet! He must have been an acrobat. I cannot, however, remember anything else about the consultation. Another, I do remember. It was with a lovely, plump, middle-aged lady who was employed as a chambermaid at the Dorchester Hotel in London. Her husband was one of many on Teesside who was now long-term unemployed as a result of deindustrialisation and she returned home for alternate weekends. This was about the time Secretary of State for Employment Norman Tebbit controversially said that under similar circumstances his father 'got on his bike' to seek work. Well, this poor lady certainly got on her bike, and it couldn't have been much fun.

On the Friday of my first week, one of the two paediatricians presented me with a baby who had congenital pyloric stenosis. Mike Cooke was appointed as a general and paediatric surgeon but did not get on with either of these ladies and my presence gave them an excuse to drop him almost completely. I had seen the operation for this condition only once and although it is a simple procedure, like everything else in surgery, one has to pay attention to detail or things can go badly wrong. The underlying cause of the problem is unknown and it affects male babies much more commonly than females, presenting with vomiting at about six weeks after birth. This is classically projectile in nature and is caused by an overgrowth of the muscle at the outlet of the stomach, the pylorus. Normally the muscle periodically contracts and relaxes to allow small amounts of food to leave the stomach for the small intestine. The diagnosis is made from the history and the ability to feel the lump of the enlarged muscle, about the size of an acorn, through the abdominal wall of the infant when it contracts after a feed. The treatment is Ramstedt's operation, in which an incision is made along the long axis of the muscle and the circular fibres are split apart by gentle teasing with forceps. The split must go down to the inner lining, which at the far end comes very close to the surface and can easily be opened inadvertently. If only a small hole is created it can simply be stitched closed, but if it goes unrecognised it can cause a silent peritonitis, which may be fatal. The condition was first described in 1888 and Conrad Ramstedt (1867-1963) devised his operation in 1911, continuing to perform it until he was eighty. My revered former boss, George Feggetter, had a brother, Stewart, a surgeon at Newcastle General, who performed more than a thousand of these procedures and was even invited to Ramstedt's funeral. The condition and its treatment had a significant mortality for many years, due to a combination of difficult anaesthesia in such small babies and lack of knowledge and techniques of intravenous therapy to replace lost fluids, but these days operative mortality should approach zero. I did more than a hundred in my first few years before it became policy to send all such cases to the Regional Centre, and I had no deaths, nor complications.

# Chapter Sixteen

# Trials and Tribulations

The contract of employment a consultant signed in those days was described as open, without a specific work plan. We were regarded as professionals in the old-fashioned definition of the word, not in the sense of paid employees as opposed to amateurs, but with a certain unwritten code of conduct. We were allowed flexibility to arrange our working hours in a way that enabled us to fulfil the exigencies of the service in a responsible manner. However, the general rule as a surgeon was to have three or four operating lists or sessions (each a half-day, but preferably at least two forming a full day to make the best use of time), two outpatient clinics and an endoscopy session, the remaining time being devoted to ward rounds, administrative work and teaching, and to partake in the emergency rota.

After the old Eston and North Ormesby hospitals closed, Middlesbrough General and South Cleveland were the primary sites and operated under separate management, provoking occasional petty rivalries about the distribution of finance. Each hospital had its own medical staff committee, which met monthly, and I was soon installed as the secretary for Middlesbrough General, mainly because I was the newest appointee and the job was rightly regarded as a chore. The chairman at the time was a laboratory-based haematologist, a self-important single woman who purported to be a devout Christian although often she did not behave like one, and who delegated as much business as she could to me, but then moaned if things did not fit with her 'busy schedule' (she did not know the meaning of the words). Fortunately for the NHS, her faith got the better of her and she soon left to become an Anglican nun, a role which heretofore I did not realise existed.

I was tasked with arranging a retirement dinner for one of the dermatologists, at which Mary and I were seated next to the senior surgeon and his wife. The latter, with whom neither Mary nor myself had previously had the acquaintance, spent virtually the whole evening informing us that young consultants such as me did not know the meaning of hard work and had been mollycoddled all our lives, her easy-going husband smiling benignly and trying to disengage himself from his wife's views by desperately conversing with the guest on his other side. The episode has remained with me because never before had I been the butt of such unsolicited blatant rudeness for such a sustained period. The strange thing is that her husband was a delightful man.

On another occasion we were invited to a dinner party at a colleague's house. The main course was game pie, my first and last experience of this dish, the pungent aroma of which seemed to permeate the whole house and so impregnated my clothes and skin that it seemed to remain in my nostrils for days. Other than the hosts, all the guests were unknown to us and at least a decade older. A lady opposite, the chairman of a local health board, was accompanied by her newly acquired second husband, a rude, aggressive Welshman, even chippier than the newsreader John Humphrys, and who clearly could not disguise his disgust that the price he had to pay for marital bliss was to reside in England. The lady to my left, a dentist's wife, had recently returned from a cruise of the Baltic capitals, but besides describing the cities themselves, in which I was interested, she seemed to have memorised every dish she had consumed on the trip, and I suddenly found myself dissolving into hysterical laughter. The combination of the pie, the Welshman and the dentist's wife made it the dinner party from hell, and I began to doubt my sanity.

***

As a newly appointed consultant surgeon, one is conscious of being on trial, and it's not only one's personality being judged, but one's skill with the knife. It was noticeable that the first operation I did, a mere groin hernia, attracted an audience. Fortunately, the theatre staff were extremely welcoming, and Ronnie (Veronica) Reed and Freda Smith, the two senior sisters, had worked at Middlesbrough General since they were student nurses. Like many hospitals, although it was an old, unattractive building, it had a loyal, friendly staff with a relatively low turnover indicative of high morale, and when it was finally forced to close in 1995, coinciding with the demise of the neighbouring Ayresome Park football ground, to be replaced by a housing estate, the nursing staff felt bereaved, even though they were moving only two miles away to a bright, airy and brand new facility.

Our two theatres were shared with the maxillofacial surgeons, whose beds were on our wards. The remaining theatres were in the 'new' block, so we were self-contained, with our own sterilisation unit next door. We had the same theatre porters for years. One was the son of a consultant elsewhere, married to a nurse, and a nicely spoken man of quiet demeanour, who hid his light under a bushel. He had been a civil engineer in Africa for some years and it was a mystery why he was now a porter, although there were rumours of a breakdown. Suffice to say, he took a degree in Philosophy from the Open University, having plenty of time to study between ferrying patients to and from theatre, and it always amused me if I popped into the nurses' restroom to see him reading Plato's *The Republic*. He was a little older than me and when he died I discovered he had climbed the Matterhorn at the age of twenty-three and was a qualified Alpine guide, achievements he kept to himself and a close-knit circle of friends.

Within a few weeks of starting, I was called one weekend to the ITU, where a man was bleeding from the large bowel. He had crashed while paragliding a couple of weeks earlier and sustained a closed head injury, from which he remained in a coma. The bleeding persisted, requiring a large transfusion, and it was clearly not going to stop. He sounded similar to my fisherman from Peterhead described in an earlier chapter. The man's prognosis from the head injury was uncertain, and after discussion with his neurosurgeon, whom I had not yet met, I performed a total colectomy and ileo-rectal anastomosis. This stopped the bleeding, but he died about a week later, the cause of death being uncertain. I attended the post-mortem, anxious to see if my anastomosis was intact or not. As is routine, the body was opened by a mortician before the pathologist arrived. Perhaps I should have warned him, but I thought I would bide my time to see what happened. Sure enough, he tore out the intestines with no regard for the implications. Because of the head injury, a neuropathologist attended and when he looked at the gut he pronounced that unfortunately the anastomosis had disrupted. I said I knew it had because I had just seen his mortician pull it apart, but there was no sign in the abdominal cavity of faecal spillage or peritonitis. This was the first of several experiences that created my somewhat guarded view of some pathologists over the succeeding years (I stress *some*—I had great faith in one colleague, but unfortunately he refused to partake in coroners' cases).

One afternoon a smartly dressed man, silver hair neatly parted and sleeked back, checked shirt and tie, tweed waistcoat with watch chain and fuchsia-coloured twills, was admitted as an emergency. He was in his mid-seventies but, unusually, his wife was much older, in her early nineties. Understandably, she no longer had either the energy nor the inclination to partake in conjugal relations, but his libido was still strong and his desire drove him to seek relief via the nozzle of an 1800-watt cylinder vacuum cleaner. As a result, to use a zoological simile, his one-eyed snake appeared to have lost a battle with a terrier. It took me some time in the operating theatre to rearrange the ragged remnant into something resembling normality, but it healed well. Sadly, however, I suspect that he would never have an erection again any further activity by such a numb member would be confined to watching him clean his shoes.

One of life's unwritten rules is that if one indulges in any form of sexual deviation in private, the gods will punish the offender in some way, *viz* the above case and previous examples of the Ladbrokes the bookmaker-embossed ballpoint pen and the insulating wire. One Sunday at about dawn I was phoned about a man who had 'lost' a dildo up his rectum. It takes all sorts! As usual, one sticks to the facts in such cases, not the motives. His wife was away for the weekend but returning by lunchtime. Was there any way she could be prevented from finding out? We certainly wouldn't tell her, but as the misplaced object could not be felt on rectal examination he would require a general anaesthetic to remove it and could not drive home. Also, there was a small possibility we might be unable to extract it from below, in which case surgery would be necessary. But if we did it straight away and managed without a problem, he could be home by lunchtime, and what he told his wife was up to him. Fortunately, with an assistant compressing from above, I managed to grasp the culprit, an enormous black silicone-rubber lifelike cast of a penis, which was handed to a goggle-eyed nurse. She received it with tentative, apprehensive, gloved hands to wash it, bag it and return it to its grateful owner. He had time to avoid it but decided to come clean and phoned his wife with the truth. I wouldn't have wanted to be in his shoes when she collected him.

In similar vein, but back in the RVI, Ross Taylor once removed an orange from a man's rectum and presented the intact object to the patient.

'But where's the other one?' came the dissatisfied response.

The funniest such case, although admittedly not for the subject, was when a young man was admitted with the cap from a deodorant impacted in the rectum. His girlfriend rammed the deodorant up his backside at the moment of ecstatic climax and the cap dislodged.

Almost the only way to meet GPs was at weekly postgraduate educational meetings. In theory, domiciliary consultations, for which the consultant received a fee, acted as another channel, the original intention of such a service being for both parties to meet in the patient's home. Although this often remained the case in rural practices, in urban areas the GP rarely attended, usually simply leaving the details with the consultant's secretary and letting him get on with it. In the days when car ownership was less common it was probably a good idea and remained so for housebound elderly patients, but the system lent itself to abuse and was time consuming for busy consultants. It was virtually phased out by Chief Medical Officer Sir Liam Donaldson in about 2005. Sadly, it seems almost impossible to get a home visit now, especially with an increasingly elderly population. When I was still in Newcastle, one RVI consultant made six domiciliary visits every Wednesday afternoon with a GP who was once his registrar but had relinquished surgery. Never five, or seven, always six. Apart from being a blatant abuse of the system, the annoying thing was he was never on reception on a Wednesday, so anyone sent in by him was treated by another firm while he collected a fee.

One Saturday at North Ormesby hospital, I bumped into a urologist, Jimmy Oldfield, whom I knew by reputation as a former senior registrar of Feg's in the 1940s. We chatted and he said that if you want a surgeon, always try a Saturday morning, and he then told me the following tale. I have already mentioned the large Irish contingent in Middlesbrough. One Saturday morning many years earlier an Irish GP phoned him asking for a domiciliary visit. The address turned out to be the GP's surgery, which was in his home, relatively common in those days. He was greeted by the GP, exuding kind words and flattery, and after seeing the patient, the host apologised for asking if he would kindly see another one, and a third, and so on, behaving as if each patient had somehow materialised without his knowledge and apologetically excusing himself with a load of blarney. But Jimmy did as he was requested, charmed by the brazen cheek of it all and by the effusive good manners of the GP. Finally, the old man remarked that he must be tired from his exertions, and would he like to come upstairs to his sitting room for a wee dram to revive him? On accepting this kind invitation he followed his host, who opened the door to reveal two or three Irish priests, all smoking cigarettes and drinking whiskey while watching horse racing on the television. One such episode would seem sufficient, but every few weeks the same scenario was repeated, almost identical to the first, the GP behaving as if he was meeting Jimmy for the first time.

Sometimes a domiciliary was requested to obtain a quick opinion on a case that was not strictly urgent, and because a fee was involved the GP often gave the impression he was doing the consultant a favour, but most of us were increasingly pressed for time. One example was an eighteen-year-old girl with a breast lump, who was clearly fit enough to be seen in hospital, which I quickly arranged, but the GP was still aggrieved that I did not see her at home.

I was soon asked to take on an extra monthly outpatient clinic at Brotton, a village almost on the coast in east Cleveland. It was held in an old grey stone-built cottage hospital, replaced in my later years by a new, larger community facility with a couple of elderly care wards and GP beds. It was like going back in time, certainly several decades, which sounds insulting but is not meant to be, more a reflection of a combination of stoicism and lower expectations in a small community apparently cocooned from the outside world. The patients were easy to deal with but often presented with late pathology. I used to say, somewhat sardonically I suppose, that something had to turn black before they would request help. Although situated only a few miles from Middlesbrough, the accent was quite different, being typical Yorkshire, with dialect to match. Generally, they were relatively poor, often badly dressed and a bit grubby in an agricultural way, but I always felt relaxed with their easy-going manner and sense of humour. The nurses, being from the same community, were also old-fashioned in a comforting way. My usual nurse was a plump, apple-cheeked lass with a heart of gold. She was married with children and the family kept a pony, a lurcher and ferrets. She once told me that her son, fifteen at the time, had requested a twelve-volt battery for Christmas. Puzzled by such a strange choice, she was told it was to power a light he and his mates would use to dazzle sea trout during nocturnal poaching expeditions to Skinningrove Beck.

With reference to Skinningrove, on one occasion close to Christmas I was asked to make a domiciliary visit after my Brotton clinic to see a lady in that village. It is on the coast and had an ironworks until the 1970s, ironstone being mined locally. The patient was a tenant in one of the new council houses built near the jetty. It was a freezing day and on being admitted to the house by her husband I was immediately taken upstairs to find her sitting upright in bed in an equally freezing bedroom. She might as well have been downstairs in the warmth, for her complaint was the complete inability to swallow, a symptom unrelieved by her present position, but when one was ill, the custom was to take to one's bed. A couple of days earlier she went to Whitby to complete her Christmas shopping and post her cards. She licked more than forty stamps and ever since had been unable to swallow, the cause of which she attributed to the glue from the stamps. She was perfectly serious, nor did her husband, who remained impassive throughout, demur. I arranged to gastroscope her the following day, the instrument sailing down without a hitch. When she recovered from the sedative, I explained the normal findings and that if the glue was responsible, the instrument had unblocked it. She drank a cup of tea and left a satisfied customer. Spasm of the gullet can be caused by anxiety, the old-fashioned term being *globus hystericus*, and this is the only explanation I have for this brief episode. Similarly, the mother of a nurse at the hospital also developed a sudden inability to swallow (dysphagia). It was clear the daughter suspected cancer, a common cause of the symptom, but at endoscopy I found a yellow, slotted plastic square used to close the cellophane wrapping of a loaf of bread at one end. It was easily extracted, but when I gave the daughter the good news she looked not only flabbergasted but positively glum, making me wonder unkindly whether she actually wanted her mother out of the way. The mother had no recollection of swallowing the unusual object.

Amazingly, nor had another patient who presented with obstruction of the small bowel requiring emergency surgery. Unlike obstruction of the large bowel, which is usually caused by a cancerous growth, tumours causing small bowel obstruction are rare. But whereas most of the large bowel is pinned back in the back wall of the abdomen, the small bowel is mobile, swinging on a curtain (mesentery) containing its blood vessels, and the commonest cause of obstruction is from adhesions or scarring from previous surgery. It can also occur if a loop is trapped in a hernia of the groin or umbilicus, but in the absence of either situation, the cause may be one of the several rarities that one sees from time to time in a professional career. In this man the cause was a solid impacted lump, which was removed by opening and then closing the short section of bowel where it was trapped. It was found to be a large piece of bone over an inch square. The mind boggles how not only had he managed to swallow such an object but had no recollection of doing so.

In another case, a lady had just popped a dried apricot in her mouth when there was a knock at the door. Not wanting to appear rude by answering the call with her mouth full, she swallowed it without prior mastication. A couple of days later she needed surgery for small bowel obstruction caused by the intact fruit, which by now had absorbed enough fluid to totally occlude the lumen, which had to be opened to remove the culprit. A high price to pay for a display of good manners!

***

I was called one Saturday afternoon to see a man in his twenties who had swallowed 154 four-inch nails, only one of which had left the stomach and was lying in the transverse colon. After the operation to remove them he was most apologetic. His was a tragic case. He was adopted as an already damaged child when he was about seven by middle-aged parents who appeared to be kind and loving. For some reason, however, he periodically indulged in self-destructive acts, although this was the first time he required surgery. I referred him for a psychiatric opinion, to no avail. He could not be treated, so should be discharged. I pleaded with the psychiatrist that the lad needed protection from himself, adding that in the old days he would have been fed and watered in an 'asylum' and put to light work under supervision, but this was now the era of 'care in the community', more truthfully described as 'neglect in the community'. He replied that there were now very few beds for long-term institutional care and in any case he would be castigated by the mental health ombudsman for taking such action. The parents were understandably upset, not knowing where to turn for help, and I sympathised wholeheartedly, as they had clearly done their best. None of us know why some individuals behave in this way, but like this young man they have usually been maltreated as young children. About a year later I was saddened, but not surprised, when I saw a report in the local paper of the inquest into his death from ethylene glycol poisoning, and the comments by his distraught parents that they felt he was let down by the NHS. And I tended to agree.

Thursday afternoon was traditionally a half-day off duty for GPs, when I presume calls from patients were diverted to the doctors' deputising service. This custom led me to curse one particular GP, who left a message with my secretary for me to do a domiciliary visit to a man with abdominal pain who lived near the hospital. I cannot recall whether I let myself in or his wife answered the door, but I was presented with two problems to solve in return for my small fee. Firstly, the man obviously had a perforated duodenal ulcer and needed urgent surgery, a diagnosis that could have been made by a medical student, and secondly, the wife was clearly severely demented. Although in severe pain, the man was able to tell me she was unsafe to leave alone, and with no relatives nearby, I would have to arrange for her to be taken into care before I could get him to hospital and operate on him. This took most of the afternoon and early evening, something the idle GP should have predicted.

Streets of small terraced houses surrounded Middlesbrough General. One man who lived alone in one of them was redecorating his living room, dressed in a boiler suit, having prepared space by stacking chairs one on top of another. He was on a stepladder to paint the ceiling when he lost his balance and impaled his backside on the leg of an upturned chair. His pain turned to panic when he realised the chair was still attached to him and he shot out the front door, only to inadvertently slam it shut on a Yale lock so he could not re-enter. He shook the chair free and staggered along two streets to Middlesbrough General, all the way refusing help from passers-by because of his embarrassment at the blood emanating from his bottom and soaking his boiler suit. He had perforated his rectum, the damage to which required a short segment excision, the join being protected by a temporary colostomy. He made a normal recovery but when I closed his colostomy three months later, an operation preceded by the usual barium enema x-ray to confirm the join had healed, one could, believe it or not, see white barium forming a perfect right angle where the chair leg had completed its journey.

My loyal and highly efficient secretary from 1980 was Olive Hitchinson. She and her husband were Salvationists and Gordon had a job in the works department of the hospital. In his spare time he managed the Salvation Army brass band. One winter's afternoon a man was wheeled straight to the theatre complex from A&E without prior warning. He had a wooden stake protruding from the left side of his abdomen, with about two feet emerging from his back, so that he was lying obliquely on the stretcher. He was fully conscious, although obviously pale and frightened, and had the presence of mind to apologise for the problem he was presenting us with. Naturally, I assured him all would be well. I glanced at my watch—it was 4.55pm. I immediately phoned Olive (the couple were diligent timekeepers) and told her to ring Gordon and ask him to bring the largest saw he had in the workshop to theatre. I knew our amputation saw would struggle to get through the stave and that unless I could cut it flush with the skin of his back I could not place him flat on the operating table. Gordon soon appeared, bewildered by the request, and nearly passed out when he saw the problem. The victim was a van driver from Barnsley who had skidded on black ice at a roundabout and crashed into a fence, a stave from which had broken off and impaled him via the windscreen. Such injuries, although dramatic, sometimes prove not as serious as they appear. Blunt objects and even low velocity bullets can be deflected by tough 'fascial planes', sheets of connective tissue present throughout the body, thereby missing vital structures. For example, the writer George Orwell was shot in the neck in the Spanish Civil War, the bullet being diverted by such fascia and missing his carotid artery and jugular vein. Our patient was not bleeding severely, but I expected him to at least have damaged intestines. We opened the abdomen, delicately exposing the stake in case its compression was preventing bleeding from a major vessel. But as luck would have it, the peritoneum containing the abdominal organs had been swept aside, and the only injury was to muscle. He did not even get a wound infection, which is unusual in such a case, even though we took precautions to avoid one. The following morning Gordon came to the ward looking like a frightened rabbit and asked how the man was.

'There he is, Gordon,' I said. 'Sitting up reading a newspaper.'

'May I go and shake his hand?' asked Gordon, and I thanked him for playing a crucial role in the procedure.

Naturally, the man was very grateful, but unfortunately, without realising he hailed from South Yorkshire, eighty miles away, the nurse who discharged him arranged a routine six-week follow-up to be sent in the post. I was therefore surprised and dismayed when I recognised his name on the clinic list in due course, not expecting him to show. But he did, and when I apologised for the error, he waved it away, saying he thought I would like to see how well he had healed, adding that when he was wheeled into theatre he thought he was a goner.

I once had a medical student from Barnsley who told me an amusing story about a miner who underwent surgery in one of the town's hospitals for haemorrhoids. For this operation the patient is placed on their back with their feet in stirrups and knees flexed to allow access to the area in question. In the male the scrotum is elevated out of the way with either Elastoplast or a rubber tube. This chap was back on the ward, gradually coming round from the anaesthetic, and feeling pain and discomfort down below, was investigating the area with his hand (where the restraining tape had been inadvertently left *in situ*).

'The bastards! The bastards! Where the hell are they?' he exclaimed in his semi-slumber, referring, of course, to his testicles.

But a passing nurse, trying to reassure him, mistook his perceived loss to being that of his dentures.

'It's all right, Mr Smith,' she said calmly. 'They're in a plastic tub on your bedside table.'

# Chapter Seventeen

# The Haunted Hospital

Within a few months of arriving in Middlesbrough a dribble of patients were referred privately and I accepted them. Providing one's gross income from private practice did not exceed ten per cent of one's salary a full-time contract could be maintained, but if it went above this level for three years, a part-time one was enforced, with a consequent reduction in salary. I had neither intended nor hoped to be in that position, because although I believed in the right for individuals, especially the self-employed, to insure themselves or pay for private treatment, I also believed such practice should take place outside of normal working hours, meaning, for practical purposes, weekends. Without wishing to sound self-righteous, I also thought that in an ideal world such a choice should be motivated by a desire for privacy and/or better accommodation, rather than what it usually was—to jump the queue. Indeed, ideally there should be no queue, but the NHS has never quite responded to demand, presumably to resist opening the floodgates, for financial reasons, and to a large extent GPs have acted as gatekeepers.

Private practice has long been a divisive issue politically, although perhaps less so now. In the eyes of some, including a previous Minister for Health, the stereotype of a consultant surgeon was a man who did a few private cases in the morning, left the rest to unsupervised juniors and spent the afternoon on the golf course, and to a lesser extent that remains the view of some people. The description may have been consistent in former years with some consultants based at the famous London teaching hospitals, but even these usually worked extremely hard and like most of those of my profession with whom I am well acquainted, put in more time and effort than was good for either their health or family life. Many consultants have part-time contracts but very few earn their living from full-time private practice. The late Stanley Rivlin was one such, but he operated solely on varicose veins, which was lucrative enough for him to drive a maroon Rolls-Royce, registration VV111. Frank Cockett was a famous vascular surgeon at St Thomas's in London who devised an operation named after him and also made a lot of money from varicose vein surgery, so much so that he named his yacht *Saphena* (varicose veins involve the long saphenous vein) and its dinghy *Varix* (the term used for a blow-out at the top of the vein).

I will be accused of having a vested interest, but in my opinion one of the worst political decisions was the banning of private beds from NHS hospitals. It was purely out of spite and potentially not only dangerous, but it also created inefficiencies in time wasting, but there it is. It seemed perfectly all right for private patients to use expensive NHS facilities such as CT and MRI scanners and be charged significantly higher sums than the examinations cost.

One of my early private patients was a deputy chairman of ICI, one of fourteen such deputies, apparently, who was now retired and living in a moorland village in North Yorkshire. He still retained a Chelsea townhouse, situated between the actors Susan Hampshire on one side and Leonard Rossiter on the other. I performed a thyroidectomy on him and a few weeks later he invited Mary and I, together with the anaesthetist, Ian Mair and his wife, Sally, to Sunday lunch. The isolated house had been extended over centuries and possessed several architectural styles, but over the stone porch was inscribed '1485', the year of the Battle of Bosworth. It seemed strange to me that a house was built in isolation at that time in such an environment. He had a wonderful rockery and a pristine croquet lawn, and after lunch we were introduced to the rules of this complicated game, played with great vigour and competitiveness by his hyperactive, or tipsy, or both, wife. He was a charming man who told me interesting tales of the early days of ICI at Billingham, north of the Tees.

My office was off a short corridor on the first floor, midway between the endoscopy unit and the female ward. As the wards had no spare rooms, relatives of very ill patients had nowhere to rest other than chairs provided in this corridor, some even sleeping there on occasions, and in those days they could smoke. One morning I opened the door to my office and met the characteristic powerful aroma of cigar smoke. I assumed it to be that of a visitor, but it seemed odd that I had not detected it in the corridor. After all, my door was kept locked, so no-one could have entered for a quiet smoke. This happened for several days in succession, each time the smell being pungent, not just a trace, but there was none in the corridor itself, a most unusual situation. Eventually I mentioned it to Olive, who immediately recoiled.

'Mr Britton-Jones,' she exclaimed in horror. 'He smoked cigars and he's supposed to haunt the hospital.'

It transpired that the aforementioned was a long since deceased surgeon and the endoscopy unit and its surrounds occupied what was originally the operating theatre. The smell disappeared, never to return. At a later date I was examining the abdomen of a man in the clinic who had an unusually large appendicectomy scar and asked him who was responsible for it.

'Mr Britton-Jones,' he replied.

I told him the latter haunted my office and explained the circumstances. He found this story very interesting because he was a spiritualist and knew Mr Britton-Jones had also been a keen follower of this religion, if it can be so termed. Curiouser and curiouser.

***

In 1983 a lady doctor was transferred rapidly from A&E, somewhat shocked from blood loss. She had been thrown from a horse and managed to hold onto the reins, only to be kicked in the abdomen. She was unknown to me at the time but became a friend. She was obviously bleeding internally, probably from the liver, over which organ she was very tender. She had, indeed, maceration of a significant portion of the right lobe of the liver and bleeding was reduced by removing the damaged tissue and closing the defect, not easy in such a friable and vascular organ, but bleeding persisted from behind. I therefore extended the incision into the chest to gain access to a torn hepatic vein, probably caused by torsion at the time of injury, and the tear was situated just as it emerged from the liver. Fortunately, I was able to apply metal clips using a special applicator and breathed a sigh of relief. Unlike the kidney, the liver has the power of regeneration and she would not miss the removed tissue, which was only about a couple of hundred grams anyway.

Horses are a menace. I knew an eminent professor of surgery, a transplant surgeon, who had two teenage daughters who, naturally, he loved dearly and to whom he was prepared to offer any gift they requested, but under no circumstances a pony or a horse. He told me that in his practice most kidney donations came from donors declared brain dead after equestrian accidents. On this subject I was asked to see a man in his mid-twenties admitted to the neurosurgical unit after a closed head injury a couple of days earlier. He was leading in a point-to-point race when he was dismounted and struck by at least one following horse. He was still unconscious but his abdomen had become distended, indicating an internal injury. At operation he had a massive retroperitoneal haematoma (blood clot behind the abdominal organs) which was tense, and after a tentative exploration I could find no obvious source of bleeding, so assumed his paralysed intestine would recover when the haematoma subsided naturally. Unfortunately, the following day bile was seen in a suction drain, and when I re-explored him and opened the peritoneum over the haematoma more extensively, I discovered an explosive perforation of the duodenum. This is a rare injury, usually caused by a severe direct blow, such as a horse's hoof, and is difficult to deal with surgically, and so it proved in this case. The site of the large disruption was at the same level as the entrance of the bile and pancreatic ducts, with their corrosive enzymes. Despite what appeared to be a secure closure, decompressed by a T-tube leading to a drainage bag as a safety valve, the repair broke down, creating a combined bilio-pancreatic fistula, with the loss of several litres of secretion daily. The whole episode, which lasted for many weeks, was extremely stressful, but thankfully, due to a combination of intravenous feeding and a drug called somatostatin—a synthetic analogue of a hormone secreted by the pituitary gland and also by some cells in the small bowel that has a potent effect on inhibiting stomach and gastrointestinal secretions—the potentially fatal fistula closed, and he went home at least two stones lighter. Within only a few weeks he regained much of this and at a later date when I could finally discharge him, he grinned and said, 'I've been on his back again.' I told him, only half-jokingly, that if he ever raced again, to please do so outwith the boundaries of the Northern Regional Health Authority, because although his own life might not have been shortened by his accident, mine certainly had, and I did not want to see him in a professional capacity again.

***

I learned a simple lesson soon after my elevation to consultant status. We had two female housemen. One was quite posh and could be snooty and made it plain at interview that we were not her first choice but that in the end she had no option. The other was a sullen girl from a poor background who made her own shabby clothes, seemingly from materials such as net curtains and tablecloths. Only a minority of medics derived from the lower social classes at that time, as had been the case when I was training. Surprisingly, not much has changed since. However, in both her dress, which seemed contrived, and her attitude, this girl was always raising the issue and clearly had a major chip. The two seemed to get on well together, but in my presence always appeared serious and unhappy, even though I tried to treat them with pleasant informality.

I made a point of always seeing my inpatients daily, even if only briefly between clinics and operating lists, but also had formal ward rounds on which I spent some time. On one occasion—and I cannot recall either the discussion or what prompted the outburst—the posh one suddenly said, 'While you're pontificating at the bedside, we could be getting on with our work.'

I was quite taken aback.

'Pontificating?' I blustered. 'I'm trying to teach you!'

'Oh,' she said. 'We didn't realise.'

And do you know? From that moment their attitude changed almost miraculously. They became pleasant and cooperative. The transition was startling. I even received postcards when they went on holiday and the posh one continued to write for a little while even after she left.

A few years later, when I was the Royal College of Surgeons tutor for our district, a position I held for ten years, I attended a presentation by Janet Grant, a Professor of Medical Education for the Thames Valley hospitals, during which the above experience came to mind. She polled the opinions of consultants in medicine and surgery and their junior doctors about the frequency of teaching, especially on ward rounds. Almost all the consultants maintained they always taught, but the juniors said teaching was minimal. Assuming they were telling the truth, they can't both have been right. It was a question of perception. The juniors, by and large, disliked formal ward rounds, firstly, because they would be peppered with questions about the patients that they might be unable to answer, and secondly, they were being delayed from doing their routine work. Prof Grant made the simple point that at the beginning of every such session, the consultant should announce that it will be a teaching round. I have since discussed the matter with several colleagues and they usually nod in agreement and say, 'It might seem obvious, but you've always got to tell them when you are teaching.'

Middlesbrough was rarely the first choice for housemen in those days. We did not routinely receive students from Newcastle, as we do now, and were at the periphery of the catchment area. Nor was the town attractive, although as one eminent professor said to me, 'It doesn't matter where you end up, you spend most of your time at the coalface, anyway.' However, one of our physicians had remained friends with a classmate who was now the Dean of Charing Cross Medical School and began sending us students for six-week stints in their final year to give them a taste of a peripheral hospital. The experiment proved a success because we were stimulated by them and spent time teaching them, while they saw a wide variety of bread-and-butter cases, instead of some of the more obscure ones which can be concentrated in teaching hospitals. As a result, the relationship became symbiotic and for some years we had housemen from Charing Cross. I think it ended when Newcastle expanded and needed to use many of the hospitals in the region, an action which prompted the names of those chosen to be appended with 'University Hospital' – as in 'St Chad's University Hospital', somewhat overblown and pretentious in some cases.

I recall one Charing Cross student in particular. Most came in pairs, but she was alone. She was pretty and beautifully dressed, with red blouse, tartan skirt, expensive-looking pearls and a terribly posh accent. She was from Sevenoaks in Kent, which we cruelly renamed One Oak because of the damage caused by Michael Fish's non-existent hurricane of 1987. On her first day we sat down together so I could describe the setup, after which she remarked that she had never been to the north before and asked what she should see. I replied she should certainly visit York, not too far south, and Durham, further north, with its cathedral and castle, and Newcastle was a fine city, with some outstanding Georgian architecture, and, of course, Whitby, on the coast. She scribbled all this down in her notebook and then looked up.

'Oh good,' she said. 'Can I see all these in one afternoon?'

Perhaps I spoke too quickly.

***

In the early 1980s we appointed a houseman, who I will call RK. An orthodox Jew from Leeds, he was anxious to adhere to the rituals of his religion, such as not working on the Sabbath, but understood this might not be possible in a fair rota with his colleagues. In retrospect he was unsuited to a career in a busy speciality, and probably to medicine itself, but he was highly intelligent, with an interest in mathematics and the newish field of computing. We tried to accommodate his needs, but it was not always possible. He assisted me one Saturday at an operation and although he agreed to hold a retractor, he turned away from the operating table, as if not seeing was equivalent to not working, which I found irritating, but never mind. He was married and lived with his parents-in-law in

Sunderland, and on free weekends in the winter months he shot off pronto on Friday afternoons to get home before sunset, the beginning of the Sabbath. Unfortunately, he was not very active in treating mishaps such as haemorrhages, expecting that the homeostatic mechanisms evolved over the millennia would save the patient without human interference. This apart, he was diligent and a pleasant chap. His parents were Russian Jews who escaped to Britain before the Second World War. RK said that every single morning since, on rising from sleep, they knelt by their bed and prayed, thanking the Almighty for saving them and bringing them to this country. I found this both touching and humbling.

My colleague Mike was keen to keep him on as a senior house officer, to which he was agreeable, because he wanted to develop a computerised database for all his gastroscopy examinations, and with RK's advice purchased a desktop computer out of charitable funds. The young man worked hard with apparently little effect until a proprietary package came on the market. Despite processing simple medical data, it had apparently taken a team several years to develop the programme, which explains his slow progress. However, through him we became known to the late Tim de Dombal, with whom we collaborated between 1983 and 1986. Tim trained as a surgeon in Leeds but transferred his attention to the new subject of so-called medical informatics, or the application of computer technology to the practice of medicine, specifically, in his case, the diagnosis of acute abdominal pain, one of the commonest surgical emergencies. We at Middlesbrough General were one of several centres to use his carefully created history and examination sheets, which could be used by junior doctors either alone or with a computer to aid in the diagnosis of such cases. Some clinicians were defensive about this procedure, suspecting the eventual purpose was to replace the doctor with a computer, but the aim was really to educate, provide feedback and act as an aid to diagnosis. For example, Tim found that at the start of their jobs, surgical housemen were about fifty per cent correct in their diagnosis of such cases based on history and examination, which improved by, say, another ten per cent following simple investigations, such as blood and urine tests and plain x-rays. Disappointingly, when tested six months later at the conclusion of their jobs, their diagnostic accuracy had not improved significantly. Even experienced clinicians were initially only seventy per cent correct, before further investigations.

The usual process is to create a differential diagnosis of a few possibilities and reduce them to a presumed diagnosis by elimination based on factors such as probability and tests. The twenty per cent or so difference in accuracy is obviously based on experience.

The senior has seen more cases, including rarities, but the intellectual process by which he or she analyses the data is complex and poorly understood. The purpose of the computer was to compare the present patient with the symptoms and signs of many others—in Tim's original programme, about 6,000—in order to discriminate in percentage terms between various possibilities. This is a more structured approach to what the experienced clinician does intuitively. But first everyone had to be speaking the same language, and this was where the standardised history and examination sheet came in. It also prevented the junior doctor from inadvertently omitting a question or a finding that may prove crucial (such as, 'When was your last period, madam?'). The commonest label (it is not truly a diagnosis), strangely enough, is what is termed non-specific abdominal pain (NSAP), which accounts for about forty per cent of all cases of abdominal pain admitted to hospital. It is a term that seemed to coincide with the computer age. Certainly it was never used when I was a junior—I suspect my ex-chiefs would have regarded it as a lazy one. But it is useful, meaning it is probably not of serious import (at present) and will not require surgery. It encompasses a whole range of possibilities—such as simple constipation, period pains, ovulation pains, irritable bowel syndrome and gastroenteritis, most of which will resolve spontaneously within forty-eight hours or so. However, when followed up, one in ten over fifties who present to hospital with such pain turn out to have a malignancy somewhere, usually in the gastrointestinal tract, so some of us developed a routine of carrying out gastroscopy and colonoscopy in such patients after discharge.

After NSAP, the commonest diagnosis was appendicitis, a condition that does not always obey the textbooks, especially in females in their childbearing years, and it can be a difficult diagnosis to make. In pre-antibiotic days a perforated appendix could be disastrous and hence surgeons were more proactive in advising surgery, with the consequence that there was a significant negative appendicectomy rate, sometimes as high as twenty-five per cent, the organ in such cases being referred to as 'lily white'. In theory, one can achieve 100 per cent diagnostic accuracy by allowing every appendix to perforate, although this would not always occur, but in practice there was a balance between avoiding removing a normal appendix on the one hand and having a low perforation rate on the other.

In the series at Middlesbrough General, conducted over three years, the first year being a baseline study, the proportion of removed appendices which were inflamed rose from sixty-one per cent at baseline to seventy-seven per cent in the first year of the test period and ninety per cent in the second. Despite this increased diagnostic accuracy rate there was a reduced perforation rate from twenty-two per cent to ten per cent, a remarkable result. Unfortunately, once the momentum provided by the study dissipated, and we all moved to one site, we allowed what should have become standard practice to wither on the vine. Frequent visits by Tim de Dombal were also motivating factors, but he became increasingly busy with similar projects elsewhere. It was a tragedy for the rapidly developing field of medical informatics when he suddenly died on New Year's Eve 1995, aged only fifty-eight, two weeks before he was due to have a coronary artery bypass.

In 1982 we had a visitor from the USA, Hiram Polk, professor and chief of surgery at Louisville, Kentucky. I think he was on a British Journal of Surgery travelling scholarship, but anyway we put on a show for him with a series of presentations and Alan Tooley held a buffet supper and cocktail party in his honour. He seemed a serious, relatively humourless individual, devoid of the famous southern charm and unfortunately patronising to his provincial hosts. His surgical reputation revolved around infections, hiatus hernia and some aspects of oncology. He got on the wrong side of me immediately by being sniffy about Franny's department, presumably out of envy. The Falklands Conflict had recently ended, but he proceeded to be remarkably condescending about the Royal Navy's role, so much so that it provoked Ian Mair to tell his Noël Coward story. Ian told Polk that 'The Master' used to say that whenever he had to cross the Atlantic he always took an American ship. Ian waited for this remark to be taken on board, to use a maritime simile, and for Polk to look smug, before delivering his crushing put-down.

'…Because if it sank, there was none of that nonsense about women and children first…'

The man was so boring and so full of himself that gradually, like woodlice seeking humidity, the men filtered towards the drink in the kitchen, leaving the ladies to politely endure the chief guest's interminable monologue. Once again, Ian Mair provided the entertainment. He suddenly bounded into where Polk was holding forth to the ladies. Then, with great skill for a man of his age, he performed a forward roll at speed, stood to attention like a gymnast in competition and smartly marched out of the room.

'Well,' said Polk to my wife. 'You'll have to explain that to me, Mary.'

But, like everyone else, she was lost for words.

# Chapter Eighteen

# Doctor in the Desert

In 1987 I finally extricated my mother from Hull to live near us, and she moved to Stockton-on-Tees. I had felt guilty about leaving her in Buckingham Street, especially after her employer retired and the shop closed, and I wrote a letter to get her rehoused in a council flat in Endike Lane in west Hull. It was an area with which she was unfamiliar, but it looked onto playing fields and for the first time in her life she possessed an indoor toilet with a bathroom to boot. Elation soon turned to disenchantment, however, when most of the flats became occupied by students, who naturally stayed up late playing loud music and banging doors at all hours. I heard about a small new development of two-bedroom flats in Stockton and thought they looked ideal. On discovering that only one was still vacant, I secured it for six weeks with a £100 deposit. Mum came up the following week and liked it, so I set things in motion. I could not pay the full mortgage, but I could contribute. Mrs Thatcher became a heroine for Mum when she increased the war widow's pension significantly. I made an appointment at the Bradford & Bingley, who advertised themselves as the pensioners' helper, only to be told almost immediately I was wasting their time and my own and there was no way they would offer my mother a mortgage. My protestations that I would stand surety in case the interest rate rose were all to no avail. Somewhat deflated and depressed, I crossed the road to the Halifax, unannounced, made enquiries, was shown into an office, and secured the mortgage within minutes. The Halifax was then still a full-time building society, the largest in the world, but later with deregulation became a bank and was ruined by the greed and negligence of investment bankers. Still, I shall always be grateful to the Halifax. Mum moved with barely a backward look and despite having never lived anywhere other than Hull, she settled down nicely and made several friends. She was hardly ever at home, exploring her new surroundings with her free bus pass.

That same year I did two two-week stints about six months apart at the Baksch Clinic in Jeddah, Saudi Arabia. The motivation was purely financial, with the added interest of an exotic location about which little was known to westerners, except those connected with the oil industry. The outpatient clinic was named after its founder, now an elderly doctor whom I met once, but the hospital of the same name was a mile or so away, modern, plush and more expensive for patients than a more basic one opposite, which fortunately most opted to use. The Baksch hospital became known to the western media in 1979 because of the controversial death of a British nurse, Helen Smith, from Leeds, whose body was found beyond iron railings below a sixth-floor balcony adjacent to an apartment in which a party had been held. The big question was, had she fallen or was she pushed? Her body was next to that of a Dutchman, who was impaled on the railings. I don't think the mystery was ever resolved. The poor girl's body underwent several autopsies and was held refrigerated in a Leeds mortuary for some thirty years at the expense of her father, a retired policeman, who remained convinced foul play was responsible for his daughter's death. He finally agreed to a funeral in 2009.

I only visited this hospital once, when we were shown round by the matron, a beautifully spoken British woman of the old school. That first morning I was picked up from the airport by a tall, ebony-skinned Sudanese man in a blue robe and spotless white turban, a delightful gent who spoke reasonable English. I later discovered that all the drivers slept in a shack at the rear of the clinic. We specialists were a mixed bunch—a Belgian neurologist, a German orthopod, an Egyptian brain surgeon, a Swiss ENT surgeon, a dermatologist-cum-'sexologist' from Luxembourg, a Chinese acupuncturist and a Swedish gynaecologist. The chap from Luxembourg was already fully booked for consultations. Continental dermatologists maintain the historical link with sexually transmitted diseases, probably because of the manifold effects on the skin of syphilis when it was common. This connection has long been abandoned in the UK by the creation of separate specialties. By a certain logic, the connection with sexually transmitted diseases can be seen to extend to male infertility and impotence, and it was mainly these two problems that attracted our new colleague's attention. I recall him saying that one man complained of his inability to have intercourse more than five times daily.

Although I was advertised as a general surgeon, I was promoted as having special expertise in haemorrhoids, or piles. Not that the Saudis were any more prone to this condition than any other nationality, but for cultural reasons beyond my understanding they associated piles with virility and were keen to have them treated, which I did mainly with injections of oily phenol rather than surgery. We were paid a basic salary, even if we saw no patients, but for every procedure we performed a percentage was added to our income, none of which attracted income tax at home because of some new rules.

We worked every day except Friday, the day for prayers, and finished at lunchtime on Thursdays, so we could go to a hotel swimming pool or the souk. We were assisted by Egyptian or Yemeni doctors who acted as interpreters and earned more in this capacity than they did by practising medicine in their own country. Our presence was advertised and patients came from all over Saudi, including Riyadh. European doctors still had a certain cachet, which may still exist, because although there is a medical school, they seemed to rely on foreigners for almost every service. I soon learned that if I asked a Saudi, through the interpreter, what he did for a living, he often looked taken aback at the impertinence and replied that he was a businessman. It seemed they often owned land, rented out to an international company and the source of their income.

I did little operative surgery, perhaps fortunately. A few anal fissures, a low-level fistula and a parotid tumour on a Yemeni tribal chieftain whom I rather took to. Another Yemeni had huge linear scars in one loin, created by comrades as a form of counter-irritation when he developed renal colic in the mountains while fighting (the British?). Kidney stones were much more common than in the UK, presumably as a result of dehydration in the desert climate, or possibly dietary. Shortly after recovering from the anaesthetic, almost every patient asked, 'When can I go with my wife again?'. Via the interpreter my reply was, 'Preferably after you have left hospital', usually received with a laugh.

I knew little about Islam when I went but I read quite a bit, although never the Quran itself. The average mosque was a simple affair and services seemed to be occupied mainly by prayer, with no ceremonial splendour led by priests. The people seemed honest—the shops in the souk were left unattended during prayers, but, of course, the punishment for stealing was draconian. I knew about the early rift between Shia and Sunni but did not appreciate its importance. Rather like that of the early Celtic and Roman church, which at least did not lead to violence, and Catholic versus Protestant, which did, these stupid schisms which have caused and continue to cause so much bloodshed are due to what Freud aptly called 'the narcissism of small differences'. I found the call to prayer by the muezzin quite moving.

In the first sentence of the abridged version of his classic *The Seven Pillars of Wisdom*, renamed *Revolt in the Desert*, TE Lawrence describes his entrance into the harbour at Jeddah at midday thus—'The heat of Arabia came out like a drawn sword and struck us speechless.' There is no better way to describe it. In the few seconds it took me to cross the road from the air-conditioned cool of the clinic to the equally cool hospital opposite, my shirt stuck to my body. However, one day it rained, causing traffic chaos. Every car had its headlights on and horns blared constantly.

The interpreters, the nurses (mainly Filipinos and extremely efficient, trained in the old British fashion before graduate status became obligatory) and the drivers seemed to look on the indigenous Saudi population with some disdain, correctly perceiving that it was essentially a slave society in terms of remuneration and working conditions, and likewise the Saudis seemed to view everyone else with suspicion. Two examples spring to mind. One man came to me with a heavy folder containing four or five CT scans, all of which showed a large tumour of one kidney and asked my opinion. I told him he needed surgery to remove the kidney. He looked surprised and replied that everyone else had told him this. That's because everyone else was right, I said. He asked if I could do it for him. Fortunately, I was due to leave in a couple of days and explained it was not possible (blood transfusion was tricky—there was no donor system and, certainly then, the family had to be relied upon). But he said finance was no problem and produced a note detailing where someone had advised him to go. It was the Cleveland Clinic in Ohio, one of the most prestigious clinics in the world. I told him that if he could arrange it, he should do so. Another man had been in a road accident and a German surgeon at one of the newer hospitals in Jeddah had done a beautiful job of fixing his fracture and performing a microvascular anastomosis, relatively new, to cover tissue loss with skin and muscle. For some reason he discharged himself and came to the clinic for my opinion. I reassured him he had been lucky to have such a good surgeon and that although he was healing well, he should return to the hospital until the surgeon was happy for his release. I suspect he was doing the rounds until he heard what he wanted to hear. One thing that struck me was how clean the patients were, despite the heat. Not all were rich, but simply for an injection of piles the clinic charged the equivalent of one month's wages for a driver.

On our day off we were driven to an area of the beach that allowed westerners to sunbathe and scuba dive in the Red Sea. I was advised before leaving England to take a facemask, snorkel and a pair of plimsolls. The latter proved a necessity, for one had to paddle out and wade for a considerable distance on almost knife-sharp coral, which would have proved impossible without protection. There was then an abrupt drop to the sea-floor, allowing the observer to enter an alien world of fascinating beauty, even with the limitations of depth constrained by a snorkel.

On my second visit we obtained permission to go to Ta'if and employed a driver for the three-hour journey to the north in the mountains, where, because of the cooler air, the king maintained a summer palace. There was not much of interest to see in Ta'if itself, but the drive was through barren, rugged, rocky terrain, which surprised those of us expecting flat, sandy desert and gave us some idea of what Lawrence and his tribesmen had to face. The road, of course, was of better-quality Tarmac than at home. Soon after leaving Jeddah, as we approached Mecca, a large green sign demanded in both Arabic and English that 'all non-Muslims turn right' (or it may have been left), to deter them from attempting to enter the holy city either by accident or design.

One of the drivers was a skinny, sullen Pakistani, one of the few who spoke no English. He always made me feel uncomfortable because he looked at us with distaste bordering on hate. I was therefore downhearted when he was my driver to the airport for my flight to London in the early hours. During my stay I acquired some Saudi riyals as spending money and had 120 left (at the time there were seven riyals to the pound). As such currency cannot either be obtained nor exchanged in the UK, when I left the car I handed them to him, thanked him in Arabic ('Shukran', since you ask) and set off to Departures. About ten seconds later my case was wrenched from my hand from behind and there was the driver, grinning as I had never seen him before and insisting on carrying my luggage to check-in. He seemed a changed man, but I then realised how much this tip was in comparison to his wages.

# Chapter Nineteen

# Crisis Management

In July 1987, Middlesbrough General reached national notoriety with the Cleveland Child Abuse crisis. I have already referred to my involvement with cases of infantile pyloric stenosis. In addition, I was called to see every child presenting by day who required emergency surgery. When I arrived in 1980 there were two female paediatricians. The elder of the two, Joan Angus, was a dour Glaswegian with the typically unbending views of many academics of that city, and a former Professor of Paediatrics at the University of the West Indies in Jamaica. She was an excellent paediatrician but was unfortunately afflicted with severe rheumatoid arthritis, necessitating a wheelchair and a stair lift in the ward. I became the 'tame' surgeon for the pair of them. One day I was doing an elective aortic aneurysm when the anaesthetic nurse came into theatre and said Dr Angus wished to speak to me on the phone. Naturally, I told her to take a message. She returned to say that Dr Angus insisted. I can only assume Pauline was so intimidated by the firm tones of the caller that common sense and initiative deserted her, so I told her to tell Dr Angus I presently had my right hand around someone else's aorta and could not come to the phone. Sometime later when I faced the good lady to deal with the problem she said, somewhat disbelievingly, that she did not realise surgeons got up to such things. I could only conclude that she imagined I sat in my office twiddling my thumbs awaiting calls from paediatricians. However, she was a sad loss when she retired in 1983. She was replaced by Geoff Wyatt, who was in his early thirties, and a very thorough and sound paediatrician. On a personal level I always got on well with him. He had a pleasant, friendly personality, but for some reason that I never fathomed, he rubbed a few people up the wrong way. Perhaps he tried to impose himself too quickly and change established routines, I don't know. Undoubtedly, Geoff worked hard and put in more hours than were strictly necessary, always going the extra mile for the benefit of the child. He was joined in 1985 by Peter Morrell, an excellent paediatrician, followed in 1987 by Marietta Higgs, a new appointment. Shortly after her arrival I bumped into Geoff and asked if his new colleague had any particular interest or expertise within the speciality.

'Child sexual abuse,' was the reply.

I must have looked surprised, for he looked at me quizzically and asked if I was the sort who did not believe such a thing existed. I said I was well aware of its existence and would expect any paediatrician to keep what I termed a 'weather eye' out for it, but to express it as a speciality interest suggested she would expect referrals, which was unlikely, or be aggressive in seeking it out. Prophetic, as it transpired.

Before the scandal occurred, one of my colleagues joined me at lunch.

'I have just met our new paediatric colleague,' he said. 'She has the glazed eyes of the fanatic.'

Once again, spot on.

One morning I went to see a child on request and found the ground floor ward like Bedlam, with children running about as if in a playground. I asked the sister what was going on. She gave a sickly half-smile and said they were all under observation for suspected sexual abuse and there was nowhere else suitable for them to go.

One of many things that were badly managed was the persistent use of the vague, undefined term 'sexual abuse'. I wonder how many ordinary people reading their newspaper realised that rather than someone 'fiddling about', it indicated anal intercourse, or buggery? How many visualised grown men performing this act (the youngest 'victim' was less than a year old) on the scale suspected? Not many, I should think.

Marietta Higgs took up her post in January 1987 and between February and July of that year, 121 children were taken into 'care', suspected of being victims of sexual abuse. The diagnoses were made by Dr Higgs and Geoff alone, based, as far as one can tell, on the test of reflex dilatation of the anus (RDA). Higgs had attended a conference in 1986 where Jane Wynne, a Leeds paediatrician, raised the test as a possible indicator of abuse, together with other suspicious features, but apparently urged caution and further research. It seems, however, that Higgs and Wyatt used it as a pathognomonic test—that is, specific for the condition.

The alarming numbers diagnosed using the technique made national news and you can imagine what the chants of the opposing supporters were when Middlesbrough FC played away from home.

A combination of parental pressure, the local media, MPs, the police surgeon and the police themselves, together with the inability of the social services department to cope with the load, culminated in the establishment of an enquiry chaired by Mrs Justice Butler-Sloss, which reported in 1988. Almost all parties were criticised, but surely the crucial issue should have been the value or otherwise of the controversial test? To my knowledge this remains unresolved. Otherwise, I think the enquiry was largely a waste of money, but at least it stopped the madness.

Of the 121 originally detained, ninety-four were returned to their parents. Sometime later a Channel 4 documentary maintained that 'independent experts' stated at least seventy per cent of the children had been abused, in their judgement, vindicating the diagnoses of Higgs and Wyatt. By this time, however, both were prevented from giving further opinions on child sexual abuse and Higgs left to work elsewhere.

I do not know who these independent experts were, but I find it perplexing how one can make such a diagnosis retrospectively. Let us assume, however, they were correct, and seventy per cent were abused. That leaves thirty per cent who were not. Considering there is no physical test, RDA excluded, the diagnosis depending on many factors, and the huge impact on the lives of everyone involved—child, parents, grandparents, etcetera—surely one must be as convinced as possible before embarking on removal of the child? One of my patients failed to attend for a follow-up appointment, a not unusual occurrence. He had arterial disease of the legs. About three months later he turned up and apologised and explained he had suffered a heart attack, again not unusual in a man with his problem. He then related how he had brought his granddaughter to see Dr Higgs because she had suffered repeated sore throats (an ENT opinion would have been more appropriate) and, after examining the child, she voiced her suspicion that she had been sexually abused. My patient was shocked and disbelieving, feeling he was being regarded as the culprit, and immediately developed crushing chest pain. When the opinion requested was for a sore throat, I wonder why this child was submitted to examination of the rectum, and possibly vagina, without consent, which, legally, the grandfather could not give, anyway?

***

During the same year, Mike Cooke and I were joined by Ben Corbett, who had a keen interest in medical informatics. Like the rest of us, he was appointed as a general surgeon and, because of the impending retirement of Frank Walker, he was asked to develop an interest in colorectal surgery, to which he was agreeable. By this year our old wards, together with those of medicine along the corridor, had been replaced by a brand new block—surgery on the ground floor with medicine above, male and female wards joined by a short arm of the main corridor. Each was divided into six-bedded units plus several single cubicles allowing a greater degree of privacy than the old layout. I was surprised when this new build was offered to us, because plans were ongoing for a new hospital either at the Middlehaven site, derelict land created by deindustrialisation near Middlesbrough Dock, where the Riverside football stadium was later erected, or, alternatively, extension of South Cleveland Hospital to create a large single site. Such plans, however, had no guarantee of fruition and it was never a question of—it could have been neither. In fact, the Middlehaven plan came to nought, but fortunately the single site eventually went ahead by extending South Cleveland on plentiful adjacent land. Our new block had a lifespan of about ten years before it was demolished, along with the rest of Middlesbrough General.

Soon after being informally recognised as the local paediatric general surgeon, I started receiving virtually all referrals for common conditions such as hernias, hydroceles, undescended testes and circumcisions. The latter is, of course, mandatory in the Jewish and Muslim faiths. While Jewish boys are routinely circumcised by a mohel shortly after birth, Muslims do not always have access to a similar religious representative, although some Muslim GPs undertake the task. Many were referred to me, often as young boys rather than babies, and I always carried out the procedure on the NHS. This was never queried until the NHS started tinkering by introducing the so-called 'internal market' with GP fund-holders and the like. The procedure could not be justified on medical grounds, but it was a religious necessity and most parents I dealt with could not afford private treatment, so my attitude was to conduct it under modern, sterile conditions with proper anaesthesia, rather than risk complications in some 'backstreet' environment. However, a significant number of referrals were on medical grounds from the wider population. The foreskin will often not retract at birth but usually does so by eighteen months of age. Some boys get one or more episodes of inflammation due to retained secretions, which are uncomfortable but self-limiting. Consequently, they were often referred for circumcision, but this is only occasionally required and should be reserved for the small minority who have a true phimosis, or inability to retract the foreskin coupled with narrowing of the outlet. It was sometimes difficult to convince the parents and I usually suggested separating the congenital adhesions and cleaning out the area under a short anaesthetic, only proceeding to circumcision if I deemed it necessary. It is well known that circumcision will prevent cancer of the penis, but this condition is so rare it cannot be justified for this reason alone. At one time it was almost routine in the United States, mainly on the grounds that it prevented urinary infections and probably as a hygienic measure. The surgical profession encouraged it—but they are paid on a fee-for-service basis. Personally, I have never seen a urinary infection in a boy who did not have some congenital abnormality of the urinary tract.

The best advice I have seen was written to a GP in 1950 by Sir James Spence, late of my *alma mater*, the RVI in Newcastle. It reads as somewhat archaic and pompous to modern eyes, but it is both amusing and instructive and I quote it in full (reproduced from *The Lancet*, October 24th 1964, page 902).

*My Dear C, Your patient CD, aetat seven months, has the prepuce (foreskin) with which he was born. You ask me, with a note of persuasion in your question, if it should be excised. Am I to make this decision on scientific grounds, or am I to acquiesce to a ritual which took its origin at the behest of that arch-sanitarian Moses? If you can give good reason why a ritual designed to ease the penalties of concupiscence amidst the sand and flies of the Syrian deserts should be continued in this England of clean bed linen and lesser opportunity, I shall listen to your argument; but if you base your argument on anatomical faults, then I must refute it. The anatomists have never studied the form and evolution of the preputial orifice. They do not understand that Nature does not intend it to be stretched and retracted in the Temples of the Welfare Centres or ritually removed in the precincts of the operating theatres. Retract the prepuce and you see a pinpoint opening but draw it forwards and you see a channel wide enough for all the purposes for which the infant needs the organ at that early age. What looks like a pinpoint opening at seven months will become a wide channel of communication at seventeen. Nature is a possessive mistress, and whatever mistakes she makes about the structure of the less essential organs such as the brain and stomach, in which she is not much interested, you can be sure she knows best about the genital organs...*

Wonderful stuff! Sir James must have had a quiet clinic that day. I have no idea what prompted the ancients to initiate and spread this ritual, but besides being a requirement for followers of two of the world's major religions, it is also practised by many Africans and by Australian aborigines to indicate the arrival of manhood—quite an ordeal, graphically described in Nelson Mandela's autobiography *Long Walk to Freedom*.

***

Stab injuries were much more common in Middlesbrough than Newcastle, where I saw hardly any (this observation may be misleading—they could have gone to Newcastle General, but I think this is unlikely as the RVI was closer to the city centre). The frequency of such injuries depressed me. I have never understood how people can contemplate carrying and using a weapon in which a matter of millimetres can determine a life sentence. I was about to leave for home one evening when I saw a man on a stretcher being wheeled into the ward. I was not on call but thought I had better investigate. From behind the curtains of the first bed I heard a man's voice.

'I am worried,' he said.

'Well, I'm not surprised you're worried,' replied a nurse.

The man repeated the phrase and the nurse gave the same reply. I poked my head through a gap in the curtains to ascertain the cause of the worry, and saw the handle of an ornate dagger, moving to and fro with respiration, the implement up to its hilt in his upper-right abdomen. He sounded sober but had apparently plunged the dagger into himself for a bet, in a pub. Oddly, the bet was for petty cash. He was fortunate, for although the liver had been penetrated, no major vessel or bile duct was severed, and he lost only about 100 millilitres of blood.

A woman in her forties was leaving a supermarket when she was stabbed from behind in an unprovoked attack by what appeared to be a youth, who dashed off. The knife pierced the lower lobe of the right lung and bleeding persisted, consolidating the lobe completely, and I had to remove it the following day when her blood oxygen levels progressively deteriorated—a procedure for which my Shotley Bridge experience ten years earlier proved valuable. Surprisingly, the culprit was identified as a fourteen-year-old girl who had short hair and was initially taken for a boy.

I was about to leave for the hospital one morning when the phone rang to say a radiologist from another hospital had stabbed himself in the chest following an argument with his wife. He was conscious and stable but when I gently popped a gloved finger into the wound, I discovered a hole in the pericardium surrounding the heart, which was beating against my finger, I must say at a rate slower than my own! Middlesbrough once had a thoracic surgeon who worked alone. After he retired, the Freeman Hospital opened in Newcastle, and we now had a named surgeon at that institution designated to visit the town if required. While I prepared the patient for surgery I asked for him to be contacted, a decision I later regretted. I explored the chest to make sure there was no active bleeding, which there wasn't, and simply closed the hole in the pericardium and drained the chest. As I was about to close, the surgeon from Freeman arrived and completed the procedure, which was routine for him. Unfortunately, postoperatively the patient developed the only hernia of the lung I have ever seen, which settled with time and compression bandaging. I should have closed the wound myself.

I can recall other stabbings resulting in the deaths of the victims—an Asian lady knifed by her husband, injuring the *vena cava*, and who died on the table. A young woman stabbed through the heart by her lover, who threw himself off a cliff afterwards. A renowned thug who was beating up a rival when someone tossed his victim a knife, giving him the tool with which he severed his assailant's axillary artery. And a schoolgirl who died in her classroom, but whose friend survived many superficial stab wounds from the same infamous attack. There were others, but fortunately with less serious results.

***

Around 1990 we appointed Peter Thomas, an Australian, and by a long chalk the best registrar I had the pleasure to work with. Peter had all the qualities that make a good surgeon—compassion, enormous stamina, thoroughness and attention to detail. He was a careful operator with a phenomenal memory. He did not conform to the stereotypical Aussie in either appearance or personality. He was tall and lean, sharp-featured with a thick beard and John Lennon spectacles, reminding me of photographs of the nineteenth-century explorer, John Hanning Speke, who discovered the true source of the White Nile. He was a voracious reader, managing about a book a week, some feat while working long hours with disturbed nights. A keen reader myself, he once queried my present book. On being told it was *To Kill a Mockingbird*, he amazed me by quoting, almost word for word, the opening lines, which made me wonder if he was one of those few people with a truly photographic memory.

Peter's wife, Ruth, was a GP, and after a few months she got a job with a practice in Easington Colliery in County Durham, then an increasingly depressed place after closure of the local pit. On her first day she had her eyes opened to certain unfortunate features of the area—firstly, she witnessed two women fighting in the street and secondly, she saw a toddler in a pushchair rocking back and forth and repeating 'bugger, bugger, bugger'.

One incident, amusing to us but not to the patient, Mr W, occurred when the latter, who surprisingly was morbidly obese (the adverb will be explained shortly) was in the recovery room after surgery. Looking down at him from either side of the trolley were Peter and Joyce Gun, a theatre sister of Chinese extraction. Mr W rolled his head from side to side and upon hearing his name called as he woke up from the anaesthetic, slowly opened his eyes. Suddenly, his head shot up and he went quite berserk, and it was fortunate that the trolley had cot sides, otherwise he might have hurled himself off it. He eventually calmed down when the reality of his true environment dawned on him. It transpired that he had been a POW in Changi after the fall of Singapore in World War II and the sight of a bearded Australian (presumably a fellow captive) and what he thought was a Japanese caused a vivid flashback. Most POWs of the Japanese that I encountered professionally never regained their former weight, having contracted tropical sprue and pancreatitis associated with starvation, but Mr W was the exception, having overcompensated at over thirty stones.

Early one morning shortly before Christmas, Peter rang to tell me a young man had been stabbed in the upper abdomen. He was stable and Peter was just about to take him to theatre to explore the wound. He did not expect to find too much, but asked me to pop my head round the door when I came in. Instead of a relatively trivial injury, the knife had entered obliquely from right to left, passing through front and back walls of the stomach and the duodenum and transecting both artery and vein to the right kidney as they joined the organ. Although he made a full and rapid recovery, he lost the kidney—a high price to pay for writing a childish love letter to a married lady to whom he had developed an affection. Her husband found the letter, knocked at his door at about six in the morning and stabbed him when he answered. Poor chap had not even managed a kiss!

Another interesting case was the only patient with tetanus exhibiting the pathognomonic sign of *risus sardonicus* that I have seen. She was an elderly lady admitted with an infected forearm in which was embedded a two-inch rose thorn and branch. The referring doctor failed to notice the 'sardonic smile' created by tonic contraction of the facial muscles due to tetanus toxin. She was transferred to ITU for ventilation and muscle paralysis, but succumbed.

Peter's drawback to further promotion was his lack of publications (not that yours truly had many), his sole contribution to medical literature being a paper on dog bites in Melbourne. During his year with us, however, Mike Cooke and I provided him with sufficient material to produce several papers, which were published. One of these, written jointly by the two of us, followed the recognition in 1985 of Vibration White Finger (VWF) as an industrial disease, and hence the possibility of compensation for those afflicted. As a vascular surgeon I was asked, like many others, to provide medical reports on claimants for local solicitors. Shipyard workers, employees of British Steel and then ex-coal miners, all of whom there were many on and around Teesside, soon came out of the woodwork because of information from their trade unions and by word of mouth. The crucial factor was the occupational history and the claimant's description of his symptoms, because often there was little abnormal to detect on physical examination. It soon became apparent that some individuals were being 'coached', presumably by their union representative, but it was usually easy to detect these.

It wasn't long before I identified what I took to be an unexpectedly large percentage of claimants with associated Dupuytren's contracture of the hands. This condition affects sinew deep to the skin of the palm, gradually clawing in the fingers, starting with the little one and progressing with time. As the name implies, it was first described by an eighteenth-century French surgeon, in a coachman, and it was naturally attributed to prolonged pulling of the reins. For many years, trades unions had sought unsuccessfully to have it recognised as an industrial disease. As a trainee I assisted Hugh Brown, a hand surgeon, at several operations to correct the deformity, but I no longer dealt with the condition. In my first 500 reports in men (there was a single female) over the age of forty-five, about twenty per cent had the condition, ranging from a single nodule in the palm to advanced contractures. I thought this figure excessive but did not know the prevalence in the population at large. The condition is almost confined to Caucasians, being commonest in Scandinavia and the British Isles, and even varies within different regions of the latter, from four to eight per cent, but at a high in our control group of 10.7 per cent, comprising patients admitted to hospital for elective surgery with no history of exposure to vibrating tools. Despite this high figure, the subjects with VWF had almost double the prevalence of Dupuytren's, at twenty per cent, rising to almost thirty per cent in those over sixty-five. The difference was statistically significant. Hence, there may be a causative relationship between the two conditions, a situation that to my present knowledge still has to be resolved.

Peter is now a successful surgeon in Wangaratta, a three-hour drive north of Melbourne, where he still reads a book a week. His hobby is collecting militaria of all ages and he stores hundreds of helmets, plus a suit of armour, in a garage. When Mary and I visited in 2006 he had just purchased the full uniform of one of Saddam Hussein's close relatives, obtained from an American general with proof of provenance, and so, naturally, I had to be photographed alongside the shop manikin that models the said uniform, complete with Saddam mask.

Another Australian, Phil Scarlett, from Newcastle, New South Wales, was one of those Aussies with a slow drawl and a languid, *'G'Dyyy'*. I once mentioned a couple from Darwin who had worked in maxillofacial surgery, or maxfax, the previous year.

'Oh, Darwin—nearly blew away in '74,' he said, referring to Cyclone Tracy, which devastated the city on Christmas Eve and Christmas Day of that year. 'Fall off your yacht in Darwin harbour and if the sharks don't get you, the crocodiles will!'
He visited Newcastle one weekend and I told him to take a good look at the Tyne Bridge. I thought he would fall for my ruse, and he did. I asked him what he thought of it and he replied it was all right, but not a patch on Sydney Harbour Bridge. I told him to examine the girders on the latter next time he went home and he would read, 'Dorman Long, Middlesbrough'—and to his credit, he did.

# Chapter Twenty

# Through the Keyhole

When South Cleveland opened in 1981, a computed tomography (CT) scanner was installed, the cost of £700,000 having been raised entirely by charitable donations. Unfortunately, it seems the purchasers obtained poor specialist advice because the machine was rapidly outdated. Understandably, none of the radiologists were practised at interpretation. The neurologists made a diagnosis of insulinoma in one patient. This is a rare benign tumour of the pancreas that secretes insulin indiscriminately, causing periodic falls in blood sugar, which can cause bizarre behaviour and even coma. The CT scans were sent to a radiologist in York who reported a typical insulinoma in the head of the pancreas and I was asked to remove it. After spending some time in the area in a futile search for this small culprit, and feeling somewhat depressed, I moved to the tail of the organ, close to the spleen, and there was an easily identifiable two-centimetre tumour. What a relief! So much for the CT report.

In the middle of a snowy night during the first winter after my arrival I had been called to Parkside Maternity Hospital by John Atkins, who had operated on a woman for what he took to be *abruptio placentae* causing haemorrhagic shock, but on opening the abdomen he found a large haemorrhagic mass separate from the uterus. It was a spontaneous bleed into an enormous tumour of the right kidney. Fortunately, because of my extensive urological and vascular experience, I found the required removal of the kidney straightforward. This seemed to impress John, and henceforth I became his preferred surgical colleague, even though I did not work at the same hospital. The tumour was an adenomyolipoma, a rare benign tumour associated with a congenital disorder called tuberous sclerosis, which has a combination of typical facial lesions, epilepsy, a predilection to similar tumours of the heart and elsewhere and, usually, mental retardation.

Shortly thereafter, John referred a pregnant lady to me who had a thyroid lump. The cardiologist, Adrian Davies, astutely diagnosed it as a medullary carcinoma on clinical grounds, aided by the obvious mucosal neuromas of the mouth and tongue and characteristic facies of this extremely rare condition, classified esoterically as multiple endocrine adenomatosis type 2 (MEA type 2) and inherited as a dominant gene. The condition also includes a dangerous tumour of the adrenal gland, a phaeochromocytoma, affecting the central part of the gland, the medulla, which secretes the hormones adrenaline and noradrenaline, which in turn have potent effects on the heart, blood pressure and circulation. The tumour, which is usually benign and only in rare cases malignant, produces these hormones to excess indiscriminately, but also in response to stimuli such as surgery, or in this case, childbirth. A massive increase in blood pressure can cause a fatal stroke or heart attack, especially in labour. As I recall, the presence of such a tumour was confirmed by the detection of raised levels of catecholamines in the blood and urine, but lateralising it (that is, right or left) was relatively contraindicated in this case because of the radiation dose to the foetus by a CT scan. The effects of the hormones were counteracted by a combination of alpha- and beta-blocking drugs and an elective caesarean section was planned, after which I would explore the abdomen and remove the offending adrenal tumour.

Unfortunately, I found large adrenal tumours on both sides, fixed and obviously malignant, plus multiple small secondary tumours in the liver. Biopsies showed the latter originated from the thyroid tumour, so there was nothing constructive that could be done for the patient other than continue with the blockading drugs to prevent the adrenal tumours from killing her prematurely. Despite the presence of spread of the cancer, such patients with these rare conditions have been known to survive for longer than would be expected if the primary tumour was of a commoner type (the late Steve Jobs, founder of Apple Computers, was afflicted by a pancreatic tumour in MEA type 1, a similar condition to our lady, but affecting different organs, and he survived far longer than if his tumour had been a carcinoma).

Our patient survived seven years, but I discovered, much to my annoyance, that not only was she subsequently referred by her GP to our senior radiotherapist, but the drugs were stopped. I found this out by chance, so was reluctant to interfere when I no longer was involved in her care, but I summoned up courage and called the GP. I politely explained that the radioactive iodine 131 she received would have no effect on the thyroid, as the cells of a medullary cancer do not attract the element, and secondly, withdrawal of the drugs could cause a fatal surge of adrenaline at any time. I might as well have saved my breath for the reception I received, which was a nonchalant, 'Well, nothing's happened so far.' At least he didn't tell me to mind my own business.

During my time in Middlesbrough I removed three more of these rare phaeochromocytomas, all benign. One was extremely unusual and occurred in a man presenting with frequent disabling, watery diarrhoea. He eventually found his way to a gastroenterologist and after all the standard investigations proved negative, frozen blood was sent to Professor Steve Bloom's lab at the Hammersmith in London, to measure vasoactive-intestinal polypeptide (VIP), which was raised. This hormone, normally secreted by cells of the small intestinal lining, stimulates secretion of water and electrolytes and hence when produced in excess by tumours can provoke the loss of several litres a day of watery diarrhoea. A CT scan showed an adrenal tumour, a needle biopsy of which under ultrasound guidance proved it to be a phaeochromocytoma. One would not knowingly biopsy such a tumour—a biopsy could provoke release of adrenaline and noradrenaline which could be potentially fatal, and there was no reason to suspect this particular one was also secreting adrenaline, but we did not wish to take any chances and blockaded him. His diarrhoea was immediately cured by surgery. I thought we might have a unique case, but Steve Bloom produced references to about 200 others worldwide.

In another case, the patient's wife kindly wrote a verse in praise of my treatment of her husband, and I quote:

*Phaeochromocytoma a condition we despise*
*Along comes Mr Clarke a super-surgeon in our eyes*
*Deftly wielding scalpel he seeks tumours hiding deep*
*Eradicating the problem hopefully for keeps*
*To finish the operation he sews a fine seam*
*Neil looks at the scar and thinks it's been a dream*
*Of course his discomfort tells him it's true*
*And we know how lucky, Mr Clarke, we met you.*

I later had a lady with the MEA type 1 constellation (as suffered by the aforementioned Steve Jobs), who presented as an emergency with profuse vomiting. We eventually diagnosed the Zollinger-Ellison syndrome, in which huge amounts of gastric acid are provoked by excessive secretion of the hormone gastrin, produced by a tumour of the pancreas, a so-called gastrinoma. When this syndrome was first described it was thought the tumour occurred in isolation, but it is now known to be associated with hyperplasia (enlargement) of all four parathyroid glands which regulate calcium metabolism, and sometimes with pituitary tumours. The gastrinomas can cause extensive duodenal ulceration with bleeding and perforation and were originally thought to be benign, but it is now known that the majority are, or become, malignant. As described in the MEA type 2 case, however, patients tend to have a longer survival than would be expected with malignant disease. Surgical cure is difficult because some of these gastrinomas can be almost microscopic and multiple, spread throughout the lining of the duodenum and the pancreas. Ideally, removal of the whole pancreas and associated duodenum should be curative, but because of the multifocality of the lesions this is not always the case. Fortunately, by the time this lady was diagnosed, proton-pump inhibitor drugs (PPIs) had become available. The next stage up from the H2-receptor antagonists, these were introduced in the 1980s to treat duodenal ulcer. Although H2-receptor antagonists reduce gastric acid secretion by eighty per cent, usually sufficient to heal a duodenal ulcer, this is not enough to deal with those encountered in this condition, but PPIs reduce acid secretion to almost zero and are invaluable in its treatment. Initial investigations failed to locate this lady's gastrinoma, but she remained symptom-free on PPIs, although I had to remove three and a half of her parathyroids to lower her blood calcium to normal, which otherwise would have caused widespread complications. At last, after several CT scans over a few years, the gastrinoma was located in the pancreas but with lymph node and adjacent liver involvement. I sent her to the pancreatic surgeon at Newcastle, but sadly she died after radical surgery.

I also carried out several parathyroidectomies for hypercalcaemia, and three adrenalectomies for aldosterone-secreting adenomas, which cause hypertension coupled with a low blood potassium, which can cause periodic muscle weakness. All this interesting endocrine surgery gradually disappeared as we all became increasingly sub-specialised. It used to be said that the average general surgeon carried out two Whipple's procedures during a lifetime. Well, I did four. This procedure involves removal of the head of the pancreas together with the duodenum which encloses it, and the lower end of the common bile duct. It's a pretty major undertaking with what surgeons call 'a lot of clockwork' around, and it requires some complicated re-plumbing to restore the anatomy. The classical indication is for a malignant tumour of the lower end of the bile duct, but these are rare and it is more commonly performed for a cancer in the head of the pancreas, although once these are diagnosed they are usually inoperable and so the procedure is still uncommon. It carried a formidable mortality, now much reduced with better anaesthesia, careful surgery and ITU facilities. Of my four, two were for a bile duct tumour, one surviving for a year, the other for seven years. Another was for a cancer of the duodenum, surviving seven years, and finally, there was one for a stomach cancer, which was clearly incurable but causing so many symptoms that I persevered until I removed all visibly involved tissue. He survived only three months.

My first ruptured aneurysm after I arrived in MIddlesbrough was a retired surgeon, Frank Walker's senior hospital medical officer (an almost defunct sub-consultant grade post even then), but he died of renal failure weeks later. One of the earliest was also the strangest—a twenty-one-year-old Asian boy known to have Behcet's syndrome who was referred from a renal physician. Named after a Turkish dermatologist, this rare and strange condition is a form of auto-immune disorder that is still not fully understood and is characterised by inflammation of various parts of the body, occasionally together with aneurysms of various arteries, which can prove life-threatening. It is very rare in Europeans, occurring mainly in the Middle East and along the old Silk Route. I managed to deal with his ruptured aneurysm, but a few weeks later the poor healing associated with the condition led to a major leak at one limb of the graft I had implanted. I dealt with this also, but a few months later a similar episode occurred, and he died before he could be transferred to theatre.

On the evening before an all-day vascular operating list, I was on the ward at visiting time. I was due to operate the following day on a man in his seventies with a large inflammatory aneurysm. Such aneurysms form a minority, and the cause of the inflammation remains unclear, but they always pose a challenge for the surgeon. They are covered with a much thicker than normal wall, glistening red and bleeding to the touch, and the planes of dissection are usually difficult to discern. A general principle of surgery is that to avoid trouble, make sure the relevant anatomy is properly exposed. But in this situation the more one dissects, the more bleeding occurs from multiple tiny vessels, obscuring the field. Difficult to explain without witnessing it. The more experienced one becomes, the less one exposes to obtain adequate control of the major vessels. I was not looking forward to this procedure but was conscious that when I had seen him in the clinic he had attended alone, and hence was relieved to see he had visitors. Two small children, a boy of about eight and a younger girl, were talking to him at the bedside, facing a window to his right. At the foot of the bed stood a well-dressed, attractive woman, probably in her early thirties. She looked in my direction and I approached her, unnoticed by the patient, who was still in conversation with the children. I introduced myself, shook hands and expressed pleasure in speaking to his daughter about the planned operation.

'No, I'm his wife,' replied the lady, much to a combination of my amazement and despondency.

The possibility of losing a grandfather was bad enough, but a husband and father was even worse. I drove home feeling more anxious than usual and slept fitfully. Fortunately, the operation went like a dream, and not a nightmare, and all was well.

Another memorable case was a man in his early eighties with a huge aneurysm and who had a pilot's licence and still flew a private plane with passengers. It's as well it was repaired before it ruptured, especially during a flight.

On the morning after an emergency admission, the occupant of one bed was lying prone, with the sheets pulled over his head. After a tap on the shoulder and a 'Good morning,' the response was a tearful, pleading voice.

'Help me, doctor, help me. I'm the lowest of the low. Please help me.'

A man in his early twenties, a drug addict, had been injecting himself with heroin in his groin. This is the chosen site by addicts after the superficial veins elsewhere have been exhausted or thrombosed. The femoral vein and artery, each about a half inch in diameter, are accessible just below the groin crease, and the pulsatile artery easily felt. Because needles are continuously reused and the personal hygiene of most addicts non-existent, the sites of injection become infected, and in the case of the artery the infected wall becomes weakened, dilated and markedly pulsatile. The medical term is a mycotic aneurysm. In the worst cases it can burst and cause sudden death, but even when treated surgically can lead to loss of the leg at a high level. Naturally occurring femoral aneurysms are uncommon, but like those of the aorta, can be easily treated by graft replacement using the fabrics Dacron or Gore-Tex. But in the presence of infection, despite even long-term antibiotics, such a foreign body becomes infected itself, eventually requiring its removal, and we're back to square one. So treatment of these addict-associated mycotic aneurysms is difficult. This man was pale and thin, having lost a lot of weight, and he was also desperate. His aneurysm was ready to burst. We managed to deal with it and save his leg. At the time of his discharge about two months later, when he had naturally been drug-free and did not seem to have suffered withdrawal symptoms, he gained two stones in weight. The blood supply to his leg was diminished and he needed a walking stick for a limp. The social workers got him a flat some distance from his former stamping ground. When I said goodbye to him, I reminded him of the state he was in on admission, and how he could have lost either his leg or his life. I used the cliche: 'Regard this as the first day of the rest of your life.' Within six weeks he was back on the drugs.

*** 

In 1991 my secretary Olive retired, a day I had dreaded. Good medical secretaries are worth their weight in gold. They are shamefully underpaid and, owing to the mysteries of the NHS pay scales, receive less than their counterparts in management, despite having to deal with patients, relatives and GPs over the phone, having specialist knowledge of medical terminology and producing letters and summaries quickly and correctly, as well as 'managing' their consultant. Luckily for me, Liz Davidson chose to move and replace Olive and remained with me until I retired in 2005.

***

At the time of the First Gulf War, a new neurologist joined us at Middlesbrough General. He was Raad Shakir, an Iraqi who was Professor of Neurology at Kuwait University and managed to extricate himself and his family before Saddam's army moved in. Raad was enthusiastic and dynamic, like a breath of fresh air, and keen for us to start carotid surgery in the prevention of stroke. I had no experience in this field. I knew that years earlier Peter Dickinson took part in a small trial comparing surgery with anticoagulants, in collaboration with RVI neurologists, but stopped at thirty or so cases after the post-surgical stroke rate was prohibitively high. However, two large international trials, one European, the other from North America, showed that in symptomatic patients, provided the combined stroke/mortality rate was less than five per cent, 'cleaning out' the fatty deposits of arteriosclerosis in the internal carotid artery could prevent more strokes than non-surgical treatment, as long as the narrowing was more than seventy per cent, as measured by ultrasound scan. The majority of strokes are thromboembolic rather than haemorrhagic. Atheromatous narrowing tends to be confined to the first inch or so of the internal carotid in the neck, just below the angle of the jaw. The friable rough area, which can ulcerate, forms a nidus on which small clots can develop and shoot off up to the brain, when they are called emboli. Such occurrences can lead to mini-strokes, so-called transient ischaemic attacks (TIAs), lasting minutes or hours in the form of numbness, weakness or paralysis and sometimes temporary blindness, all warning signs that a permanent disabling or even fatal stroke is imminent. If such patients are referred pronto and receive a duplex ultrasound scan of the neck showing a tight narrowing of the artery, then removal of the 'plaque' (the technical term for the segment of narrowing), is indicated.

After going to Liverpool to visit Peter Harris, who demonstrated the operation, we started our own series—that is, once I could persuade the authorities to release (can you believe it?) £750 to buy the extra surgical instruments required. This was because of the wonderful new directive from management that any new service provided had to be costed and approved before it could go ahead. In fact, the main expenditure was the radiology, the hospital stay and theatre time, not the £750 for instruments, but they were already provided for as part of the surgical budget.

Technically, the operation is not difficult, but it is unforgiving of even minor unforeseen problems, which can hardly be called errors, for the artery has to be exposed and controlled before it can be clamped and opened, and inadvertent dislodging of just a tiny piece of friable loose atheroma or clot from the diseased segment can cause a stroke. At my retirement I had conducted more than 250 carotid endarterectomies with a combined stroke/mortality of 2.8 per cent. Initially, every case was discussed at a weekly conference, when we decided which line of treatment to follow, but after a few short years Raad was headhunted by Charing Cross Hospital. Subsequently, nearly all cases were referred to me fully worked up by a neurologist, as opposed to direct requests from GPs.

Also in the early 1990s we started doing laparoscopic cholecystectomies—removal of the gallbladder by the minimally invasive or 'keyhole' technique. Gynaecologists had been conducting visual examinations of the pelvic organs for decades. A pioneer was Patrick Steptoe, who was responsible for the world's first test-tube baby, and not from a major London teaching hospital but the more mundane Oldham Royal Infirmary. He also pioneered operative procedures via the laparoscope. It was another gynaecologist, Mouret, who did the first laparoscopic cholecystectomy, in France in 1987, combining an instrument with a rod-lens system and microchip that enable the surgeon to view the magnified operative field on a TV screen and perform the dissection using fine instruments passed along five-to-ten-millimetre cannulae (hollow steel tubes). Word travelled fast in the rest of Europe and, of course, the United States, where some 600,000 cholecystectomies are done annually, making it probably the commonest elective abdominal procedure, as gallstones affect around ten-to-fifteen per cent of the population, although not all are symptomatic.

Videos of the procedure and instrument salesmen from various companies (none British, of course, despite the rod-lens system being invented by Harold Hopkins, a British optical physicist) were present at the annual Association of Surgeons meeting in Cardiff in 1992, and I remember accompanying Professor Johnston, my old chief in Newcastle, as we wended our way around the trades exhibition.

'It's a gimmick,' he said dismissively. 'It won't last.'

But how wrong he was.

Shortly afterwards I attended a training course in Leeds, the trainers being from the USA, but none of them from prestigious institutions. Naturally, the British organisers pronounced that during the infancy of this new procedure all cases should be confined to teaching hospitals, as if by divine right, and yet there was no logic behind this statement, as few individuals had built up any experience. As one of the Americans said, 'If you don't do it, someone else up the road will'—but the incentive was much greater in a private insurance-based US system, less so in the NHS. As I have described earlier, the most feared complication of cholecystectomy is damage to the bile duct, and within a couple of years of the laparoscopic technique being introduced it was reported that the incidence of such injury in the States was five times that of the conventional open method. This was clearly a warning to proceed with caution and the National Institutes of Health in the USA advised all surgeons to do their first fifteen under supervision.

The Irish had the best system. Surgeons at the Beaumont Hospital in Dublin trained their 150 colleagues in the country, a relatively small number over time, with the additional advantage that it is legal in that nation to practise (as compared to experiment) on animals, the chosen species being the pig. Indeed, although those used were anaesthetised, there was no requirement to sacrifice them, but I am unaware whether they subsequently commanded a fee for their pork as well as for their service as 'guinea pigs', so to speak.

Nevertheless, there was still a race to proceed, driven partly by an expectation that the companies might be overwhelmed by requests for instruments and develop a waiting list. Mike and I put in an order using funds from charitable donations (there was no way the local management would have agreed to fund us), but it had to be processed via the usual channel. After months of waiting, due, as we thought, to the reasons just highlighted, Mike inquired at the stores department, only to find the written request still on someone's desk. So we had some catching up to do when the equipment arrived. One of Mike's contemporaries, Chris Royston, came from Hull to take each of us through an operation. He was already experienced and started branching out into other procedures, such as hiatus hernia and even groin hernia repairs.

The main advantage of laparoscopic cholecystectomy is that it replaces a single large incision which cuts through muscle with four small ones, each only five-to-ten millimetres, with the consequent reduction in postoperative pain and healing, a shorter hospital stay and no permanent scar. Of course, every surgeon knows the anatomy, but the approach requires different hand-eye coordination to the open method. For it to be possible, the abdominal organs need to be easily visible and manipulated, by temporarily filling the abdominal cavity with $CO_2$ gas, a so-called pneumoperitoneum, created at the beginning of the operation by piercing the abdomen with a Veress needle. This simple but ingenious device, being spring-loaded, reduces the risk of injury to underlying organs by retracting the sharp point as soon as it enters the cavity. Gas is then insufflated to distend the abdomen to resemble a full-term pregnancy. The laparoscope/camera can then be safely introduced via the umbilicus, giving an excellent view of the internal organs, and the three narrow trocars required to perform the procedure can be inserted in turn under direct vision.

***

For ten years since the mid-eighties I had been the surgical tutor, which involved attending six-monthly meetings at the Royal College of Surgeons in Lincoln's Inn Fields in London and organising teaching for local FRCS candidates. I held a session every Wednesday evening and in addition taught general surgery and physiology to ENT junior doctors, required for their diploma exams.

For a few years beginning in 1992 I organised an annual symposium entitled Current Management and New Developments in South Tees, aimed at both GPs and hospital doctors. It was prompted by the idea that we know about advances in our own fields but not necessarily in those of other specialties, and from the practical aspect it referred to changes or new services or techniques now available locally, of which colleagues may not be aware. I was reminded of how a university common room can act as a stimulus for new collaboration when experts from different fields mingle socially for refreshment. With increasing technological innovations, I was intrigued to know how, for example, a physicist knew an ITU doctor or anaesthetist would want to measure the partial pressure of oxygen in the blood, and that this could be estimated by colorimetric means.

The aforementioned Harold Hopkins was prompted to invent a prototype fibre-optic instrument as early as 1951 after a chance meeting with a gastroenterologist, who remarked that views with the old-fashioned rigid brass gastroscope were limited by blind spots around bends, and more importantly, were potentially dangerous to pass. Later, on meeting a urologist who wanted to take photographs of bladder pathology via a cystoscope, he devised the rod-lens system, presently used in laparoscopes, and which increased illumination fifty-to-eighty-fold over the instruments it superseded. Sadly, but I'm afraid, predictably, Hopkins failed to persuade any British manufacturer to develop his prototype, which went, as usual, to the USA and Germany. Disgracefully, as a further kick in the teeth, this modest genius received no national honour. He did, however, receive an honorary fellowship of each of the medical royal colleges. He should be on the fourth plinth in Trafalgar Square, alongside another neglected genius, Sir Geoffrey Hounsfield, who invented the first commercial CT scanner in 1971. At least Hounsfield was knighted and shared a Nobel Prize. What a digression! Well, we didn't expect such distinguished collaboration, but the point I am making is that a medical community needs a periodic central focus of communication so we can all be informed about changes and improvements over a wide range of services. The symposium occupied a whole Saturday, the proceedings were published, and it proved very popular over the years I organised it.

***

The year 1992 brought our silver wedding anniversary and we literally pushed the boat out by taking a Caribbean cruise out of Fort Lauderdale with the Holland America Line, the mix of the crew being along old colonialist lines—the officers being tall, blond Dutchmen in white tropical uniforms and the rest being almost all Indonesian. Most of our fellow passengers were American. One, seated at our table, was a retired senior executive with the Pfizer drug company who remarked after a few days, 'I'm tired of shacks and sugar cane', and later praised us with, 'The British islands are better kept than the French ones.' When we entered and left the American Virgin Islands (purchased for $25m from Denmark in 1917), all non-US citizens had to line up and go through passport control, an action we took in our stride but deeply resented both visually and verbally by the handful of Canadian passengers, and quite rightly so.

With both boys away at university, Mary and I were alone for the first time in nearly twenty years. Mary was now working as a part-time school nurse. For some time I had been troubled by the sight of a mass of manila folders in a compartment of my desk in my study, the records of my research with Dr Moore all those years before. Some of the results had been published, others were presented at meetings and published in abstract form, but the bulk of my own studies remained unpublished. One reason was lack of time and other priorities on my return to the UK, but the main one was the practical difficulty of compressing all the data into the limited form necessary for publication in a scientific journal. I had kept abreast of the literature over the years and no similar work had been published, so I sought the advice of my old chief, Professor Johnston, to see whether he thought an MD thesis would be accepted, despite the long gestation period. He proved enthusiastic and very helpful, so I went ahead and produced the thesis entitled *Studies on Whole Body Nitrogen Turnover, Protein Synthesis and Breakdown in Man using N15 Glycine* in 1994. I was duly awarded the degree after a *viva voce* with three examiners.

It was during one of my visits concerning the thesis that Joan Kehoe, the prof's long-standing secretary, whom I had known since I was a medical student, boosted my ego by telling me that her boss had remarked he should 'never have let Dave go to Middlesbrough'. A bit late in the day, perhaps, but never mind.

So I am one of the few surgeons to possess both the MS and MD degrees. We British are proud of the number of letters after our names. I knew a GP in Whitby who had two lines of letters after his—so many that it paradoxically diminished the proposed impact, certainly to the *cognoscenti*, who knew that most of the diplomas with several letters were relatively easily acquired.

In early 1997, after spending Christmas with us, my mother became vaguely unwell, losing her appetite and sense of taste. Her GP proved pretty useless and after a while I carried out a full examination, which proved to be normal, but I also took some blood tests and one evening in February I got a call from one of our haematologists telling me she had acute myeloid leukaemia and to admit her the next day. She spent a few days in hospital and was told she had 'cancer of the blood' (the word leukaemia was not used), a diagnosis she received with equanimity, and she received a course of chemotherapy. After suffering an unpleasant and uncommon reaction, an allergy rather than the expected side-effects, she did well until September, when she began to look unwell. The night before a routine appointment Mary and I visited and I noticed, but did not comment upon, the ominous sign of petechial haemorrhages on her cheeks, indicative of a low platelet count. The following morning I was giving a seminar before an operating list when I received a call from the neighbour who had offered her a lift. She was not answering the door. I knew what to expect when I drove to her flat. She was lying on her back, next to her bed, dead, but still warm. From the signs it appeared she had risen from her bed feeling sick, gone to the bathroom and in the process banged her head on the sink, for she had a bruise on her forehead. I suspect she then sustained a haemorrhagic stroke from the low platelet count, which prevented her from getting back into bed. She did have asymmetry of her face, although she had managed to drag a pillow under her head. I was saddened she had died alone, but relieved that her end was swift.

Since her diagnosis I had visited almost daily and become an expert on the various soaps she watched—*Corrie*, obviously; *Brookside*, *Emmerdale* but never, ever, *EastEnders*. She asked me to make an appointment with a solicitor to make her will and insisted that I accompany her, but otherwise never referred to her impending death, except on one occasion when, out of the blue, she simply complained that 'I'm taking a long time dying.'

I think her ten years in Stockton were reasonably happy—her health was good until her final illness and she made a few good friends. A friend from Hull stayed several times. Her flat was pleasant and quiet and she was finally secure financially.

Mary and I had taken both our mothers to Sorrento for a week in 1990 and they saw Pompeii, Capri and the olde worlde splendour of the Hotel Tramontano. So there were a few consolations at the end of a life which, although not exactly miserable, by modern standards was one of relative poverty, monotonous, largely lonely (especially after I departed), and blighted by early widowhood, which may not have had the impact it did had I not made an appearance. No doubt she would have found someone else and perhaps had a fulfilling life. She was house-proud, always well dressed, and she dutifully visited Aunty Elsie in Grimsby every weekend during that lady's final illness, as well as caring for her own mother for fourteen years until her death in 1968. I was fifty-five when Mother died, at the age of eighty-one, and although I think she was proud of my success, she never said so in my presence, and to her dying day was not averse to giving me a good telling off, usually over some mild indiscretion.

# Chapter Twenty-One

# The Rocky Road to Retirement

I continued as a general surgeon until only a few years before my retirement, when I became committed full-time to vascular surgery, apart from a small paediatric component. Here are a few memorable cases and events...

One of my patients was a middle-aged nurse on whom I did a mastectomy for breast cancer. She worked in what was amusingly called the 'new block' (that is, from the 1950s) at the Middlesbrough General, so I never saw her except for follow-up appointments every few months. For a few years she remained well, but then felt vaguely unwell. I could find no evidence of recurrence of her cancer and a biochemical screen was normal. Unknown to me, her GP sent her to a physician who thought her symptoms might be menopausal. She never wore makeup and had the typical parchment-like skin of a heavy smoker's face, always looking somewhat careworn. At one appointment she seemed transformed. She had always treated me as a friend, once presenting me with a patterned earthenware pot she had made at a night class. But on this occasion she was positively beaming, bright-eyed and bushy-tailed, with a new blonde hairdo, streaked instead of a lank dun colour, and glossy red lipstick.

'I've found out what's wrong,' she said. 'I've got ME. I've seen a specialist at Bishop Auckland.'

More like a quack, I thought, but did not say. I said how pleased I was—and I was—to see how well she looked, but I had my doubts. Sadly, not much later, we discovered secondary deposits from her breast cancer, from which she eventually succumbed. The moral of the story, if there is one, is that some patients like having a label. They can cope with the certainty of a diagnosis, even if unpleasant, rather than the uncertainty of not knowing.

One of our theatre sisters was fond of saying, 'The only luck some people have is bad luck'. A solicitor asked me to give a medical report on a man of twenty-six. He had been the front seat passenger in a car driven by his best friend, their wives seated in the back, when it collided with a lamppost. The driver and the women sustained only minor injuries, but the subject of my report was left paraplegic (paralysed from below the waist), with a permanent colostomy because of injury to his bowel and an indwelling urinary catheter. Since the accident his wife had divorced him and he now lived alone in a bungalow, confined to a wheelchair, receiving assistance from carers, morning and evening. What bad luck, and what a miserable existence.

I did a home visit at the request of a GP to a lady in her forties who had a very swollen abdomen. She was lying on a sofa downstairs. A brief examination revealed an enlarged liver and a large volume of fluid in the abdomen (called ascites), indicating secondary cancer in the liver from an as yet unknown primary. I admitted her to hospital, where a fuller examination found a very large, pigmented mole on her back, obviously a malignant melanoma, but that would only be visible to the patient in a mirror. She had been aware of it, however, and had drawn a previous GP's attention to it some years earlier, to which he had apparently commented, 'If it ain't broke, don't fix it'—which, if true, seems almost unbelievable. Very sadly, her short remaining time on earth was blighted by subsequent blindness caused by spread of the tumour to the brain.

An Irishman in his early twenties was admitted one evening with pain in the groin. He bore the scar of a biopsy of his right testicle carried out in Hull a few days earlier. He was a member of the Traveller community. The biopsy revealed a malignant tumour, so I told him he needed to have the testicle removed. His response was, 'If you remove my testicle, doctor, I shall do you harm.' A trifle taken back, I said I could not do so without his permission, but then explained his situation in some detail. It was like talking to a brick wall. His parents came the following day; both very down at heel, his father small and hunched, with terrible dentition, and the appearance of a man in his seventies rather than the likely fifties. However, perfectly politely, he explained that with no offence to me, they wanted to take him to Ireland to seek a cure at the hands of a seventh son of a seventh son, a remedy previously unknown to me. The day after, the police rang me asking his whereabouts, as he was wanted by the police of two counties for various crimes. A few days later I received a call from a female surgeon in the south of England. Her opening remarks were, 'I have a delightful young Irishman as a patient here...'—the word 'delightful' sounding sincere rather than sarcastic. I briefly put her in the picture.

It's interesting how some procedures can turn full circle. One Christmas Day, assisted by a female locum, I operated on three patients with acute large bowel obstruction, one after the other, each procedure taking about three hours. Large bowel obstruction is common, and the cause is usually a cancerous growth. Except for a loop towards its end, the colon is fixed to the back wall of the abdominal cavity. It begins in the right lower abdomen as its widest part, called the caecum, where the small bowel enters at its termination, and from which dangles the appendix. Here, the contents are semi-fluid. It then continues straight up to just below the liver under the ribcage, turns at a right angle and crosses in a slight downward bow as the transverse colon to the spleen on the left side under the ribcage. It turns down as the descending colon, then forms a free loop like a letter 'S', called the sigmoid colon, and finally for its last twenty centimetres lies deeper in the pelvis and is now called the rectum. The colon's primary function is to absorb water from the intestinal contents. It plays no part in digestion and propels the final almost solid product, the faeces, for evacuation. Cancers can occur anywhere in the colon but are commonest on the left side. They tend to be like constricting collars and because the faeces at this level is more solid, obstruction is more common here than on the right, where tumours are often cauliflower-like, the bowel more capacious, and the contents semi-fluid. In theory, the obvious surgical treatment for an obstructed colon is to remove the portion containing the tumour and join the divided ends together to restore continuity. However, many years ago this method was found to be potentially disastrous, mainly because of breakdown at the join (anastomosis), leading to death from peritonitis. A variety of reasons could be responsible, some fairly obvious, such as operating on unprepared bowel (that is, full of faeces), which was also dilated. Over time, on the grounds of safety, a staged procedure was developed. Although safe, it required three operations. Stage one was limited to making the diagnosis and relieving the obstruction by creating a transverse colostomy (bringing a loop of the transverse colon to the surface and opening it so the contents emptied into a bag). At a second operation a couple of weeks later, the tumour was removed, the cut ends joined together, healing of the join protected by the colostomy. This itself was closed by a relatively minor procedure, perhaps three or so months later when the patient was fully recovered and home. A modified approach removed the tumour at the first operation, but closed off the bottom end, bringing the upper end as a terminal colostomy, rather than a loop. About three months later the colostomy was detached and the bowel re-joined. So the first operation could be definitive and at best, curable, at the price of a colostomy. Follow-up studies showed that, for a variety of reasons, a significant number failed to have the bowel restored to continuity. Hence, what now seems to me like recently, but was in fact forty years ago, the idea of removing the tumour and doing a primary anastomosis was revisited. Simple, really—it just took a bit of courage to try it. Hugh Dudley and colleagues at St Mary's Hospital in London removed the tumour in the usual way, stapled off the lower end and, using a large urinary catheter inserted via the appendix and sterile corrugated plastic tubing at the cut end, flushed out the faecal contents into a receptacle, using several litres of saline solution. The two ends were then joined. Postoperative anastomotic breakdown was at the same level as in elective operations, and the method soon became accepted. This has been a long-winded summary, but it is an important issue. Colon and rectal cancer is common. There is now a national screening programme, based on testing faecal samples for occult (that is, hidden) blood, and it is hoped that in time the condition will be diagnosed before it becomes symptomatic.

On another occasion, my registrar and I were on call on Christmas Eve. Her family home was in the Midlands and I took over early on Christmas Day so she could drive to have a festive lunch with her parents. The only new patient was a 'wimp' with abdominal pain, she said. Shortly after she left, I encountered the wimp, a man in his early thirties, bent double holding his belly after he left the toilet, and I removed his acutely inflamed appendix a couple of hours later. On her return, I asked my registrar if she had enjoyed Christmas, and after a pause, said, 'Oh, by the way, the wimp had appendicitis.' Instead of an embarrassed, spluttered apology, she greeted the news with a mere shrug of the shoulders. If that had happened to me at her stage, I would have received a serious bollocking and have had to hang my head in shame.

As we all know, appearances can be deceptive. It has been inculcated into generations of medical students to maintain decorum in dress. One afternoon I was teaching a group on the ward and proudly showing them a man in a side room whose aortic aneurysm I had repaired a few days earlier. Naturally, he had a full-length abdominal incision. After my presentation and description of the pathology and surgical procedure, a rather scruffy young man, wearing a ponytail, an earring and a purposefully loosely knotted tie, brazenly expressed his opinion that what I had done amounted to butchery and surely there must be some less invasive way of doing the procedure. He spoke so confidently that rather than be offended, I asked if he could think of an alternative. Presumably thinking on his feet, he queried the possibility of inserting some form of expandable graft from below, via the femoral artery in the groin. His fellow students looked embarrassed at his cheek, but I praised him for his ingenuity and explained that an Argentinian vascular surgeon, Juan Parodi, had in fact devised such a graft, which was now being developed commercially. I never saw that lad again, but he had an original mind and was not afraid to challenge the status quo. As I said, appearances can be deceptive.

We were prompted to use aortic stent grafts by one of our vascular radiologists, Bill Leen. Bill (or Guillaume, as he was baptised) was an Aberdeen graduate, from Mauritius and of Chinese origin, and was a highly skilled interventional radiologist (that is, he performed diagnostic and therapeutic procedures requiring manual dexterity). He was also very intelligent and always willing to go the extra mile. These new stents were expensive. They were basically the Dacron grafts we routinely used, woven in different sizes on essentially early twentieth-century textile looms, which normally cost a couple of hundred pounds or so, but they were collapsed within a skeleton of nitinol wire (an alloy with a memory), and inserted on a special introducer, taking the price up to circa £4,000. Nevertheless, this was still cheaper than the conventional method, with its attendant ITU and ward stay, and more comfortable and less risky than the conventional open approach. The femoral arteries in the groin were exposed in the x-ray department, under either general or epidural anaesthesia. Bill would then take over, inserting an introducer over a guide-wire and using x-ray control with intermittent injections of small amounts of contrast liquid, identifying the precise anatomical position of the stent, which was then deployed and dilated with an inflatable balloon and retained in position by wire hooks impacted into the wall of the aorta.

We were fortunate that I persuaded the chief executive, Bill Murray, to fund the first dozen cases, realising that if we developed the expertise early, and the procedure took off as we expected it to, we would become an established centre and attract cases from elsewhere, who would be funded accordingly. In the first year, 1999-2000, we performed twenty-one aortic stent grafts. For anatomical and technical reasons, only about forty per cent of aneurysms were suitable, but with continued development of both grafts and skills, by 2014 I believe that up to eighty-five per cent could be treated. In the main, however, ruptured aneurysms still need open operative surgery.

***

I had planned to retire at sixty, in 2002, a decision based largely on well-known but probably out-dated statistics showing that medics who retired at the normal age of sixty-five on average survived for only two years, whereas those who left at sixty lived to seventy-two. Reasons for the discrepancy were not speculated upon. Did the extra five years kill you, or was it the attitude of mind of those going early which preserved them? Nobody knows, nor do I know what the present figures reveal, suffice to say that at sixty I still felt fit and enthusiastic and as big changes were taking place, I stayed on and split the difference by going at sixty-two.

It is interesting that the generation before mine nearly all retired at sixty-five and had that age not been a statutory requirement, many would have hung on. I can think of two main reasons why. Firstly, they had been through the war, which had curtailed their income for six years, and of course, the NHS was not founded until 1948, so they would not receive a full pension until they had worked for forty years. Secondly, my fellow senior registrars and I kept them in their beds. In other words, we did all the night work. At the time I eventually retired, in 2005, I was working an average week of just under sixty hours and considered it easy compared with before 2002, when I reluctantly relinquished general surgery to concentrate on vascular surgery and my paediatric component, by now a formal commitment.

With the change in junior doctors' training, coupled with the European Working Time Directive, senior registrars were abolished and replaced by specialist registrars (SpRs). Even though they were only allowed to work up to an average forty-eight hours per week, they were fast-tracked to become consultants in about eight years, compared to fourteen years for me and most of my colleagues.. We had to deal with more emergencies personally and/or supervise the SpRs more closely, both of which are marked improvements in patient care and training, providing the emergency rota is not too onerous. But each SpR expressed a speciality interest, which predicted the eventual doom of the so-called general surgeon. In addition, if I was on call for vascular surgery, but the SpR on duty was a budding upper gastrointestinal surgeon, which often happened, I could end up at weekends trying to fit in lower limb amputations, a bread and butter operation, which in former days would have been performed perfectly competently by a registrar.

In 2002 it was decided to centralise all vascular surgery in the greater Teesside area (population circa 600,000) at South Cleveland Hospital. Alex Clason and I dealt with south of the river, as before, and Chris Wood continued serving Hartlepool, seeing outpatients there but with beds and operating at South Cleveland, and a new surgeon, Andrew Parry, served North Tees.

On a personal level, I was sad to lose the wide variety of interesting and often challenging cases I had dealt with for more than thirty years, but it was inevitable. As our late-lamented Dean of Medicine, Henry Miller, and my own mentor, Francis Moore, both said, independently, 'Everyone is against specialisation except the patient', and it is true that better patient outcomes are achieved by specialists, performing a limited range of procedures at which they become increasingly proficient. The drawback is there is still a need for the generalist who can coordinate treatment in patients with multiple pathologies.

In February 2002 I was called out of a seminar to be told the dreadful news that my old friend and colleague, John Farndon, had collapsed and died of a heart attack the previous evening. John was Professor of Surgery at Bristol, editor of the *British Journal of Surgery*, holder of several honorary degrees and at the peak of his career. I always regarded this effervescent, handsome man with his apple cheeks and cheeky grin as being like a Greek god and somehow indestructible, and even now can hardly believe he was cruelly taken from us at only fifty-five. We had some happy times together in the good old RVI.

The following month both the Queen Mother and the legendary rugby commentator, Bill McLaren, died, in the same week that my first and longest-serving colleague, Mike Cooke, retired. The chief executive, Bill Murray, an engineer by training, was one of the first to directly involve clinicians in management and Mike served as the chief of service for the Division of Surgery, encompassing the specialties of general surgery (including its subspecialties), urology, ENT and ophthalmology. Each of these four directorates had its own clinical director. Other major specialties were divided up accordingly. The clinical directors controlled their own budgets, in close cooperation with a divisional manager, and was responsible to the chief, who attended the weekly management group meetings, the composition of which was larger than that of the Cabinet! I was already clinical director for general surgery and was asked to take over from Mike as chief of service. I was ambivalent about this—it massaged one's ego, but in reality one did not have much leeway to control a budget. The bulk of the expenditure was on staff salaries and senior NHS management expected annual 'efficiency savings' of a few per cent, so 'new money' to improve or develop a service was almost impossible, certainly in my speciality, in which contracts with the 'purchasers' expected us to deal with everything they threw at us. However, the trust was embroiled in exciting times, having won the contract to provide cardiothoracic surgical services in the south of the North-East region to support the Freeman Hospital in Newcastle, and with the prospect of a single-site hospital under the private finance initiative (PFI) scheme. In addition, when I realised who might get the job if I declined, I accepted. On becoming a whole-time vascular surgeon my caseload fell substantially, and I could devote the time needed to attend the plethora of meetings that ensued.

The first hurdle in the PFI process was to develop a business case that could be accepted by the Treasury, and it was then put out to tender—in our case, two consortia placed bids. The design for the business case created by the trust, at our own risk (expenditure that could have been put to alternative use but would be wasted if the bid failed), was planned by a Californian company. The extremely articulate, enthusiastic and knowledgeable American responsible, who had dealt with world famous hospitals, amused us all when he produced his computer-derived proposed site drawings, showing one of Middlesbrough's main thoroughfares, Marton Road, lined on both sides with palm trees!

The single site went ahead, taking forty-four months for completion and having just over 1,000 beds. Middlesbrough General was closed, demolished and, together with Middlesbrough Football Club's ground, Ayresome Park, is now a housing estate. I wonder if the house on the site of my old office occasionally smells of cigar smoke?

The new complex was renamed the James Cook University Hospital after the great navigator, who was born only a few yards south of the location. On one site are all the recognised specialties, apart from transplantation and specialist paediatric surgery. The jewel in the crown is the cardiothoracic centre, which is world class, and one of the first to offer immediate angiography and clot-busting therapy, angioplasty and stenting for coronary thrombosis by consultant staff, twenty-four hours a day, seven days a week. The design of most new hospitals seems to include an atrium, situated fairly close to the entrance and presumably aiming to copy the original Roman domestic purpose of being a focus for meeting. It was in the atrium at James Cook that Prince Andrew officially opened the single site, with all the local dignitaries in the plum seats, even though most had contributed nothing to the project. I recall the prince giving a look of astonishment when he entered and saw the size of the audience. The people at the coalface are usually excluded from such events, so it was a pleasant surprise for the chiefs of service to be invited and introduced afterwards to the prince, with whom we had a brief conversation.

A few years earlier I managed, for once in a blue moon, to leave for home early in the afternoon and was briefly held up in traffic. Approaching was a motorcycle police escort followed by a Rolls-Royce containing the unmistakable figure of Diana, Princess of Wales, being driven quite slowly. On arriving home a few minutes later, I consulted the previous day's *Evening Gazette* to learn that she was opening a new cancer centre at my own hospital and later a frozen food factory on a nearby industrial estate. I quickly phoned my mother, a fervent royalist, picked her up and took her to the factory, where we joined only about fifteen people, all ladies as I recall, and most in headscarves. There was also a single policeman. We were confined to the corner of the short road, off the main one, and not allowed closer than about 200 yards from the entrance. But Diana obviously asked the driver to slow down, wound down her window and, with her head and an arm outside, glided past as if in slow motion so we could all get a good look. What a trooper! Unforgettable.

My last vascular operation before I retired in 2005 was a long *in situ* saphenous vein bypass of a femoro-popliteal block for limb salvage. I had no particular sense of finality. I agreed to continue a monthly clinic and operating list for children, ending in December, when it was anticipated that a replacement would have been found.

***

In May, Mary and I took the popular train journey through the Canadian Rockies, followed by an Alaskan cruise. We imposed ourselves on Bill and Pat Cookson for a week at their retirement home in Stony Plain, Alberta. Bill and I were housemen together on the Dickinson Unit in 1966. Like me, Bill originally had surgical ambitions, but he seems to have been persuaded that the UK was 'finished', and two weeks after he and Pat married they took off into the unknown for a GP-cum-surgeon job in Drayton Valley, a small community surrounded by nodding donkey oil extractors. Professionally, his job proved fulfilling. With the nearest city, Edmonton, being a ninety-minute drive away, the practice had its own small hospital, with access to most basic investigations, and both obstetrics and minor surgery could be conducted locally. The work was more rewarding than being a GP back home and each partner had their own speciality. All were British (it seems Canadian graduates were not interested in such isolated communities).

Bill came to a couple of five-yearly reunions, and we kept in touch at Christmas. With each card he usually appended an invitation to visit, but I think I still took him aback when I phoned asking if we could stay. The logistics meant it would have to be a week, three days longer than the time relative strangers are generally supposed to tolerate one another without some form of fallout, but I am pleased to say they seemed to enjoy seeing us.

I feel guilty stating that I was disappointed with the Rockies, but once one became accustomed to the scenery it was unvarying and we only saw one wild animal, a dozy elk having a snooze. The luck of the draw, I suppose. The electric blue of Lake Louise and its backdrop glacier did not disappoint, however. I was moved to see that every small town we visited had immaculately maintained war memorials to those Canadians who fought for King and Empire in two world wars. After all, they could simply have washed their hands of both affairs—the sheer distance would have saved them, if not us.

Our Alaskan cruise was more rewarding in terms of wildlife. We saw leopard seals, large aggressive creatures that prey on their smaller cousins, and went on a wonderful boat trip during which a male and female orca, with calf protected in-between, played with the vessel, diving underneath from one side to the other, almost as if they were trained to do so. Finally, just as the captain said we needed to return to the harbour, after fruitlessly searching for humpbacks despite seeing their blowouts from a distance, we were rewarded with one that appeared only yards from the boat and, almost in slow motion, dived to reveal the magnificent telltale fluke, which seemed to remain stationary in the air, before giving a farewell wave and joining the rest of the body underwater. A moment to treasure.

Mary and I were pleasantly surprised to receive an invitation to a Buckingham Palace garden party in July 2005. Blessed with glorious weather, we saw all the members of the royal family who attended, the only absentees being Charles and Camilla. We actually got very close to HM herself as she was introduced to a pair of guests at a time, the spectators being politely held back at a discrete distance by courtiers. It is said that such introductions are made at random, but I doubted this when we saw the tiny, ageing figure of Sir Harold Evans, ex-editor of the *Sunday Times* (and, incidentally, the Darlington-based *Northern Echo*, his first paper) accompanied by his glamorous blonde wife, Tina Brown. I was amused to see him attempt a flustered curtsey rather than a bow, and a bit miffed that he was allowed such a privilege since he left our shores for New York, especially now he was an American citizen. Not only that, but the following week he had an article in the *Mail* describing his transatlantic voyage on the QE2 to London for the party, obviously all *gratis*.

We stayed at the Royal College of Surgeons and as we were dressing, a newscaster announced an amber alert on the Tube. As a result, almost all the passing taxis were occupied, and we finally managed to hail one much later than planned. Rather as in films when someone in a chase tells the driver to 'Follow that car' and he replies he has always wanted to hear that, ours, when asked to take us to Buckingham Palace, similarly said it was the first time he had received such a request. We mentioned the amber alert to him, but it was obvious something was amiss because police sirens could be heard in every direction. It was only a few weeks after the 7/7 bombings, and London was hypersensitive. Anyway, this taxi driver certainly used the Knowledge, the famous preserve of black cabbies, because he took us every which way. Each time he saw obstructed traffic he seemed to find a way round, all the time chatting in a friendly manner. I confess to briefly thinking he might be taking us on a wild goose chase to elevate the fare, but suddenly recognised Birdcage Walk, and my guilt prompted a generous, well-earned tip. It was a marvellous feeling walking through the red gravel of the palace forecourt and then a large room at the back leading into the gardens, with two military bands playing alternating numbers. Apart from military guests, the great majority were understandably 'of a certain age', but there were some young people from the dominions—apparently they can apply to their embassy and stand a high chance of success because the opportunity is not widely known.

***

One Sunday in mid-October 2005, I received a phone call from Stella Leen, who in a calm, softly spoken voice, informed me that Bill had died suddenly the previous afternoon. He returned home after a vigorous game of indoor tennis complaining of indigestion, went upstairs for a shower and a rest and minutes later, when she went to check, Stella found him dead. Slim, a lifelong non-smoker, careful with his diet and taking regular exercise, Bill was about the last person one would expect to suffer a heart attack. He was only fifty-one. Like Johnny Farndon, the other friend whose death hit me like a thunderbolt, Bill was at his peak. Highly intelligent and cultured, he had extraordinary manual dexterity and whatever the hour was always willing to take on cases when my colleagues and I felt needed his help. His premature death was a serious blow to the hospital and much more so to his bereft widow and their three daughters.

Since my retirement Mary and I have visited India and Australia, as well as Canada, and taken two cruises, to the Baltic capitals and down the Danube and Rhine, as well as enjoying holidays with my younger son Paul and family to Dorset and Cornwall, both of which were glorious weather. From just after retirement until the pandemic, I joined another group of retirees who were taught to row by Tees Rowing Club. The Tees is a lovely river, upstream of Stockton, and it was a pleasant way of keeping fit each week. I joined the Old Hymerians association and every two months attend a lunch at the school. Now co-educational and independent, it has new blocks containing music departments and a swimming pool, but is still recognisable as the place I loved and which at one time, like the RVI later on, I never wished to leave.

I have always been a keen reader on a wide variety of subjects, but tend to concentrate on history, biographies and the Victorian novel. I have even read *Ulysses* and all six volumes of Proust! I made it my first task upon retirement to tackle all those unread books already on my shelves, some of which were bought enthusiastically but remained neglected because of the exigencies of my NHS work. I have made a great deal of headway, but continue to be diverted by persuasive press reviews, although I hope to succeed before the Grim Reaper calls. Mary and I are also keen on art and have visited many galleries and exhibitions and seen most of the Bard's plays performed. Since 2007 we have had a static caravan on a farm in the Lake District. We now know the central and eastern fells well and will continue to walk them while we remain fit enough. Wordsworth was seventy when he last climbed Helvellyn and Wainwright persisted for even longer, until his eyesight, rather than his legs, let him down. Responding to a request broadcast on the BBC's *Look North* local evening news programme, I became a steward and later a guide at Durham Cathedral, the wonderful world heritage site and iconic symbol of the North-East, the history, countryside and culture of which means so much to me.

**We'd like to ask you a big favour — it will only take you a few moments but will make a huge difference to us.**

If you enjoyed reading David's story, please leave a review or even just a rating on Amazon. Positive reviews help independent publishers get their voices heard and sell more books in a crowded marketplace.

We read every review and are so grateful to you for taking the time to help.

To leave a review, search for the book on Amazon and scroll down the page, or scan this QR code:

**Opening Up, Volume I**
**The Making of a Surgeon**

**The remarkable journey of a war widow's only child in bombed-out Hull as he embarks on a distinguished career in surgery.**

Experience David Clarke's formative years, including winning a public school scholarship and his medical and surgical training.

Join him on his professional journey, where he shares fascinating anecdotes about the colourful and distinguished characters he meets.

Delve into his digressions on surgical history and marvel at the progress made during a single professional lifetime.

A snapshot of a golden era of Britain's NHS, a treasure trove of medical detail and a tribute to figures who shaped modern medicine.

With heartwarming stories and vivid descriptions, this compelling memoir offers a unique glimpse into the world of surgery.

Search on Amazon or scan this QR code:

## The Man Behind the Mask
## The Autobiography of a Pioneering Orthopaedic Surgeon

**The compelling story of the steelworker's son who transformed thousands of lives by bringing joint replacement to the North-East of England.**

John Anderson CBE was inspired to become a surgeon after seeing their heroism at close quarters when he spent a year in hospital as a teenager.

In the decade years before he started his work, 12 knee and hip replacements were carried out in Middlesbrough by surgeons trying out emerging techniques. By the end of his career, Anderson was performing that many each week.

Loved and respected by everyone who knew him, as a friend, patient or colleague, this is the story of The Man Behind The Mask.

Search on Amazon or visit https://mybook.to/8GYTK

**Married to the Man who Washed Himself Away**
**A Memoir of Motherhood, Marriage and Obsessive Behaviour**

**This extraordinary true story will move you to tears and inspire you to never give**
**up.**
Set in North-East England in the 1950s and 60s, it follows the life of a lively teenager who
falls for a handsome older man.
Joan dreams of a romantic future, but her husband's obsessive-compulsive disorder stands
in the way of creating a normal home for their growing family.
She must find a way to overcome the formidable challenges that stand in her way as she
tries to find happiness.
Immersed in the warmth, love and hardship of a working-class community, Joan's story
of heartbreak, adversity and resilience will stay with you forever.
**"Exquisitely written, this story touches your heart and stays in your**
**soul"——Sacha TY Fortuné**

Search on Amazon or use this link: https://mybook.to/marriedtotheman